The absence of a professional police force in the city of Rome in classical times is often identified as a major cause of the collapse of the Republic. But this alleged 'structural weakness' was not removed by the Emperor Augustus and his successors, and was in fact shared with other pre-modern states: a specialized police force is a modern invention. In this critical new study of the system of law and order in ancient Rome in both Republican and Imperial periods, Wilfried Nippel identifies the mechanisms of self-regulation which operated as a stabilizing force within Roman society. This case-study of ancient Rome has a comparative dimension and will interest legal historians of other pre-modern societies as well as ancient historians, anthropologists, sociologists and political scientists.

KEY THEMES IN ANCIENT HISTORY

Public order in ancient Rome

KEY THEMES IN ANCIENT HISTORY

EDITORS

Dr P. A. Cartledge
Clare College, Cambridge

Dr P. D. A. Garnsey
Jesus College, Cambridge

Key Themes in Ancient History aims to provide readable, informed and original studies of various basic topics, designed in the first instance for students and teachers of Classics and Ancient History, but also for those engaged in related disciplines. Each volume is devoted to a general theme in Greek, Roman, or where appropriate, Graeco-Roman history, or to some salient aspect or aspects of it. Besides indicating the state of current research in the relevant area, authors seek to show how the theme is significant for our own as well as ancient culture and society. By providing books for courses that are oriented around themes it is hoped to encourage and stimulate promising new developments in teaching and research in ancient history.

Other books in the series

PUBLIC ORDER IN ANCIENT ROME

WILFRIED NIPPEL

Professor of Ancient History, Humboldt-Universität, Berlin

CAMBRIDGE
UNIVERSITY PRESS

Published by the Press Syndicate of the University of Cambridge
The Pitt Building, Trumpington Street, Cambridge CB2 IRP
40 West 20th Street, New York, NY 10011–4211, USA
10 Stamford Road, Oakleigh, Melbourne 3166, Australia

First published 1995

Printed in Great Britain at the University Press, Cambridge

A catalogue record for this book is available from the British Library

Library of Congress cataloguing in publication data
Nippel, Wilfried
Public order in ancient Rome / Wilfried Nippel.
p. cm. – (Key themes in ancient history)
Includes bibliographical references and index.
ISBN 0 521 38327 7 (hardback). ISBN 0 521 38749 3 (paperback)
1. Law enforcement – Rome. I. Title. II. Series.
HV8212.N56 1995
363.2′0937 – dc20 94–45107 CIP

ISBN 0 521 38327 7 hardback
ISBN 0 521 38749 3 paperback

F P

Contents

Preface

This book is about the maintenance of public order in ancient Rome, with special reference to the period of the Republic. It deals with the methods by which the rules designed to secure peace in the community were enforced. It elucidates the characteristic Roman responses to issues of public order, such as arose in the case of rule-infringements which could not simply be left for settlement (of whatever kind) between the parties concerned or to the decision of a court that one of the parties could call upon, but had to be dealt with through communal means of enforcement.

Scholars who have investigated problems of law and order in the Late Republic have often argued that the lack of a strong and politically impartial police force was a serious, structural weakness in Roman society. It turns out that the Roman Imperial period, with its new governmental agencies, did not remedy the alleged deficiency. Moreover, the same point could be made at the expense of virtually all pre-modern societies. The establishment of a police force in the sense of a specialized and impartial law-enforcement agency was an innovation of the eighteenth and nineteenth centuries. It was the product of fundamental changes in individual and societal attitudes towards, and demands for, public order. This book rejects the notion that modern standards of policing are 'natural' and indispensable to the proper functioning of a political community, and sets out instead to identify the functional equivalents of a police force in a 'policeless' society.

I should like to thank Peter Garnsey and Paul Cartledge for their encouragement, help and patience. Barbara Metzger carefully and skilfully edited my text and transformed it into intelligible English.

Dannenberg/Elbe, Germany

Abbreviations

ANRW   *Aufstieg und Niedergang der römischen Welt*, ed. H.
Temporini and W. Haase. Berlin and New York,
1972–

CIL   *Corpus Inscriptionum Latinarum*

FIRA   *Fontes Juris Romani Anteiustiniani*, ed. S. Riccobono *et
al.* 2nd ed. Florence 1940–43

ILS   H. Dessau, *Inscriptiones Latinae Selectae*, 3 vols. Berlin
1892–1916

ML   R. Meiggs and D. Lewis, *A Selection of Greek Historical
Inscriptions to the End of the Fifth Century B.C.* Rev. edn.
Oxford 1988

ORF   H. Malcovati, *Oratorum Romanorum Fragmenta*, 2 vols.
4th edn. Turin, 1976–9

PG   *Patrologia Graeca*, ed. J.-P. Migne. Paris, 1857–66

Journal titles are abbreviated according to the system of *L'Année
philologique*, ancient sources according to the *Oxford Classical Diction-
ary*. Dates are BC except for those indicated as AD and others which
are quite obviously so.

Introduction

Societies differ both in their perception of public order and in the methods of its enforcement that they consider appropriate, and, of course, both may change over time in any given society. Modern societies have become accustomed to specialized law enforcement agencies called police that are authorized to regulate social conflicts, if need be, by employing physical force. They represent the state's claim to the 'monopoly of legitimate physical violence' (Weber 1972: 29, 183, 516) with respect to internal relations, whereas the army does the same with respect to the outside world. The establishment of a police apparatus that is supposed to guarantee impartial enforcement of the rules of public order and become functionally differentiated from the military forces is, however, a rather recent achievement from the perspective of universal history. The breakthrough to this solution during the eighteenth and nineteenth centuries arose out of new demands on public order but met with considerable objections as to the political dangers and the repercussions upon societal self-regulation that it would imply.

One of the leading proponents of police reform in late-eighteenth-century England, Patrick Colquhoun, called 'police in this country ... a new science; the properties of which consist not in the Judicial Powers which lead to punishment, and which belong to Magistrates alone, but in the prevention and detection of crimes, and in those functions which relate to internal regulations for the well ordering and comfort of Civil Society'. An anonymous opponent criticized Colquhoun's proposal, however, as calling for 'a new engine of Power and Authority, so enormous and extensive as to threaten a species of despotism and inquisition hitherto without a parallel in this country'.[1] All of the police reformers argued,

[1] Colquhoun's tract, *A Treatise on the Police of the Metropolis*, first published in 1796, was by 1800 already in its sixth edition; the anonymous critic quoted takes issue with this edition. The quotations are taken from Philips (1980: 155).

with John Fielding, that 'the government of a City or Country, so far as regards the Inhabitants ... must always be suited to the Nature of the Government and Constitution of the Country', and that 'the police of an arbitrary government differs from that used in a Republic, and a Police proper for England ... must always be agreeable to the first nation of the Liberty of Subjects'.[2] This did not, however, dispel the fear that the example of French absolutism might be followed in England.

These quotations should suffice to stress that the case of ancient Rome should not be approached from a point of view that assumes not only the existence of a police force, but also a degree of public order analogous to that which (in theory at least) is achieved in modern developed societies. To detect the rationale that may underlie the Romans' attitudes and methods, we must instead look for the correspondence of these attitudes and methods with fundamental features of their political and social structures and values. We must also consider how 'functions which relate to internal regulations for the well ordering and comfort of civil society' can be fulfilled without employing any substantial governmental apparatus.

A most conspicuous difference between the ancient and the modern experience is illustrated by Colquhoun's argument about the 'prevention and detection of crimes'. That (apart from cases of high treason) the state itself should assume such a task and not leave it to the vigilance of its citizens was a notion quite foreign to the Romans, at least during Republican times (Mommsen 1899: 297). Not only did the authorities as a rule decline to engage in prevention, detection and public prosecution of everyday criminality, but Roman criminal law itself covered a much more restricted scope than that of modern societies: theft, damage to property, assault and slander were considered torts and subject to civil proceedings, which, however, issued in fines in addition to the property value concerned (Strachan-Davidson 1912: I, 39). We do not even know to what degree (if at all) the Roman authorities undertook the prosecution of murder. It is unclear whether in ordinary (not politically dangerous) cases in the Early and Middle Republic such crimes were really prosecuted by magistrates before

---

[2] *Extracts from such of the Penal Laws as particularly relate to the Peace and Good Order of this Metropolis* ... London (1768) 3.

the popular assembly or if even that was left to suits on private initiative, or whether the jury courts of the Late Republic, whose action presupposed charges brought by a citizen, were the only place in which criminal proceedings occurred.

As is so often the case in ancient history, the selectivity and bias of our sources are serious problems. There are only a few chance or indirect references to the treatment of everyday conflicts, and down to the first century B C we know almost nothing about public order in the municipalities which became part of Roman Italy. There is of course ample evidence with respect to the issues of public order connected with the political turmoils of the Late Republic, but we can only broadly compare this evidence with that for earlier periods. The annalistic tradition provides for the Middle Republic only a few details on decision-making processes, and (whatever their merits for the outlines of constitutional history) the embellished accounts of the Early Republic are probably furnished with projections from Late Republican scenes. Liveliness and love of detail are inversely proportional to authenticity. We can learn more from comparison with the situation of Imperial times, which shows that the emergence of important governmental agencies only to a certain degree implies an increase in the objective level of public order; rather, decisions whether action should be taken and what means were appropriate had become subject to the often erratic discretion of individual rulers and governors.

We cannot fill the lacunae of our evidence with comparative materials, but comparison can indicate the range of possible solutions to structurally similar questions. This helps us to avoid the modernist fallacy of assuming governmental response instead of societal self-regulation, and to indicate which of the features that we encounter were concomitants of unique Roman political and social structures and which have nothing at all to do with Roman peculiarity, much less Roman failure. Finally, comparison should also help us guard against a certain overestimation of our subject: problems of law and order are a basic component of the crisis of the Republic, and they also reflect the achievements and (old and new) deficiencies of the Empire, but they cannot be held responsible for the fall of either. That the subject deserves close study for its historical as well as current interest should, however, become clear from the following pages.

CHAPTER I

Republican principles of policing

THE DISPLAY OF MAGISTERIAL AUTHORITY

In the political order of Republican Rome, the higher magistrates, because of their overall responsibility for the *res publica*, had at their disposal means of enforcement that were only to a limited extent available to the magistrates specifically entrusted with particular police duties. Furthermore, a fundamental principle of the Republican constitution was the distinction between the city and the world outside (Rüpke 1990: 29–51). The sacred boundary (*pomerium*) constituted the city of Rome (*urbs*) as a pacified sphere from which military power was excluded (Gell. *Noctes Atticae* 10.15.4; 15.27.5; Varro, *De re rustica* 3.2.4); the *auspicia* taken for the field became invalid once the returning magistrate had crossed the *pomerium*. Keeping the army out of the city was understood as an aspect of political freedom (Cic. *Philippicae* 5.21). Thus the higher magistrates, although possessing both civil and military responsibility, were not allowed to use military means to maintain law and order within the city. In this the Roman Republic was fundamentally different from many other pre-modern states, which, although lacking a police force in the strict sense, could still mobilize military force as a last resort (Finley 1983: 18–23).

Rome in fact had no standing army, only a militia that (probably until the mid-second century BC) was dissolved and newly recruited annually (Gschnitzer 1981). The distinction between the military and civil capacities of the magistrates precluded any recourse to conscripts within the city, subject to military discipline by virtue of their oaths (Dion. Hal. *Antiquitates Romanae* 11.43.2; cf. Livy 7.16.8; Tondo 1963; Nicolet 1976: 141–9). Instead, in a crisis the Roman authorities were dependent on volunteers, who were likely to appear in sufficient numbers only if they were convinced of the reality of the danger.

There was also no specialized magistracy chiefly or exclusively responsible for maintaining public order. During the first centuries of the Republic, the system of magistracies became progressively more differentiated as new offices were created to perform particular functions once entrusted to the highest magistrates. The differentiation of functions was more a matter of a routine division of labour than of a clear-cut allocation of legally defined competences, and the chief magistrates retained their overall responsibility. It was they, too, rather than the lesser magistrates, who commanded the most powerful means for enforcing obedience.

Coercitio

The special instrument of enforcement which a magistrate possessed was what is called *coercitio*, a coinage of modern scholarship designed to cover the various measures a magistrate could apply to enforce obedience without instituting legal proceedings.[1] Included under it were scourging and execution (exclusively associated with the *imperium* of the chief magistrates: that is, their comprehensive military and judicial power), arrest and imprisonment, and the imposition of fines up to a certain maximum. Higher fines could result from a formal trial before the People in which the magistrates assumed the role of accuser. It was understood that only magistrates with *imperium* could issue orders to a citizen, summon one or have one arrested without the magistrate being present in person (Varro quoted by Gell. *NA* 13.12.6; Giovannini 1990: 432–3).

This catalogue of possible measures is not an enumeration of legally defined powers: a magistrate might impose any other measure he thought appropriate but in that case would face the possible objection that he was acting without precedent. For instance, the consul Gabinius' deportation order against a Roman knight in 58 was sharply criticized by Cicero as without foundation in previous practice (*Epistulae ad familiares* 11.16.2; on expulsion of foreigners, see Mommsen 1871–88: II, 139, n. 4). Even more extreme was Mark Antony's ploy as consul in 44, when he threatened Cicero with the destruction of his house if he refused to attend a

---

[1] See, however, Cic. *De legibus* 3.6 and, for technical usage by jurists, *Digesta* 1.2.2.16; 1.16.6pr.

Senate meeting (Plut. *Cicero* 43.7). In certain cases, for example, with respect to the public water supply, the use of *coercitio* could even involve intrusion upon the property rights of private persons.[2]

The most severe measures, scourging and decapitation, were banned once the plebeians had succeeded in establishing the right of appeal to the popular assembly (*provocatio*), instead of being subjected to the arbitrary action of the magistrates. This is not the place to deal with the vexed question of the development of *imperium* and *provocatio* during the so-called Struggle of the Orders (Martin 1970; Lintott 1972; Humbert 1988). It will suffice to state that from the Middle Republic onward – say, from the passage of the *lex Valeria de provocatione* in 300 – a ban on scourging and execution within the city was formally recognized and that later, with the *leges Porciae* of the early second century, it was supported by the introduction of a penalty for the violation of *provocatio* and the exemption of citizens from these measures in Italy and the provinces as well, the tendency of some provincial governors to ignore claims notwithstanding (Cic. *2 In Verrem* 5.163; *Fam.* 10.32.3; Lintott 1993: 68). Exemption from the humiliation of corporal punishment underlined the distinction between citizens and Roman subjects (including Italian notables, as some scandalous second-century cases show: see quotations in Gell. *NA* 10.3), as well as between citizens and slaves (Saller 1991). Thus, *provocatio* had become an essential aspect of *libertas* (Livy 3.45.8; Cic. *2 Verr.* 5.163).

Decapitation with the axe was preceded by scourging with rods, probably a sacral rite serving to expel the delinquent from the community and avoid polluting citizens (and the scourging lictors) with his blood (Gladigow 1972: 311–12). Some well-known cases in which this sort of capital coercion was applied show that its primary purpose was to enforce military discipline (Val. Max. 2.7.6).[3] This was the case with mutinous soldiers (e.g., in the Spanish theatre of war in 206: Livy 28.29.11), and in a spectacular way when an example was made of a member of the aristocracy itself. The famous story of the execution of his son by T. Manlius

---

[2] As a rule the magistrates would, however, arrange for adequate financial compensation (Pennitz 1991).

[3] Cf. the suggestion by Timpe (1990: 379–9) that the original purpose was to impede private warfare. On *disciplina militaris* as complementary to *imperium*, see Lind (1986: 61–7).

Imperiosus Torquatus in 340 (below p. 31), and the tradition of political conflicts in which a *dictator* threatened to use *coercitio* against his *magister equitum*, reported for 325 and 217 (Livy 8.32.8–10, 22.27.3), provide conspicuous illustrations. There are also some cases of exemplary punishment in which the property of citizens was confiscated or even the persons themselves sold into slavery for having refused to respond to a levy or to declare their property at the census or for having deserted the colours (Livy, *Periochae* 14, 55; Varro quoted by Nonius p. 28 L; Val. Max. 6.3.4; Dion. Hal. *Ant. Rom.* 4.15.6). The first recorded instance is in 275; magistrates probably had developed this practice as a sort of substitute for the measures banned by the laws of *provocatio* (Drummond 1989: 221).

Additional power to enforce military discipline against groups of citizens lay with the censors, who could demote persons charged with neglect of their duties; for example, four hundred knights were deprived of their public horses in 252 (Val. Max. 2.9.7; Frontin. *Strategemata* 4.1.22), and two thousand ordinary citizens were reduced to the status of *aerarius*, which probably meant loss of voting rights and/or liability to increased taxation, in 214 (Livy 24.18.7–8). In 204 one censor even threatened to treat in this way the members of all but one of the thirty-five tribes (Livy 29.37.13). In other cases censors enforced rules concerning public land and water supply by fining trespassers (who probably belonged to the higher social classes) and removing buildings which had been illegally erected.[4]

In the great majority of cases reported from the Middle Republic onward involving measures such as temporary imprisonment, fining or seizing a pledge (*pignoris capio*), it was a matter of conflict within the ruling élite: a higher magistrate opposing a lower one (Livy 42.9.4) or debarring a candidate for office who was not properly qualified (Val. Max. 9.7.1), a consul disciplining a senator who refused to appear (Varro quoted by Gell. *NA* 14.7.10; Stroux 1938), or a consul in the chair confronting a senator who tried to obstruct the proceedings (Ateius Capito quoted by Gell. *NA* 4.10.8).[5] Examples include the clash between the consul L. Marcius Philippus and the former censor L. Licinius Crassus in 91 (Cic. *De oratore* 3.4), and Caesar's attempt in 59 to stop Cato's filibuster

[4] E.g., in 184 (Cato, *ORF* no. 8, fr. 99–105; Livy 39.44.4) and in 169 (Livy 43.16.4–5).
[5] For cases in which the *sella curulis* of a praetor was smashed by order of a consul or tribune, see David and Dondin (1980).

by having him imprisoned (Suet. *Divus Iulius* 20.4). As a rule, these political demonstrations were quickly abandoned either voluntarily or upon the intervention of tribunes. Although the enforcement of general rules by way of *coercitio* was subject to highly erratic decisions arising from conflicts between individual officials, even their rather idiosyncratic employment underlined their general validity.

The censors similarly supervised morality (*regimen morum*), whether formal rules such as the sumptuary laws or simply the generally accepted standards which the Romans liked to ascribe to ancestral tradition (*mos maiorum*) (Polay 1971; Astin 1988; Baltrusch 1989). Public morality in the Roman Republic was not (or not primarily) a matter of disciplining the bulk of the citizenry. In practice, senators and knights were the chief objects of censorial punishment, which took the form of loss of membership of the Senate and of public horses respectively (see Livy 4.8.2). Apart from the dramatic cases mentioned above, these measures would as a rule be applied to small numbers – an individual senator or a few dozen knights – and only at intervals of five or often more years. The underlying assumptions were that the upper classes ought to control themselves and that their proper conduct, on the one hand, and the loss of honour for some of their members, on the other, would set an example for the citizenry as a whole (Cic. *Leg.* 3.28–9). Thus the story went that during the censorship of Tiberius Sempronius Gracchus in 169 people put out their lamps when the censor returned home after supper in fear of being suspected of indulging in drinking bouts (Plut. *Tiberius Gracchus* 14.3). Some censors are known to have addressed the general public on public morals (for example, Gell. *NA* 5.19.15 on Scipio Aemilianus).

There was no defined catalogue of offences which the censors might punish, and there were no theoretical limits to the spheres of conduct which they might review. Greek observers were amazed that not even the most private spheres were excluded from censorial scrutiny – that censors' authority, as Dionysius of Halicarnassus (*Ant. Rom.* 20.13.3) put it, extended even to the bedchamber. The Greeks (with the possible exception of the Spartans) knew no real equivalent: freedom from intervention in the private realm had always been characteristic of Athenian democratic ideology and practice (Thuc. 2.37.2). Even institutions such as the so-called *gynaikonomoi* (supervisors of women) as they are known from Athens under the autocratic régime of Demetrius of Phalerum (317–307 BC) and from other Greek cities, though they were apparently used to enforce specific rules regarding banquets and the public appearance of women, did not, as far as we know, violate the boundary between public and private spheres in the way the Roman censors appeared to do (Athenaeus 245a–c; 521b–c; cf. Arist. *Politics* 1322b37–23a5; Wehrli 1962; Gehrke 1978). This impression had obviously been created by certain incidents which, though unusual, had become part of the stock of examples associated with the censorship, for example, the elder Cato's expulsion of a senator for having kissed his wife (or having embraced her more intimately) in broad daylight in front of his daughter (Plut. *Cato Maior* 17.7). Erratic decisions and, indeed, measures primarily motivated by political or even personal concerns, could be considered part of the rationale for the institution provided they were presented as based on generally accepted standards.

The censors could not, however, systematically scrutinize the private and public conduct of senators and knights. Compliance with the sumptuary laws, with their detailed rules about numbers of guests, annual outlays for dinners, etc., was unverifiable (Gruen 1990: 172–3). As a rule the censors would respond only if illicit behaviour had become a matter of common knowledge or at least rumour, or if fellow-citizens had denounced it (Macrob. *Saturnalia* 3.17.1). It was for the censor to decide whether to act on his own initiative or wait for a member of the public to come forward with a specific accusation (Val. Max. 6.2.8). Scipio Aemilianus declared in 142 that he would not proceed against a knight suspected of perjury if no one was prepared to accuse him (Cic. *Pro Cluentio* 134; Val. Max. 4.1.10); this was apparently an unusual proceeding, again demonstrating the range of discretion that the censors could exercise. They would, as a rule, give the accused person a formal hearing, but could proceed without one (Tatum 1990a: 38). Like that of *coercitio*, the public effect of censorial punishment depended not on its blanket application to the greatest possible number of violators of public order, but on its exemplary and unpredictable use especially against members of the upper classes.

The same pattern recurs with respect to the tribunes of the people, who could also have recourse to a sort of coercive action (see catalogue of cases in Thommen 1989: 187–91). These powers, however, like their function as public prosecutors (Bleicken 1968: 106–49), stemmed from the sacrosanctity which had allowed them to usurp rights during the Struggle of the Orders (when in their confrontations with the patrician magistrates the tribunes had been backed up by the plebeians' oath to slay anybody who touched a tribune). As a consequence, they could employ their equivalent of *coercitio* only directly and in person; for example, they could arrest citizens on the spot but were not entitled to issue summonses (Labeo and Varro cited by Gell. *NA* 13.12.4, 6). The most spectacular actions – throwing someone from the Tarpeian Rock or consecrating his goods to Ceres, the goddess of the *plebs* – revealed most clearly the origin of these powers in the tribunes' primitive function of defending individual plebeians, as well as the rights of the plebeian community as a whole, against encroachments by the then exclusively patrician magistrates (Dion. Hal. *Ant. Rom.* 7.17.5; Cic. *De domo sua* 123–5). From the Middle Republic onward, the tribunes had also undertaken to curb obstinate members of the ruling élite on behalf of the Senate (Bleicken 1968: 83–94). Thus in 109 a censor whose colleague had died in office was persuaded to abdicate only by the tribunes' threat to imprison him (Plut. *Moralia* 276F), whereas the same course of action against the censor Ap. Claudius Caecus in 310 had failed because three tribunes had accepted his appeal (Livy 9.34.26). In most cases the use of coercion by tribunes was simply a component of conflict within the political élite; as a rule its ultimate consequences were avoided, if need be, by the intervention of another tribune. The intercession of colleagues, even if there had been no formal appeal to them, was the only remedy available against a tribune who exceeded the specific competences of this peculiar magistracy. Thus, for example, in 131 C. Atinius Labeo was restrained from carrying out the archaic ritual on the Tarpeian Rock against the former censor who had declined to appoint him to the Senate (Livy, *Per.* 59; Pliny, *Historia naturalis* 7.143).

The tribunate performed an ambivalent role as at once the defender of the people's rights and liberty and the arm of the Senate. Tribunes were entitled to prevent any coercion (even in connection with private law suits) of a citizen initiated by another magistrate (Thommen 1989: 233–41). Helping the individual citizen, even in cases in which the magistrate's action was not excessive and the tribunate as a whole would not be prepared to intervene, was the rationale for the institution. Thus, apparently, ran the argument of the tribune of 58 who supported a henchman of

Clodius against a praetor although he himself had been assaulted by the Clodian on a previous occasion (Asc. p. 47, 1–9 (Clark)). The tribunate also provided scope for patronage: thus the dramatic clash between P. Rutilius and the censors in 169 is ascribed to the tribune's intervention on behalf of one of his own freedmen (Livy 43.16.4). Again, the conflict in 138 between two tribunes and the consuls, which led to the consuls' imprisonment, originated in the tribunes' demand to nominate ten exemptions from military service each (Livy, *Per.* 55). It was also on the occasion of an unpopular levy that both consuls had been imprisoned in 151 by tribunes who had failed to obtain exemptions (Livy, *Per.* 48; Taylor 1962).

As a rule, the tribunes would proceed against other magistrates and against private citizens only if someone had shown contempt for the office (see Plut. *Caius Gracchus* 3.3; Pliny, *Epistulae* 1.23.2). Nevertheless, they alone were in a position to decide that a citizen should be subjected to coercion. In the first place they could reject a citizen's appeal and submit the case to the Senate.[6] Such a grave decision was apparently for the tribunes as a college to make, and it would hold only if every one of them adhered to it.[7] In extreme cases, the imprisonment of persons, as a rule only a temporary measure, might thus be prolonged for years (Pliny, *HN* 21.8) or perhaps even indefinitely (Livy 39.18.3). For example, a leading centurion (*primipilarius*) arrested for homosexual intercourse with a youth died in prison because the tribunes had refused to release him (Val. Max. 6.1.10). At the same time, the power of tribunes to free prisoners could amount to a veritable obstruction of justice.[8] Secondly, tribunes could act on their own whenever they saw a danger to public order[9] and/or a threat to the liberty of the

---

[6] In the affair of the alleged Numa books in 181, the tribunes refused to support the owner against the praetor, who wanted to burn the books, and submitted the case to the Senate. The Senate voted that the tribunes should participate in the decision about financial compensation (Livy 40.29.11–3). For further examples from the Middle Republic, see Bleicken (1968: 84). There is, however, no evidence for such a procedure in Late Republican times (Thommen 1989: 235).

[7] When L. Cornelius Scipio, after his conviction, refused to pay the heavy fine imposed on him, the decision of one tribune to have him imprisoned was approved by eight tribunes but annulled by the tenth (Gell. *NA* 6.19; Livy 38.60).

[8] Gladiators who had confessed to acts of violence were set free in 57 (Cic. *Pro Sestio* 85); in 52 a slave who had probably been involved in the murder of Clodius was returned to Milo, his master (Asc. p. 37, 13–6).

[9] In 104 the tribune Cn. Domitius Ahenobarbus arrested and later returned a slave who had sought to give evidence against his master, whom the tribune had indicted before the assembly (Cic. *Pro rege Deiotaro* 31).

People. In 102 a tribune (in opposition to the opinion of the Senate) prevented a Galatian priest of the Magna Mater cult from prophesying a Roman victory over the Cimbrians in front of the assembly (Plut. *Marius* 17.5–6). The tribune Trebonius took action against Cato for trying to obstruct legislation by way of the filibuster in 55 (Plut. *Cato Minor* 43.2–4). It was tribunes who in 44 removed a diadem from Caesar's statue, and arrested the person who had fixed it there along with the claqueurs who had hailed Caesar as king when he returned to Rome from the Latin Festival (Nic. Dam. *Caesar* 20.5; Plut. *Caesar* 61.8). Alas for them, Caesar's angry reaction led to a bill which deprived both tribunes, L. Caesetius Flavus and C. Epidius Marullus, of their offices (Kloft 1980).

All in all, *coercitio* appears to have been more an instrument for controlling members of the ruling class than a means of disciplining the man in the Roman street. This reflects the Roman aristocracy's willingness to submit itself to rules which demonstrated its commitment to the public interest on the assumption that the docility of the lower classes would follow. This picture may, of course, be partially due to the bias of our sources, which tend to report spectacular instances rather than everyday practice, but any estimated number of unknown cases in which coercion was employed has to be balanced by a complementary assumption about intercessions by the tribunes. Furthermore, examination of the role of the magistrates' auxiliaries underlines the point that this assessment of the role of *coercitio* is not simply a function of the perspective of our sources.

Auxiliaries

The magistrates had at their disposal a staff of permanent and relatively well-paid public servants (*apparitores*), organized in corporations (*decuriae*) of scribes, lictors, criers and summoners (Jones 1960; Eck 1978: 43; Purcell 1983; Cohen 1984; Badian 1989). They included both free-born citizens and freedmen, for whom membership might mean a considerable increase in social status, reputation and income; a magistrate might even fill a vacancy with a client of his own (Livy 40.29.10). In addition, there was a sizeable number of public slaves who performed a variety of tasks, especially in the maintenance of public buildings and property (Eder 1980). However, it was apparently considered inadmissible for public slaves to carry out even moderately coercive measures against citizens.[10]

The Romans' attitude towards using public slaves was strikingly different from that of the Athenians. For more than a hundred years from the earlier fifth century onward, Athens made use of a body of Scythians who as public slaves assisted the presiding magistrates or councillors in maintaining public order during assemblies and court proceedings (Pl. *Protagoras* 319c; Aeschin. 2.173).[11] Being dragged away from the platform by barbarian slaves must have been particularly humiliating (Hall 1989: 44–7); unfortunately, there is no convincing explanation why the Athenians nevertheless made such use of them. The references to the Scythians in the Aristophanic comedies give a contradictory picture; in some instances they are said to be feared, in other cases laughed at (Long 1986:104–7). In any case, their functions were later taken over by subdivisions of the citizenry (Busolt-Swoboda 1920–6: II, 980, 995; Hunter 1994: 145–49).

The lictors carried the fasces, probably of Etruscan origin (Sil. *Punica* 8.483–4), bundles of rods with projecting axe-blades which served as instruments as well as symbols of physical coercion (*insignia imperii*) (Livy 1.8.2; Gladigow 1972; Marshall 1984; Drews 1972; Schäfer 1989). They are said to have produced terror, especially in the subjects of Roman domination abroad (e.g., Cic. *De lege agraria* 1.9), whereas within the city the axe-blade was removed from them (Cic. *De republica* 2.55). Magistrates with *imperium* never appeared in public without their lictors (twelve for consuls, two or six for praetors), even when they were going about for purely private reasons. Hence the warning – however seriously meant – to a praetor that being thus accompanied to the threshold of a brothel would violate the dignity of his office (Sen. *Controversiae* 9.2.17).

The lictors, again, could fulfil tasks which might imply coercion only when the magistrates were present. (Serving a summons was the task of a *viator*.) This means that they could not relieve the magistrate of the duty of physical confrontation with the recipients of his orders. Walking in single file in front of the magistrate, they

---

[10] In the provinces magistrates could also make use of bailiffs such as the *Bruttiani*, men from Bruttium who because of their alliance with Hannibal were not treated as *socii* (Gell. *NA* 10.3.17–9), or temple slaves such as the Sicilian *Venerii servi* (Eppers and Heinen 1984).
[11] Their suggested identity with the Scythian archers probably bought for military purposes (Andoc. 3.5, 7) is dubious (Plassart 1913).

did not even serve as an effective bodyguard. The armed body-guards ascribed to tyrannical kings and the *decemviri* of 450 (the committee of ten that had been installed for the codification of law but then assumed arbitrary power) are clearly differentiated from the lictors in the sources (e.g., Livy 1.15.8; 3.48–9). The rule that no one was allowed to step between the last lictor and the magistrate, except his underage sons (Val. Max. 2.2.4), indicates that this arrangement was thought to create a taboo zone. The lictors had primarily a symbolic function, to 'represent the magistrate's legitimate claim upon reverence and obedience' (Mommsen 1871–88: 1, 376).

This was especially the case after the establishment of *provocatio*, but the annalistic accounts (which may be coloured by Late Republican experience) suggest that it applied as well to the Early Republic. Confronted by the plebeian masses, magistrates found themselves unable to single out a ringleader for exemplary punishment when the person concerned was backed by the crowd or protected by a tribune's intervention. This was not just a matter of the crowd's outnumbering the lictors. Rather, they were never employed to disperse a crowd, and there was no question of their using their rods (*virgae*) indiscriminately to apply physical force. The rods were untied, on the magistrate's explicit order, only when the delinquent had already been seized, stripped of his clothes and bound to a stake. This grim ritual required acceptance of the lictors as representatives of the magistrate's authority: hence sometimes only one lictor was disposed to seize a ringleader (*dux seditionum*; Livy 2.27.12). In his account of the Volero Publilius conflict in 473, Livy has the crowd reason that the lictors' power consisted solely in the plebeians' respect for them (2.55.3).

By clearing the way and exacting reverence for a magistrate, the lictors constantly evoked citizens' deference to the authorities. The breaking of their fasces by an angry crowd, as is reported for the Late Republic (e.g., Dio Cass. 38.6.3; Asc. p. 58, 14–24) and supposed for the Struggle of the Orders (e.g., Livy 2.55.9, 3.49.4), symbolized flagrant disregard for the authority of the magistrates concerned.

The symbolism associated with lictors and fasces is underlined by a number of rituals and traditions. For example, the lictors changed their dress from toga to military cloak according to the *habitus* of the magistrates they served (Cic. *In Pisonem* 55); at a funeral, lictors represented the offices that a defunct *nobilis* had occupied during his lifetime (Polyb. 6.53.8); the *dictator* had twenty-four lictors at his disposal (Polyb. 3.87.7); the consul of the Republic's first year, Valerius Publicola, is said to have acknowledged the supremacy of the People by lowering the fasces in front of the assembly (Livy 2.7.7; Cic. *Rep.* 1.62). It is worth stressing that the lictors were also regarded as symbolizing, so to speak, the magistrates' civilian as opposed to purely military authority (see Pliny, *Panegyricus* 23.3; Claudianus, *De quarto consulatu Honorii* 1–17). Thus Mark Antony was reproached for having been accompanied as master of the horse (as the *dictator* Caesar's deputy in 48 and 47) not only by the six lictors assigned to this office but also by soldiers; this was held to have revealed his tyrannical aspirations (Dio Cass. 42.27.2).

Stressing the primarily symbolic function of lictors does not entail denying them a practical role, but one should not conclude on the basis of standards of modern policing that they constituted too small and inefficient a force. They and the other groups of *apparitores* did, of course, assist the magistrates in maintaining order at public assemblies, trials in the Forum, in front of the Senate's meeting place, and during public festivals. In addition, the magistrates were regularly accompanied by privately recruited helpers, retainers and clients, who, however, tended not to be employed for direct coercion (see Val. Max. 9.5.2). Supervision of voting and the counting of votes were entrusted to persons of high reputation, especially members of the panel of jurors or even senators (Pliny, *HN* 33.31; Cic. *Pis.* 36; *Post reditum in Senatu* 28; Plut. *Cat. Min.* 46.2). Candidates were entitled to nominate watchers at the ballot-boxes, as is known from an incident during the elections of aediles in 50, when one such *custos*, who had apparently tried to tamper with the box, was delivered to the consul by supporters of other candidates (Varro, *Rust.* 3.5.18).

In general terms, controlling the crowds at these public events presented no serious problems. Forum and *comitium* were the places in which rulers and ruled met (Witt 1926; Millar 1989; Patterson 1992: 190–4), in which political decisions were justified, debated and formally ratified, and in which citizens exercised their right of participation – a right of which not even the poorest, however irrelevant his vote for the final result, was deprived (Cic. *Rep.* 2.39–40; Livy 1.43.10). Magistrates and senators needed no protection

from their subjects, and the Senate even met regularly with the
doors left open. Disputes in the Senate might, however, provoke
tumult outside (see Livy 1.48.2). Noisy interference from bystanders might lead to the dissolution of a meeting (Cic. *Epistulae ad
Quintum fratrem* 2.1.3), and in a turbulent scene in 56 tribunes of the
people had to prevent demonstrators from entering the chamber
(Dio Cass. 39.28.2–3). Special guards were thought necessary,
however, only under extreme circumstances (e.g., in December 63
at the height of the Catilinarian conspiracy), and no one considered
banning the public from the area round the Senate's meeting
places. Finally, there were no politically, religiously or ethnically
constituted parties or permanent factions whose members were
likely to clash.

This is not to paint an idealized picture of the Roman political
process, but only to underline that public mass meetings, necessarily involving a certain degree of noise if not disorder, were a
routine affair. They were not extraordinary demonstrations that
would require authorities to take precautions against popular
violence. We will see how the authorities could react if serious
disturbances did for any reason occur.

EVERYDAY POLICE FUNCTIONS

Maintaining public welfare and order was partly the responsibility
of the aediles and various boards of minor magistrates. Some of
their tasks were derived from those of the higher magistrates, while
others were conferred on them in particular; some were permanent
and others the result of ad hoc commissions by the Senate and the
higher magistrates. They combined a variety of functions which in
Greek cities and especially in democratic Athens – always very
anxious to define carefully the competences of magistrates
(Aeschin. 3.14–5, 29) – were entrusted to boards that had the
power to impose minor fines (Aeschin. 3.27; Arist. *Pol.* 1299b14–8,
1321b6–27; *Athenaion Politeia* 50–1; Pl. *Leges* 763c–e; Stanley 1979;
Hansen 1980; Klingenberg 1983; Owens 1983). The most detailed
information on such officials is, however, provided by a Pergamum
inscription containing a law on city controllers (*astynomoi*) from the
Attalid period (Austin 1981: 352–6; cf. Hansen 1971: 191–8).

The Roman aristocracy's principle of making do with a small
number of magistrates without any clear hierarchy of responsibility

(Martin 1985: 224) produced a certain amount of overlap of functions between aediles, on the one hand, and the censors, praetors, quaestors and minor magistrates, on the other.[12] Responsibility for fire prevention and fire-fighting, for instance, was shared by the aediles and the *tresviri capitales*, but in especially serious cases the consul was expected to appear on the scene (Cic. *Pis.* 26) and even the tribunes are said to have been involved (*Dig.* 1.15.1).

In addition to the corn supply and public games, the aediles were responsible for urban order (*cura urbis*) – the supervision of markets, public baths (Sen. *Epistulae* 86.10), eating houses, taverns and perhaps brothels (see Sen. *De vita beata* 7.3),[13] and the cleaning, maintenance, repair and accessibility of streets, public places and temples (Frei-Stolba 1989; Robinson 1992: 59–82; cf. Sonnabend 1992 on traffic regulations). It is difficult to see how they could have adequately performed so many functions. They had no *imperium* (and accordingly no accompanying lictors), were not authorized to summon or arrest citizens, and enjoyed no immunity with respect to civil proceedings during their term of office. In the lawsuits with regard to market transactions in slaves and cattle over which they presided, they lacked the power of the praetors to implement their decisions (Kaser 1963).

In general, the aediles were not supposed to have the higher magistrates' indisputable claim to obedience and reverence, although certain incumbents in Late Republican times tried to exact it (Suet. *Nero* 4; Varro quoted by Gell. *NA* 13.13.4). In addition to their *apparitores* they could employ public slaves (Varro quoted by Gell. *NA* 13.13.4), but we do not know much about the use they made of them in everyday practice. It does not follow, however, that they had no effective means of disciplining individuals who violated the rules of public order. I leave aside their role in prosecuting a number of Middle Republican cases which resulted in extremely high fines that were then spent on public buildings or festivals. The variety of offences involved in these cases

---

[12] See, e.g., the responsibility of the quaestor posted in Ostia (established by 104) with respect to the corn supply and its transportation to Rome (Cic. *Sest.* 39; *De Haruspicum responso* 43) and the involvement of praetors in corn distributions (Asc. p. 59, 18–19).

[13] This does not mean the compulsory registration of prostitutes; the application for such registration by women of rank seeking to avoid the Augustan penalty for adultery was prohibited under Tiberius (Tac. *Ann.* 2.85; Suet. *Tiberius* 35.1; Daube (1986) and McGinn (1992: 281–4).

– from profiteering by money lending and corn speculation through illegal occupation of public land to sexual misconduct – can only partly be understood as deriving from their administrative functions. In other cases there must have been an ad hoc demand to prosecute scandals (like Claudia's insulting the Roman people in 246; Gell. *NA* 10.6), and the aediles assumed responsibility for bringing the cases before the popular assembly (Lintott 1968: 96–8; Bauman 1974b; Garofalo 1989: 99–140).

The aediles were capable of imposing fines up to a certain sum (Tac. *Annales* 13.28.2), confiscating false weights (Juv. 10.100–2; Persius 1.129–30) or shoddy goods (see Plaut. *Rudens* 372), and removing obstacles to traffic (*Dig.* 18.6.13). Measures probably varied with the status of the person involved. Respectable persons would have been able to quarrel with an aedile (see Cic. *Fam.* 8.6.4; Frontin. *De aquae ductu urbis Romae* 76). As a rule the aedile would have been somewhat feared in the milieu of the brothels and seedy eating-houses (*popinae*), which also served as gambling dens (Sen. *De vita beata* 7.3; Mart. 5.84). But not even persons of dubious reputation would necessarily put up with an aedile's grossly over-stepping his authority. This is revealed by the story of the harlot who had violently repulsed a drunken aedile's attempt to force entry into her house; the tribunes intervened to prevent his bringing a suit against her before the People, declaring that the woman had acted rightfully (Gell. *NA* 4.14). One should also consider the revealing report from AD 22 that the petty tradesmen who operated *popinae* managed to avoid penalties by claiming to be Roman knights (which, ultimately, led to a redefinition of who was entitled to wear a knight's golden ring; Pliny, *HN* 33.32). In general, the office of aedile did not amount to an agency for regulating the conduct of the lower classes.

One effective means of enforcing the rules of public order may have been to make violators financially liable. Each aedile was responsible for the streets in one of the city's four regions; the assignments were made by agreement or by drawing lots (*Tabula Heracleensis* 24–8). They were supported in this task by the sub-magistrates called *quattuorviri viis in urbe purgandis* and *duoviri viis extra urbem purgandis*. The amount of work would have increased considerably with the growth of the city and the improvement of its infrastructure: the first paving of city streets was initiated by the censors of 174 (Livy 41.27.5). The magistrates were authorized to shift the responsibility for street maintenance onto the adjacent house-owners. If one of these neglected his duties the aedile would award the job to a contractor and charge the house-owner with the costs (*Tab. Her.* 29–31).[14] The aediles also appointed two residents or property owners in each quarter (*vicus*) to oversee the public fountains (Frontin. *Aq.* 97).

The role of citizens

Some rules may have been enforced through the lawsuits which citizens could initiate whether their interests were directly at issue or not (*actiones populares*).[15] Thus regulations published by the aedile's edict concerning the conduct of funerals (Cic. *Phil.* 9.17; cf. Ovid, *Fasti* 6.663–4) may have been enforced by the threat of indictment by another citizen.[16] There is, however, no direct evidence for this; we can only infer it from municipal laws.[17] For example, a clause of the *Tabula Heracleensis* (17–19), which for purposes of municipal legislation selects relevant ordinances from various Roman laws down to Caesar's time, reveals that a suit could be brought against an official charged with violating the rules for the public distribution of corn. It does not, however, say how a person who illegally obtained corn should be prosecuted. The recently discovered *lex Irnitana* (75) of Flavian times (González 1986; cf. Galsterer 1988) contains a provision against the buying up and hoarding of foodstuffs which may be based on earlier Roman precedents. The *Tabula Heracleensis* and the Caesarian charter for Urso (*lex coloniae genetivae Iuliae Ursonensis*) have several such provisions, aimed both at holding municipal officials to the letter of the law, and at enforcing citizens' observance of rules such as the reservation of special seats for councillors (*decuriones*) at the public games (*lex Ursonensis* 125).

One incentive for bringing a suit on behalf of the public interest

---

[14] The passage refers directly to the rules of the city of Rome; compare the corresponding Hellenistic law from Pergamum referred to above.

[15] Since Bruns (1882) and Mommsen (1907), however, there has been scholarly controversy over the interpretation of this category.

[16] Desecration of graves could be prosecuted by any citizen and was punished by large fines (*Dig.* 47.12.3; Behrends 1978).

[17] See the inscription from Luceria, *ILS* 4912, and the charter for Urso 73–6 (Johnston 1989).

is of course a reward for the accuser,[18] and such a provision is known from a decree of AD 11 regulating the public water-supply for the city of Rome (Frontin. *Aq.* 127) and from municipal charters in connection with certain building-regulations (Garnsey 1976: 133–6). The general problem with such provisions is that they may also be an incentive for abuse. Complaints about informers who allegedly made a business out of bringing a suit, especially in cases which involved financial interests, are a standard subject of Athenian sources.[19] The *quadruplatores*, known from Plautine comedy (*Persa* 62–74) and mentioned in another source as accusers of gamblers (Ps.-Asconius, p. 194, 11–13 (Stangl)), were apparently, though not beyond doubt, a Roman equivalent (De Martino 1955; Danilovič 1974).

During the reign of Tiberius, the problematic reliance on informers was discussed with respect to the sumptuary laws, the doubtful efficacy of which is indicated by their repeated re-enactment from the Middle Republic onward (Macrob. *Sat.* 3.17). Tiberius rejected an initiative by aediles pleading for better enforcement of these rules, which in the Republican period had from time to time been supported by the sanctions that censors could impose upon senators and knights. Caesar employed special watches over markets as well as soldiers and lictors to enforce his sumptuary law of 46 (Suet. *Iul.* 43.2). This was an extraordinary and apparently a temporary measure; in any case, it did not prove a great success (Cic. *Epistulae ad Atticum* 13.7.1). The view taken by Tiberius was that the efficacy of the sumptuary laws was a matter of self-regulation within the élite; otherwise one would have to resort to informers and put up with all the negative consequences of this (Tac. *Ann.* 3.54, 56.1). This argument shows that even during the Principate one might be prepared to accept certain deficiencies of law enforcement if improvement would have unpleasant implications. It was quite another matter that, despite complaints, informer-accusers in cases of treason were considered indispensable

---

[18] Compare the provisions of the criminal law: *praemia* were apparently not offered for all kinds of criminal prosecution, but were especially established for cases (such as electoral bribery) in which no victim (or other person on behalf of a victim) was likely to undertake prosecution (Alexander 1985).

[19] See the definitions of *sykophantes* quoted by Ath. 74e–f (MacDowell 1978: 62–6). It is difficult, however, to assess the social reality behind the complaints; compare the divergent accounts of Osborne (1990) and Harvey (1990).

by Tiberius and his successors, and that senators would denounce each other as a way of winning the emperor's favour (Flaig 1992: 114–15). Similarly, the benefits for informers provided by the Augustan marriage laws were upheld for fiscal reasons (Brunt 1971: 566; Nörr 1977: 316; Wallace-Hadrill 1981),[20] irrespective of all the complaints they provoked and of exemplary measures against informers in fiscal matters (Gaudemet 1980; Brunt 1984: 479–80; Giovannini 1986).

It is impossible to assess the degree of effectiveness achieved by the aediles or the way in which the combination of magisterial supervision, the practical work of auxiliaries, and societal self-control operated and changed during the Republican period and the early Principate. However, the foregoing discussion should caution us against judging them by modern standards.

Aediles and crowds

As the magistrates responsible for the majority of public games (until 22 BC, when this task was transferred to the praetors), the aediles had to ensure the proper conduct of both actors and audiences.[21] They were authorized to punish actors physically (Plaut. *Trinummus* 990; Suet. *Divus Augustus* 45.3–4). Actors were usually non-citizens; a citizen who became an actor (or even a gladiator) would be declared infamous (Cic. *Rep.* 4.10; *Dig.* 3.2.2.5), which involved various restrictions of his civil rights (Ducos 1990; Leppin 1992: 71–83; Barton 1989: 9–11; Gardner 1993: 110–54).[22] Probably more important were the agreements the magistrates made in advance with the directors of the companies, especially concerning the choice of plays, since these might inflame the audience. (Direct attacks on individuals were forbidden and could be answered with a charge of *iniuria* by the person

[20] On structural parallels in early modern England, see Elton (1958), Beresford (1958) and Winslow (1975).
[21] On the maintenance of order in the Athenian theatre, see Pickard-Cambridge (1968: 273).
[22] Arena and stage performances by senators and knights (first attested in 46 BC) were prohibited in the early Principate; thus attempts by members of the higher orders to evade the prohibition by engineering their infamy (Suet. *Tib.* 35.2) were excluded (Daube 1986: 3–5; Levick 1983; and Lebek 1990a on the Larinum inscription which contains a Senate decree from AD 19). Nero, however, not only performed himself but also induced and compelled knights and senators to do so (Tac. *Ann.* 14.14.4, 14.20.3–4; Juv. 8.183–210).

concerned; *Rhetorica ad Herennium* 1.24, 2.19.) If trouble did occur, director and company would have to face financial sanctions, annulment of salary, and loss of the opportunity to perform in the future (Gizewski 1989: 96–8). Private organizers of gladiatorial games were reminded by the aediles that they had to ensure proper conduct on the part of the spectators; hence the revealing edict of 56, which provided that only fruit and not stones might be thrown into the arena (Macrob. *Sat.* 2.6.1).

The aediles and the minor magistrates had difficulty coping with refractory crowds, as an event of 213 reveals (Livy 25.1.6–12; cf. Bauman 1972). After protests from indignant citizens and after censure and exhortation by the Senate, the aediles and the *tresviri capitales* took action against the practice of foreign cults in public places, and only narrowly escaped violence when they tried to eject the crowd from the Forum and to destroy the places of worship which had been installed there. The Senate responded by placing the urban praetor in charge of the suppression of the cults, and he was apparently successful in enforcing a ban on the public practice of foreign cults and the confiscation of all books on those rites. The alertness of those 'better' citizens who had already shown their irritation about the incidents certainly contributed greatly to this resolution of the affair. The story in itself shows that, although the minor magistrates were supposed to prevent such public nuisances, in tense moments the authority of the higher magistrates was needed. In cases in which the aediles and the *tresviri capitales* organized special guards or carried out arrests and searches, they acted under a special mandate from the Senate and the higher magistrates (below pp. 27–8).

The tresviri capitales

The three-man board known as the *tresviri capitales*, commonly understood as police magistrates of a kind, was established shortly after 290. Its name was derived from its supervision of the jail (used primarily for detaining accused persons awaiting trial) and of the executions which took place there (*Dig.* 1.2.2.30). Their best-documented task is the organization of a night fire-brigade composed of public slaves (*Dig.* 1.15.1). Neglect of this duty on one occasion – probably during the great fire of 241 – led to the condemnation of a college of *tresviri* by the People (Val. Max. 8.1. damn. 5). In this task they may later have been supported by the *quinqueviri uls cis Tiberim* if we assume that these officials, of whose existence we learn only in connection with the emergency measures of 186 (Livy 39.14.10), became a permanent institution (*Dig.* 1.2.2.31; Pailler 1985).

It is sometimes argued that in connection with their night patrols the *tresviri capitales* also fulfilled a sort of general police function, especially as they were somewhat feared by the ordinary people in the milieu Plautus depicts (e.g., *Aulularia* 416–17). The *tresviri capitales* were indeed authorized to arrest and punish runaway slaves (Plaut. *Amphitruo* 153–62; Asc. p. 37, 8–16), but this does not necessarily mean that they searched for them. Nothing is definitely known about the status and functions of the underlings at their disposal – 'eight strong men' according to Plautus. It is inadvisable to generalize on the basis of certain extraordinary situations (see Pliny, *HN* 21.8 on an incident during the Second Punic War), or moments of crisis in which the *tresviri capitales* acted by special command of the Senate and the chief magistrates. This is not of course to say that they were weak officials, or to rule out the possibility that their functions were more comprehensive in scope than the sources directly reveal.

The idea that the *tresviri capitales* (as auxiliaries of the praetors in this respect) exercised summary criminal jurisdiction over ordinary citizens and slaves was developed by W. Kunkel as part of his re-interpretation of the development of Roman criminal law (1962: 71–9). Exploiting the scarce and equivocal hints of criminal pro-ceedings before the *tresviri* in the sources (esp. Cic. *Clu.* 39–40; *Divinatio in Caecilium* 50; Ps.-Asconius, p. 201, 20–1 (Stangl)), Kunkel hypothesized that ordinary crimes were not subjected to the cumbersome, time-consuming proceedings in the popular assembly (and later in the jury courts) but prosecuted *ex officio* by the *tresviri capitales*, and that the latter could impose and execute the death penalty even on citizens of humble origin.

This conjecture implies that the nobility would have sacrificed the principle of citizens' equality before the law to cope with the problems of law and order. It also suggests – against the available evidence down to the Principate (Robinson 1981) – that consider-able numbers of slaves were no longer under the control of their masters, so that slave delinquency could no longer be dealt with in domestic trials (e.g., Plut. *Cat. Mai.* 21.4; Val. Max. 8.4.1) or by noxal action against their owners, who had the choice of either paying compensation or handing over the slave to the plaintiff (Mommsen 1899: 8–9, 16–26; Nicholas 1962: 233–4). Furthermore, it does not take into account that in a great number of conflicts victims were primarily interested in the restoration of property or financial compensation and that a patron might enter into arbitration (between clients) or negotiation (on behalf of his client with the patron of the adversary party), with the result that a considerable number of cases could be resolved by extrajudicial means. Admittedly, such procedures would have worked best in the smaller Italian communities; assumptions as to its functioning within the city must, of course, be subject to our uncertainty with respect to the extent and strength of patron–client ties.

Kunkel explicitly assumed that without this summary criminal jurisdiction Rome would not have been able to cope with the wave of criminality which allegedly was a necessary consequence of the city's growth and of the increasing number of slaves and urban proletariat after the second century BC. It is in my opinion highly doubtful, however, that the Roman élite of the second and first centuries believed that things had degenerated to that extent. With their numerous retainers they were able to protect themselves against ordinary criminality. Even if we assume a rising crime rate,[23] it does not follow that the ruling élite would have reacted in the way Kunkel suggests. Comparison with the English experience of the eighteenth and early nineteenth centuries shows that there is no automatic correlation between criminality and its suppression, on the one hand, and an inclination to improve the efficiency of law-enforcement, on the other (see Epilogue below). Furthermore, whereas the English criminal law of this time imposed the death penalty for a great number of criminal offences, the harshness of the law tended to be mitigated by commutation of the penalty into deportation, and convicts often managed to avoid actual transportation (Radzinowicz 1948, index s.v. 'transportation').

The example also cautions us against accepting Kunkel's assumption that the Roman authorities would not have allowed lower-class criminals to go into exile because they would then have had to face the problem of their illegal return, even if they had been

---

[23] Kunkel's suggestion is based on the new penal law against carrying weapons with offensive intent (see below p. 55).

formally outlawed and thus at least in theory made liable to execution by anyone who chanced upon them (Mommsen 1899: 936). Societies may put up with such circumstances (see Bowsky 1967: 13 on late-medieval Siena, and Cozzi 1973 on Renaissance Venice), as, for instance, the Athenians did, relying on the remedy that any citizen could arrest an outlawed person and hand him over to the magistrates for execution (Dem. 23.31–2; Lycurg. *Against Leocrates* 121). Thus, Plato complained that in democracies persons condemned to death or exile could walk about freely (*Republic* 558a). Under the Empire Pliny, as governor of Bithynia, was embarrassed when he saw criminals who had been condemned to forced labour or to participation in gladiatorial games being employed as paid public slaves by cities such as Nicomedia and Nicaea, even when it was far from clear that they had obtained official pardons (*Ep.* 10.31 and, for Trajan's reply, 10.32).

In sum, I cannot prove that the Romans did not see ordinary criminals as a major problem, but I can call into question the supposed universality of such rules as those on which Kunkel's hypothesis is based. It should be added that the sources give no hint that in the Republican era the threat of the death penalty and especially of public executions was used to deter potential criminals. Spectacular executions in full view of the citizens (Hinard 1984) are associated, as far as we know, with various forms of proceedings against persons charged with high treason (*perduellio*; see especially the tradition on the legendary case of Horatius and the procedure which was abortively revived in the trial against C. Rabirius in 63; Livy 1.26.6–12; Cic. *Pro Rabirio perduellionis reo* 11, 16). They were also employed against those declared public enemies during the Sullan era (see below pp. 66–7). Another exemplary punishment (depicted in detail by Pliny, *Ep.* 4.11) was the burial alive of a vestal virgin found guilty of unchastity and the public scourging (to death) of her lover (Beard 1980: 16; Cornell 1981; Hampl 1983).[24] That comparable exemplary proceedings are not reported as a means of disciplining the capital's criminals of humble origin probably indicates that the authorities saw no urgent need to deal with street criminality in this way. The contrast to the development of criminal law during the Imperial period,

---

[24] Guilt was assumed rather than established by any sort of examination (Linderski 1984b: 176).

which aimed at deterring criminals by spectacular physical punishment, is striking, though admittedly an argument from silence.

An alternative hypothesis for explaining the role of the *tresviri capitales* in criminal matters might be developed from a comparison with the functions of the Athenian equivalent, the Eleven, similarly responsible for the public jail and executions. A procedure called *apagoge* called for the delivery to the Eleven of a thief caught red-handed and probably also of an exile who had returned illegally (Hansen 1976; Cohen 1983: 52–61; Carawan 1984). If he confessed, he would immediately be put to death; if he denied the deed, he would be tried by a court, but in the meantime imprisoned unless three citizens were prepared to stand surety for him (Arist. *Ath. Pol.* 52.1; Aeschin. 1.91, 113).

There is some circumstantial evidence that the *tresviri capitales* presided over comparable proceedings. First, there is the account of a criminal case in Cicero's *Pro Cluentio* (38–39) in which freedmen and friends of a missing person delivered the alleged murderer to the *triumvir*; he confessed but named someone else as instigator. Cicero does not say what happened to the confessed murderer. He is only interested in the case of the alleged instigator. The *triumvir* had interrogated him but then did not proceed further. Cicero asserts that the magistrate had been bribed, but it seems probable that the accused did not confess. Second, Valerius Maximus (8.4.2) has the story of a slave who would not confess, though he had been tortured six times, but was condemned and then executed by the *triumvir* as if he had pleaded guilty.[25] Of course, it may be objected that a procedure whereby confession resulted in self-conviction was not likely to be often successful. But one should not exclude the possibility that a culprit caught *in flagrante* was inclined to confess and that the accusers and the magistrates could exert considerable pressure to extract such a confession, especially since slaves could be subjected to torture.

Again, the comparison does not prove anything; it only points to the possibility of reasonable alternatives to Kunkel's interpretation. Thus with respect to the existence of summary criminal jurisdiction over Roman citizens we have to be content with a *non liquet*.

[25] The text differentiates, however, between the judges and one named *triumvir* who carried out the execution; it is thus relevant to a possible juridical role of this magistrate only if we accept Kunkel's (1974: 155, n. 17) assumption that the *iudices* mentioned were the magistrate's *consilium*.

CONSPIRACIES AND ILLEGAL ASSOCIATIONS

A system of maintaining public order that relies on the daily confrontation of magistrates and citizens is especially suspicious of any organization of citizens which is not under the authorities' control. The sources reveal a feeling of vulnerability to conspiracies and a distrust of organizations.

Night meetings were considered the core of the independent organization of the *plebs* in the Early Republic, and *coetus nocturnus* was allegedly banned by the Twelve Tables (8.26) and by a dubious *lex Gabinia* of (?) 139 (Porcius Latro, *Declamatio in Catilinam* 19). Clandestine meetings in private houses are reported as being the origin of conspiracies aimed at a restoration of the Tarquins in the first year of the Republic, and at the establishment of tyranny by Sp. Maelius in 439 and by Manlius Capitolinus in 384 (Livy 2.3.7, 4.13.10, 6.20.4). Slave risings, sometimes in connection with attacks from abroad, during the earlier periods of the Republic (in 501, 500, 460 and 417), were also interpreted as conspiracies (Hoben 1978). The authenticity of almost all these cases may be doubted, but the important point is that the annalistic tradition reflects an almost neurotic sensitivity on the part of the authorities to the putative danger of conspiracies.

Such an attitude also governed the reaction of Senate and magistrates in certain cases during the Middle Republic: disturbances and conspiracies involving slaves and war captives in 259, 217 and 198, the mysterious incendiarism of 210,[26] and the famous Bacchanalian affair of 186 and the Catilinarian conspiracy of 63. We might compare here the even more drastic measures recommended by Aeneas Tacticus (10–11) in the fourth century BC for a typical Greek *polis* facing the constant danger of internal conspiracy supported by exiles or foreign enemies (Winterling 1991), and the measures including a sort of curfew taken by Athenion at Athens in 88, which in Posidonius' biased account are pilloried as tyrannical acts (Ath. 214; Bugh 1992). Typical responses of the Senate included ordering the minor magistrates – the *tresviri capitales* and other boards such as the five-man one mentioned for 186 – to summon special watches to prevent arson. In the Bacchanalian affair (Livy 39.9–19) additional watches were employed to arrest

---

[26] Zonar. 8.11; Orosius 4.7.12 (on 259); Livy 22.33.1–2: Zonar. 9.1 (on 217); Livy 26.27.1–9 (on 210); 32.26.4–18; *Per.* 32; Zonar. 9.16 (on 198).

persons trying to flee the city, and the aediles were instructed to
search for the priests of the cult. We may assume that in this
instance the magistrates' auxiliaries had to be assisted by citizen
volunteers (as implied by Livy 39.16.13), since hundreds of people
were arrested and later summarily tried (Finley 1983: 21; Bauman
1990: 344). The volunteers employed within the city were quite
distinct from the regular troops (see Cic. *Leg.* 2.37) used for the
suppression of the cults in southern Italy.

The detection of a conspiracy would in most cases depend on
information supplied by a fellow-conspirator or one of his intimates. A significant countermeasure employed in all the cases
under discussion was the giving or offering in advance of indemnity
(and security against revenge; Livy 39.13.5–6), as well as rewards
to informers, money for citizens, and both liberty and money for
slaves (David 1986). Sums of 100,000 sesterces (Livy 32.26.14 and
39.19.4, referring to the crises of 198 and 186 respectively) would
elevate the informer to membership in the first census class as
compensation for the loss of a patron which would ensue from his
denunciation. Offering liberty to slave informers meant not only
interfering with the property rights of slave-owners not involved in
the case (who, however, were financially compensated by the state;
Livy 32.26.14), but also providing an incentive for the denunciation
of masters by slaves. The establishment of such an exemption from
the rule (vital for a slave-owning society) that slaves cannot give
evidence against their masters (Cic. *Deiot.* 3) is a significant demonstration of just how seriously alleged conspiracies were taken (Liebs
1980; Schumacher 1982: 39–68).[27] Comparable reactions by the
Athenians include their interpretation of the profanation of the
Mysteries and the mutilation of the Herms as revealing a great
conspiracy in 415 (Thuc. 6.27.2; Andoc. 1.11–33), and the Thasian
decree concerning a reward for informers in a conspiracy, which
probably also dates from the late fifth century (ML no. 83). The
testimony of women was taken seriously when they proffered information which might lead to the unmasking of a conspiracy, as in
the cases of Hispala Faecenina in 186 (Watson 1974) and Fulvia in
63 (cf. the general remarks of Papinian in *Dig.* 48.4.8).

The informer, however, took the risk that the authorities would
individually decide on the correctness of his denunciation and

---

[27] The other exemption concerned *incestum*, unchastity in a vestal (Cornell 1981).

might even construe it as a confession of his own guilt, as happened to Vettius in 59 when he reported an alleged attempt on Pompey's life (Cic. *Att.* 2.24.3). The magistrates would confront further suspects with the evidence given by the informers, and that could produce more confessions (see Livy 26.27.8–10). In summary trials (*quaestiones extraordinariae*), in which the chief magistrates acted as both prosecutors and judges, confession by the culprits was probably often the basis for condemnation; certain actions may also have been construed as a sort of guilty plea by implication, as happened with those who tried to flee the city after the eruption of the Bacchanalian scandal (Livy 39.17).

The case of 186 (Pailler 1988) is revealing of the motives which guided the authorities beyond the suspicion that the Dionysiac cult had led to orgies of sex and crime. The suppression of the foreign, private cult as such was apparently not the main aim. The decree of the Senate did not necessarily exclude any form of individual worship of the god provided that official permission was obtained. A comparable policy of keeping a Dionysiac cult under official control is known from a decree from Ptolemaic Egypt, probably from the reign of Ptolemy IV Philopator (Select Papyri 208). The Senate's decree (which is known from an inscription: *CIL* I, 2², no. 581 = *FIRA* I² no. 30) forbade without any qualification the keeping of common funds and prohibited *magistri* and male priests. The crucial aim seems to have been the destruction of associations which cut across sex roles and status and age categories and might estrange parts of the citizenry from their 'natural rulers' (North 1979; Scheid 1981: 158–9). Bacchic initiation was seen as potentially creating particularistic loyalties and, especially, rendering initiates unfit to take the military oath (Livy 39.15.13). Cult associations with hierarchies of their own appeared to undermine the integrative functions of the official state cults and to provide opportunities for the organization of groups beyond the control of the authorities, thus constituting almost a state within the state (see Livy 39.13.14). Given that the city had outgrown the dimensions of a face-to-face society (Livy 39.9.1), it was especially important that meetings took place only under the direction of the appropriate authorities (Livy 39.15.11).

This pattern of response to suspicious associations was destined to persist. The Late Republic and the Principate saw various attempts to control *collegia* suspected of organizing citizens beyond the authorities' reach (see below pp. 72–3 and 82). This suspicion was the greater if political and religious ties (of an apparently sacrilegious character) seemed to be combined: thus, the Catilinarians were accused of having sealed their allegiance by means of human sacrifice (Dio Cass. 37.30.3 in comparison with Sallust, *Bellum Catilinae* 22 shows the progressive aggravation of the charge). Similarly, charges of ritual murder, cannibalism, incest and promiscuity became standard reproaches against Jews and Christians who were suspected of forming illegal associations (Henrichs 1970; Marasco 1981; Nippel 1990: 27–8).

Alertness to conspiracies in Italy would also provoke Roman magistrates to interfere in Italian communities, for example, in Capua in 314 (Livy 9.26.5–7) and in the course of the Bacchanalian affair (Gruen 1990: 42–5). The same happened if certain other crimes could be understood as endangering Roman interest in Italy (Polyb. 6.13.4–5, and Cic. *Brutus* 85–8 on murders in the Sila Forest in 134). As a rule, however, maintaining public order in the municipalities was left to the local authorities.[28]

CITIZEN INITIATIVES

The magistrates' role in maintaining order can be understood as complementary to the mechanisms of social control underlying the authority of both the magistrates and the Senate. It is, however, easier to make plausible assumptions about these mechanisms than to demonstrate their operation (see Flaig 1993). Originally, military discipline must have been important in a society which was almost constantly at war and regularly called up considerable parts of the citizenry. Citizen-soldiers were subject to the discretionary power of their commanders to punish any conduct which could be understood as undermining military discipline (Jung 1982: 963–75). Constitutional rules excluding the military from the city notwithstanding, people knew that the magistrates and senators would act as their military commanders as well. The importance of this awareness for internal relations is indicated by the tradition that in

---

[28] Our meagre evidence allows no unequivocal statement on the scope of local criminal jurisdiction (Simshäuser 1973: 145–56; Galsterer 1977: 74–6; Salmon 1982: 138; Cloud 1994: 527–8). The execution of death penalties is known from a first-century Puteoli inscription (Bove 1967) but may have concerned only slaves (De Martino 1975).

early times the patricians employed levies to discipline the *plebs* (e.g., Livy 2.28.5; 3.10.10–14; 3.41.6–10), and by the story of the troubles in the popular assembly over a triumph for Aemilius Paullus in 167, when citizen-soldiers were finally impressed by an appeal to military discipline (Livy 45.36.7; 45.37.14; Plut. *Aemilius Paullus* 31). This would no longer have happened in the Late Republic, however, because structural changes in military organization meant that the urban citizenry was no longer regularly called to arms.

With respect to the nobility, military discipline was also enforced by the use of paternal authority (Thomas 1984; Harris 1986).[29] The right of a father to put his son to death (Gell. *NA* 5.19.9; Cic. *Dom.* 77) was employed especially to enforce military and political discipline (Dion. Hal. *Ant. Rom.* 2.26.4–6; Polyb. 6.54.5). In the alleged cases of the first consul Brutus in 509 (Dion. Hal. *Ant. Rom.* 5.8; Plut. *Publicola* 6.3) and the *dictator* Postumius Tubertus in 431 (Livy 4.29.5) and in the most famous instance, that of T. Manlius Imperiosus Torquatus in 340 (Livy 8.6–8; Cic. *De finibus* 1.23), the execution was ordered in virtue of magisterial authority, but the sources (with exceptions such as Livy 2.5.8 on Brutus) stress its congruence with paternal authority (Verg. *Aeneid* 6.820–4). With regard to the Sp. Cassius case of 486, different traditions coexisted, according to which the would-be tyrant was condemned either in a public trial or by his own father (Livy 2.41.10–11). In historical times a senator prevented his son from joining Catiline's camp and executed him by virtue of his *patria potestas* (Sall. *Cat.* 39.5; Val. Max. 5.8.5; Cass. Dio 37.36.4). The father's right applied only to a son under his *potestas*. T. Manlius Torquatus in 140 obtained permission from the Senate to try his natural son D. Iunius Silanus (who, having been adopted by someone else, was no longer under his authority) instead of having an official investigation on the charge of provincial maladministration. Having been dismissed from his father's sight, the son duly committed suicide (Cic. *Fin.* 1.24; Livy, *Per.* 54; Val. Max. 5.8.3). During the Bacchanalian affair, convicted women were turned over to their relatives or to those who had authority over them so that their executions could take place in private, provided that a suitable person was available (Livy 39.18.6). The important point is that paternal authority and

---

[29] In everyday life *patria potestas* was of much less importance (Saller 1986, 1988).

domestic punishment were generally considered auxiliary measures for enforcing public authority. Whereas fathers sternly insisted on maintaining public order, the *avunculus* (mother's brother) was likely to express familial emotions (e.g., Collatinus at the sight of his nephews: Plut. *Publ.* 6.1; Dion. Hal. *Ant. Rom.* 5.9; Thomas 1984: 513). A delicate conflict could, however, arise from a clash between the exercise of paternal authority and the dignity of a magistrate. The case of the tribune C. Flaminius, whom his father tried to remove from the *rostra* to block his agrarian legislation in 232, was discussed as a collision between *patria potestas* and the *potestas* conferred on the tribune by the people, the infringement of which might constitute a case of lese-majesty (Cic. *De inventione rhetorica* 2.52; cf. Val. Max. 5.4.5; Bauman 1984: 1286–7). In another famous instance a man on horseback approaching a consul who was his son was very pleased when he was finally ordered by the last lictor to dismount (Livy 24.44.9–11). At least from the Middle Republic onward it was generally believed that in such a case the dignity of the public office should prevail.

It is extremely difficult to assess the role of the state religion in this context (cf. North 1990: 17). That *nobiles* occupied the colleges of priests, that *imperium* was indissolubly associated with the taking of auspices and that almost all political action took place in a religious context surely enhanced the nobility's authority. In addition, the spectacular funeral procession for a deceased *nobilis* displayed the *insignia* (including the *fasces*) of all the public offices he himself and each of his ancestors had occupied (Polyb. 6.53; Pliny, *HN* 35.6). The religious substratum of political authority might under certain circumstances cause the populace to be awestruck by the display of a magistrate's or senator's priestly dignity as well. Cicero (*Brut.* 56) recalls the story of M. Popillius Laenas, who as consul in 359 quelled a seditious assembly wearing his priestly robe. In 133 Scipio Nasica's habit as *pontifex maximus* seems to have contributed to the Gracchans' reluctance to attack senators (below p. 58). In later times the *plebs* no longer showed such deference. That they were engaged in cult activities of their own is complementary to this development.

The vexed problem of the importance of patron–client relations (see Wallace-Hadrill 1989; Brunt 1988: 382–444) cannot be discussed in all its dimensions here. The point at issue is whether considerable parts of the populace were so closely tied to the nobility that in crises they would join the 'forces of order'. This is aside from the fact that individual clients of magistrates might be appointed as *apparitores* or in some situations even be employed instead of an official assistant. It is imagined that in the Early Republic clients supported magistrates or the patriciate in serious confrontations with a politicized *plebs* (e.g., Dion. Hal. *Ant. Rom.* 7.21.3, 9.41.5), but it is difficult to identify clients in this role with respect to later conflicts (Brunt 1988: 431–5). There were of course always persons who for material and sentimental reasons were closely attached to the great houses of the nobility (see Tac. *Historiae* 1.4.3), and at least they can be assumed to have been part of the 'loyal mobs' that helped the nobility to win the upper hand in the confrontation with the great *populares* of the late second century. But these cases only prove the relative strength of the nobility in a crisis rather than suggesting that they could count on sufficient support under other circumstances. After all, this pattern did not repeat itself during the disturbances of the first century, except that in some cases, as in 100 (Cic. *Rab. Perd.* 22) and 56 (Cic. *QFr.* 2.3.4; cf. 1.2.16), dependants from the countryside were brought to the city.

As to the urban masses, it must have been simply a question of numbers that in a populace of at least 750,000 (Brunt 1971: 376–88) only small groups could be in so close a relationship to the *nobiles* that, on the one hand, they could rely on material support and expect to obtain money, grain, or free lodgings if need be, and, on the other hand, they were ready to support them unconditionally in political matters. There were chances to earn a living by calling on high-ranking persons during the morning levee (*salutatio*) and by accompanying candidates in public, but this did not by any means imply steady relationships with mutual obligations (Q. Cic. *Commentariolum petitionis* 35). The introduction of subsidized corn distributions by C. Gracchus (which were subject to changes, abolition and re-establishment during the following decades) did not necessarily weaken existing patron–client bonds, but the free distributions that came into effect in 58 brought particular relief, which probably enabled the more respectable elements of the *plebs* to exercise some sort of patronage over the very poor (Garnsey 1988: 213–4). However appropriate to earlier times, the relations between nobility and *plebs* in the Late Republic can no longer be adequately understood in terms of a comprehensive patron–client model. The emergence of an intermediate leadership capable of organizing and mobilizing considerable parts of the urban masses (below pp. 73 and 78) is convincing evidence of this.

The foregoing remarks are not intended to suggest that the social preconditions for the magistrates' and the nobility's authority had completely broken down during the Late Republic, but they do explain to a certain degree the growing difficulty of exercising it in critical situations of political unrest. Compliance with the orders of a magistrate would not be a matter of course but would depend on a convincing appearance combining resoluteness with flexibility; this placed especially great demands on his eloquence (see Val. Max. 8.9.1). The establishment of jury courts and the introduction of secret voting in the assembly since the mid-second century had institutionalized the demand for oratorical competence (see Cic. *Rep.* 5.11). *Contiones*, in which magistrates addressed the people without submitting formal proposals, became events at which people responded directly to effective rhetoric (Cic. *Orator ad M. Brutum* 168). These meetings became so frequent that rules concerning the competition between meetings called by different magistrates had to be developed (Gell. *NA* 13.16; Lintott 1987: 43).

First of all, the new style of politics allowed the pursuit of anti-senatorial policy by the great *populares*, all of them credited with rhetorical mastery (e.g., Cic. *De or.* 1.38; *Brut.* 125–6, 224; Tac. *Dialogus de oratoribus* 36.3; David 1980; Achard 1981). But this weapon was of course not monopolized by one side; Tiberius Gracchus' opponent Octavius is said to have convened daily *contiones* (Plut. *Ti. Gracch.* 10.4). Under certain circumstances even apparently popular proposals could be defeated by an opponent's eloquence (see, e.g., Cic. *De amicitia* 96 on an instance in 145). Cicero projected this constellation back to the struggles of the Early Republic by attributing to leaders of the state the ability to pacify the *plebs* by persuasive oratory (*Brut.* 54). With respect to his own times he asserted that eloquence was more important than jurisprudence to the consulship, since a consul had to be able to stop seditious tribunes and calm the passions of the people (*Pro Murena* 23–4; Bauman 1985: 15–24). Boasting of his role in the Catilinarian crisis, Cicero again and again asserted that by his eloquence alone he had achieved success beyond the great military victories of the past and equal to those of Pompey the Great (e.g., *In Catilinam* 3.26; cf. Pliny, *HN* 7.117; Nicolet 1960).

Self-help

The absence of a law-enforcement agency and even of any demand for one reflected the assumption that in cases in which public order was not at issue citizens were themselves able and prepared to protect their lives and property. Broad scope for legitimate self-help, however, had to be balanced by precautions against the employment (by those who were professedly protecting their rights) of means which themselves threatened public order. This applied even to the old legal provisions for the treatment of manifest thieves. The Twelve Tables allowed the immediate killing of a thief who came at night or carried a weapon (8.12–3; Cic. *Pro Tullio* 50–1), and this was more than the natural right of self-defence. Justified killing was vindicated by an immediate calling (*endoplorare*) upon neighbours whose attendance would exclude the possibility that the burglary was merely faked to conceal a murder plot. A manifest thief who was not apprehended under the aggravated circumstances just mentioned was to be brought before the magistrate, who after a summary proceeding could hand him over (for enslavement) to the plaintiff. A fleeing suspect was legally considered a manifest thief if he was immediately followed with the help of neighbours and proof of his guilt adduced by a search of his house. The search took the form of a solemn ritual (the intruder being naked) which ensured all parties concerned against misconduct and overreaction (Wieacker 1944, 1988: 244–5; Horak 1963; Wolf 1970; Maxwell-Stuart 1976). A number of parallels in Indo-European law show the same rationale – licence to execute the law on the spot in certain cases requiring a call for the assistance of fellow-citizens to prevent gross abuse (Schwerin 1924; Schulze 1933: 160–89; Hammerich 1941; Kaufmann 1979; and, on Greek evidence, Lintott 1982: 20–2; Bain 1981).

These procedures had become obsolete by the Middle Republic, though exceptional treatment of manifest theft (which now could be prosecuted by an action for a fourfold penalty) persisted, and special action was made available against the owner of premises in which stolen goods were discovered (Gai. *Institutiones* 3.183–94).

The search for runaway slaves was a special case. The public interest demanded some support for owners in addition to the arrest of fugitives by the *tresviri capitales*; this could consist of permission to search urban premises in the presence of a public slave

(Eder 1980: 78–9). Searches for runaways in the countryside were performed by professional slave-catchers. Possessed of hiding-places, they were in a position to arrange for flight and afterwards offer to buy the alleged fugitives from their owners for a low price; they may also have been involved in outright kidnapping. Late Republican provisions were aimed against these practices, but the corresponding civil suit was probably insufficient to suppress them (Mommsen 1899: 780–1; Daube 1952; Bellen 1971: 44–64; Watson 1987: 64; Rilinger 1988: 249–50). Provincial governors would support the recovery of runaways according to their discretion; access to official assistance depended mostly on personal connections (Bradley 1989: 32–8). The record of a late-second-century Sicilian governor who praised himself for having restored exactly nine hundred and seventeen runaways to their Italian masters surely reflects an extraordinary situation (*CIL* I² 638; Verbrugghe 1973).

In the political and social context of the Late Republic, more problematic implications of the general rule of self-protection emerged. The nobility's capacity to protect itself at home was limited by the social necessity to allow almost anyone free access (see Vitr. 6.5), though, of course, doormen exerted a certain control (see Sen. *De constantia sapientis* 14.1–2, 15.5). The murderers of Livius Drusus in 91 took the occasion to mingle with the crowd that had accompanied him home from the Forum (Vell. Pat. 2. 14. 1). An attempt on Cicero's life in 63 was planned for the morning *salutatio* (Cic. *Cat.* 1.10; Sall. *Cat.* 28.1). The Catilinarians allegedly viewed the Saturnalia as an appropriate time for a series of assassinations, since houses were kept open throughout the night to accept the gifts which clients customarily sent their patrons on this occasion (Diod. 40.5). An aristocrat's usual entourage of slaves and freedmen would also serve as a bodyguard in confrontations in public places; its employment often constituted a borderline case between appropriate self-defence and illegitimate offensive use. A Late Republican restriction on the number of followers (*sectatores*) who attended upon candidates for public office (Cic. *Mur.* 71) may have been not only a measure against electoral corruption, but also the reflection of a concern to limit the opportunity for violent clashes (Kinsey 1965).

Citizens were, of course, supposed to protect their houses themselves. The Senate's decision in 57 that the higher magistrates should take measures to protect the reconstruction of Cicero's city house reflected the recognition that in this particular case, an attack on private property involved issues of constitutional and augural law (Cic. *Har. Resp.* 16) (below p. 75). In emergency situations which affected all of the citizenry, magistrates organized patrols to prevent large-scale arson, but they otherwise could only exhort citizens to post night watchmen, as Cicero did during the Catilinarian conspiracy (Cic. *Cat.* 2.26, 3.29). Of course, the well-to-do could employ their slaves and retainers for this purpose (see Livy 23.3.2; Dion. Hal. *Ant. Rom.* 11.22.3), whereas ordinary people had to rely on neighbourly help. With considerable numbers of underlings at their disposal and with the possibility of using armed force, the upper classes were able to defend their lives and property in situations of extreme danger, such as when a riotous mob attacked the houses of those suspected of involvement in the murder of Caesar in 44 (Cic. *Phil.* 2.91; Plut. *Brutus* 20.7–8; Nic. Dam. *Caes.* 17.50; App. *Bella civilia* 2.147.614), or when attempts at burglary and plundering were made during a civil war (*Laudatio Turiae* 2.9a–11a). Of course, those who were best prepared to defend themselves with trained fighters were also likely to use these forces for political purposes, as Milo was notorious for doing (see Asc. p. 33, 12 on the defence of his city house in 52).

The problematic aspects of self-defence within the city had certainly become more apparent during Late Republican situations of acute crisis, but the violence in the Italian countryside that was a by-product of the unresolved agrarian question represented a much greater, almost endemic problem (Brunt 1971: 555–7; Gruen 1974: 433, n. 122). Complaints about big men forcibly ejecting peasants from their land to consolidate their large estates had already been made in connection with the Gracchan agrarian legislation (App. *BCiv.* 1.7.29; Sall. *Bellum Iugurthinum* 41.8). During the first century the problem had apparently increased, especially in regions affected by the massive redistribution of landed property as a consequence of the Sullan proscriptions and veteran settlement (Cic. *Leg. agr.* 3.13–14; *QFr.* 1.1.21; *Paradoxa Stoicorum* 46). Armed gangs made up of slaves and clients were used to terrorize neighbours and violently seize landed property; herdsmen clashed over pastures (Cic. *Pro Tullio* 18–22; *Pro Caecina* 20–2, 57; *Clu.* 161; *Pro Quinctio* 28; *Pro Sulla* 71; *Pro Milone* 74; *Phil.* 14.7). New legal remedies instituted in response to this development (Lintott 1968: 124–31; Labruna 1972; Frier 1983; Annequin 1992) could hardly dam the flood of violence.

It is true that compensation for damages was increased in comparison with the *lex Aquilia* (the statute regulating damage to property) if they were caused by armed gangs, and a new interdict was directed especially at the employment of armed men, whether the employer had title to the property in question or not. Speedy and effective proceedings before a jury of three or five 'recoverers' (*recuperatores*), capable of officially summoning witnesses, was made available for such actions, reflecting the public interest in settling them (Schmidlin 1963: 45–50; Kelly 1976: 53–70; Lintott 1990). The remedies developed by the praetors during the seventies made the legal situation somewhat intricate, however; apparently the right of one who had been driven off by force to re-install himself by the same means was not completely ruled out (Cic. *Fam.* 7.32.2) until the *leges Iuliae de vi* (*Dig.* 48.6.2, 48.7.5).[30] In any case, improved legal remedies against the use of armed force in property disputes were incapable of solving the general problem that law enforcement in these cases was based entirely on private initiative, and that the chances of obtaining justice and having judicial decisions executed were unevenly distributed according to the social standing of the parties concerned (Kelly 1966).

Disturbances in the countryside aggravated the problem that security during journeys was exclusively a private matter. Prohibitions on carrying weapons did not exclude the right to employ an armed entourage against the notorious threat of highwaymen and brigands (Asc. p. 50, 7–9; Cic. *Att.* 7.9.1; *Phil.* 12.25; Varro, *Rust.* 1.12.4), as is stressed in the accounts of the bloody clash between Clodius and Milo on the Via Appia in 52 (Asc. p. 31, 21; Cic. *Mil.* 10), and in the report that Spartacus and his first followers armed themselves with weapons taken from people on the roads (App. *BCiv.* 1.116.540). Here again, armed retainers (of landowners and professional slave-catchers) would be used not only for legitimate self-protection but also to kidnap people and to carry them off to work-houses (*ergastula*) where they had to work as slaves (App. *BCiv.* 4.30.130; Suet. *Aug.* 32.1; *Tib.* 8; Brunt 1971: 292–3). Herdsmen, who were necessarily trained in using weapons, often acted on their own, as is indicated by their part in slave insurrections (Brunt

---

[30] See also Sallust's exhortation to Caesar (*Ep.* 1.8.4–5) to proceed against violent property conflicts. The inclination to take up arms, for example, in boundary disputes, remained, however, a well-known phenomenon in the Principate (Sen. *Brev. vit.* 3.1).

1971: 552; Yavetz 1983: 152–4). Governors in Sicily after the crushing of the slave rising about 100 regularly made it a capital offence for slaves to possess weapons; uncompromising enforcement regardless of circumstances could, however, be perceived as undue severity (Cic. *2 Verr.* 5.7; Val. Max. 6.3.5).

Popular justice

Various forms of collective action were presented by their participants as expressing willingness to assist in the execution of justice (Usener 1913; Lintott 1968: 6–21; Veyne 1983). This popular justice included both community support for the claims of individuals and sanctions against the violation of common interests. Again, it varied in degree from legitimate pressure to taking the law into one's own hands.

The enforcement of certain rules beyond formal law by public denunciation, and the willingness of authorities to turn a blind eye to them, are well known from a great many Byzantine, medieval and modern examples. Charivaris ('rough music'), insulting, shouting, noise-making and mockery in front of the houses of unpopular persons often by the young men of a community and especially at night appear in typical situations: the widower who marries a young girl, the wife who deceives or beats her husband, the miser who does not invite the community to dinner on the occasion of a wedding or a funeral, are likely victims. In less obvious cases, an accusation of illicit behaviour may be brought by someone who has a quarrel with the person concerned. Threats with violence, especially the destruction of the accused's house, may be implied, though as a rule the accuser stops short of carrying them out. The effects of such sanctions range from relatively harmless admonition to the destruction of reputation which may force the party concerned to leave the community.[31] Other forms, such as leading someone naked on an ass, appear especially in cases of

[31] Alford 1959, Pinon 1969 (on terminology); Meuli 1975: 445–69, 471–82, Le Goff and Schmitt 1990 (comparative materials from antiquity to modern times); Davies 1990 (Greek antiquity); Gauvard and Gokalp 1979 (Middle Ages); Davis 1971 (sixteenth-century France); Weber 1976: 399–406 (nineteenth-century France); Thompson 1972, Kent 1983, Ingram 1984, Shoemaker 1987 (early modern England); Conley 1991: 15–43 (Victorian Kent); Wyatt-Brown 1982: 435–61 (on charivari and lynch law in the southern states of America); Johnson 1990 (on the American Midwest).

adultery but also as abusive punishment in political cases and often as part of official sanctions (Bury 1958: I, 224; II, 67, 73; Patlagean 1981: 124; Mellinkoff 1983; Schreiner 1989; cf. also Schwerhoff 1992). Especially during carnivals, rituals are performed mocking social superiors and local authorities – a channelled licentiousness which, however, in situations of social tension may lead to serious disturbances (Le Roy Ladurie 1981; Burke 1978: 178–204, 1983; Villari 1987). Adaptation of charivari forms to express social and political protest is also a common phenomenon and may cause the authorities to abandon their usual moderation.[32] Under certain circumstances charivaris are staged to defend a community against representatives of demands from outside, for example, tax-collectors.[33]

With respect to classical antiquity, the occurrence of charivaris directly enforcing particular rules of conduct in everyday life is known only from chance references. Examples include the mock rituals to which bachelors in Sparta were subjected (Plut. *Lyc.* 15.1–2; Ath. 555c–d) or the sanctions in Cumae against adulteresses, who were pilloried and led on the back of a donkey (Plut. *Mor.* 291F).[34] Plautine comedy has several hints at the use of abusive chanting in everyday conflicts about property and sexual relations, and also reflects the connection with the nightly revelry of drunken young men (Usener 1913; Hendrickson 1925, 1926). Furthermore, there is evidence of the employment of this type of popular justice in legal and political contexts. Certain forms of public denunciation could be understood as supporting the course of law.

[32] See Harris (1986): London apprentices during the seventeenth century rather regularly staged ritualized attacks on brothels on Shrove Tuesday, but one held unusually during Easter Week of 1668 met with massive repression because it was understood as attacking the crown's religious policy as well.

[33] See Bercé (1974: 177–84, 206–33) on seventeenth-century France; in eighteenth-century England Methodist preachers were sometimes driven out of a community in this way (Walsh 1972; Thompson 1972); on charivaris in the insurrection against British rule in nineteenth-century Québec, see Greer (1990).

[34] For further parallels, see Herter (1960: 79), Latte (1968: 291–2), and Schmitt-Pantel (1981). On the Greek legend that as punishment for losing her virginity a father locked his daughter in with a horse that caused her death, see Ghiron-Bistagne (1985). It also seems possible that the Roman Lupercalia ritual included charivari elements to denounce the disorderly sexuality of women (Hopkins 1991: 479–83). On sexual humiliation during public executions of female Christians, see Shaw (1993). Charondas, the early Locrian lawgiver, had allegedly established that deserters should be publicly exposed for three days in the market-place dressed in women's clothes (Diod. 12.16.1–2); on a similar practice in the Byzantine hippodrome, see Guilland (1966: 304–5) and Cameron (1976: 172).

The Twelve Tables (2.3) on the one hand allowed one to waul [wail] (*obvagulare*) before the house of a witness who otherwise would not appear, but on the other hand made it a capital offence to chant abuse in public (*occentare*) which would amount to destroying the accused person's social existence (8.1b = Cic. *Rep.* 4.12; Brecht 1937; Momigliano 1942). Later law acknowledged that in certain situations the natural support of kin and neighbours needed to be supplemented by that of a wider range of fellow-citizens, but that respect for personal reputation required restrictions (Drummond 1989: 157). It equated *occentatio* with *convicium* (Festus p. 192 L), defamation, against which action for *iniuria* (meaning physical as well as verbal assault) was available when the public insult was *adversus bonos mores* and caused loss of honour (*infamia*) for the person attacked (*Dig.* 47.10.15.2).[35] By implication, public denunciation was under certain circumstances legitimate if it conformed to accepted standards, and a person who was already considered infamous would have no opportunity for legal action (Raber 1969: 23–39).[36]

That public munificence was demanded by charivari is known from attempts at Pollentia, Siena and Verona in the first century AD to force notables to hold funeral games (Suet. *Tib.* 37.3; Tac. *Hist.* 4.45; Pliny, *Ep.* 6.34.1–2). It is especially revealing that this took place with the acquiescence of the local magistrates even though extorting a promise to hold games by means of *iniuria* was forbidden by law (*Dig.* 48.6.10). In Rome itself such occurrences were probably rare because of the number of public games and of gladiatorial games (and funeral banquets; Purcell 1994: 685) put on by the nobility. The same holds true for the grain riots which functioned elsewhere as a special kind of popular justice, aimed at the fixing of a 'just price'.

Popular justice could also be employed in the context of political protest. Thus weddings with politically scandalous implications such as that of Sulla in 88 (Plut. *Sulla* 6.10) and that of Pompey in

---

[35] The same holds true if the customary mourning *habitus* of a defendant was intended not only to mobilize permissible public support but also to arouse aggression against the plaintiff (Daube 1951; Lintott 1968: 16–21). The emperor Claudius, however, recommended mourning rituals as useful means in preventing protraction of lawsuits (Stroux 1929: 61–70; Woess 1931).

[36] It was admissible to point to a debtor in default by placing a poster on the *Columna Maenia* (Weiss 1949).

86 (Plut. *Pompeius* 4.2–3) led to such reactions from the populace.[37]
Strong charivari elements are detectable in confrontations between
Clodius and his enemies in the fifties (below pp. 76–7). Playing on
the sexual habits of politicians was also a feature of the mock verses
about generals which soldiers sang on the occasion of a triumph
(Suet. *Iul.* 49.4; 51), and it was a common ingredient of political
invective; see, for example, the verses of C. Licinius Calvus on
Pompey (Sen. *Controv.* 7.4.7), various references to Caesar's stay
with the Bithynian king (Suet. *Iul.* 49) and Cicero's speeches and
letters with respect to Clodius (Richlin 1983: 85–6, 96–8). Such
personal attacks were also part of the standard repertoire of law
court speeches and would be considered, depending on their
coarseness or elegance, as Cicero (*Pro Caelio* 6) puts it, either *convicium* or *urbanitas*. Parallels with the carefully crafted allusions to
particular public figures during stage performances (Cic. *Sest.*
118)[38] make it clear that at least in the Roman case resort to
charivari forms is not to be understood as expressing a popular
culture clearly distinct from an élite one.

Another form of popular justice was lynching, which might be
resorted to when people felt that someone was obviously guilty and
the immediate execution of justice was appropriate, especially
when due process was unavailable or thwarted (see Livy 3.13.3). In
contrast to the historical experience of the American frontier which
has given the phenomenon its name (Cutler 1905; Coker 1933),[39]
in Rome (and in other ancient societies)[40] lynching occurred only
in cases that aroused outrage, for example, a madman's seizing the
crown of Caesar and putting it on during a festival in 31 (Dio Cass.
50.10.2), and a knight's attempted killing of his son by scourging in

---

[37] This motive was repeated in the insults inflicted on Sulla during his siege of Athens in 88
(Plut. *Sull.* 6.12; 13.1). On a charivari directed at a Roman delegation in Tarentum in 282,
see Dio. Cass. fr. 39. 5–9; for parallels in Renaissance warfare, see Trexler (1984).

[38] A more serious incident is known from Asculum in 91, when a political allusion by an
actor provoked his lynching by the Roman part of the audience (Diod. 37.12; Rawson
1985: 98–9).

[39] Apart from ephemeral lynch mobs, organized vigilantes during the eighteenth and nineteenth centuries claimed the right to take the law into their own hands (Brown 1979).

[40] Sen. *Controv.* 3.8 discusses a case from fourth-century Athens in which, when a man
declared that his son had been raped at a party, the house and the party guests, including
the alleged victim, were burned. In Egypt (*c.* 59) a Roman embassy member was lynched
because he had (accidentally) killed a cat (Diod. 1.83.8). The Jerusalem temple carried
warning inscriptions that any alien who entered the holy area would immediately be put
to death (Bickerman 1946/47).

Augustan times (Sen. *De clementia* 1.15.1). Politically motivated lynchings in Republican times include the murder during his trial in 98 of the former tribune Furius, who had enraged people by becoming a turncoat in the conflict about Saturninus (Dio Cass. fr. 95.3; App. *BCiv.* 1.33.148). Gabinius and the jury that acquitted him in 54 were seriously threatened (Dio Cass. 39.62.2, 63.1).[41] At Caesar's funeral the tribune Helvius Cinna was lynched because he was mistaken for the praetor Cinna (Suet. *Iul.* 85), and the incident led the tribune Casca to issue an edict that he should not be identified nor held to be in agreement with the other Casca who had participated in Caesar's murder (Dio Cass. 44.52.2–3). The sources show great sympathy with the behaviour of the crowds in these cases. When C. Fabius Hadrianus, governor in Africa, was burned to death in his official residence in 82 by Roman citizens (Livy, *Per.* 86), the deed was not prosecuted, according to Cicero, because everyone believed that he had deserved his fate. Cicero suggests that the same would have happened if a similar attempt on the villainous Verres' life by a Sicilian community had been successful (*2 Verr.* 1.68–71).

The claim of legitimacy which underlay ritualized collective killings could also be expressed by the *modus operandi* chosen. In Greek and Jewish culture this was especially the case with stoning, which might on the one hand be the collective execution of legal punishment, and on the other hand be the result of action which though spontaneous was understood to be the immediate execution of justice, the public and communal punishing of manifest crime (cf. Apul. *Metamorphoses* 10.6.3; Hirzel 1900; Pease 1907; Gras 1984; Rosivach 1987).[42] Collectively stoning a person to death (as opposed to mere stone-throwing) was not a genuine Roman tradition except in *fustuarium*, the clubbing and stoning to death of deserters by their comrades,[43] and the stoning by mutinous soldiers of officials (Livy 4.50.5–6; Plut. *Sull.* 6.9). The Roman way of demonstrating that a killing was to be understood as popular jus-

---

[41] In other cases of alleged obstruction of justice, verbal attacks by crowds (Cic. *Clu.* 79) or hissing in the theatre (Cic. *Fam.* 8.2.1) were to be expected.

[42] On related forms of execution in Greek antiquity, see Gehrke (1985: 32, 251); on ritualized killings of human scapegoats, Burkert (1977: 139–42).

[43] This sort of execution was also employed when a whole unit was punished by 'decimation', making an example of one out of every ten soldiers, the one being selected by lot (Polyb. 6.37–8; Livy 5.6.14; Cic. *Phil.* 3.14; Tac. *Ann.* 3.21.1; 14.44.4).

tice was expressed in the formula that the victim had been 'torn to pieces at the hands of the crowd' (*manibus discerpere*). This is the label the sources applied to almost all the lynchings of Republican and Imperial times (Gnilka 1973; Schetter 1984). The procedure is also assumed in the Late Republican legend that Romulus was killed by senators inside the *curia*, the Senate House (Livy 1.16.4; Florus 1.1.17; Val. Max. 5.3.1; Plut. *Romulus* 27.5; Ungern-Sternberg 1993: 101–2).[44] In certain cases it was said that the participants were certain to have acted in the public interest as defined by the consensus of the ruling class, for example, in the murder of Saturninus (App. *BCiv.* 1.32.145; Florus 2.4.5–6),[45] or in accordance with official decisions in connection with the Sullan proscriptions (August. *De civitate Dei* 3.28).[46]

Making public the events within the *curia* (by analogy with the Romulus case), and open acceptance of responsibility for it, was supposed to guarantee that the action of Caesar's murderers would be understood as being in the public interest (App. *BCiv.* 2.114.476–7), but this proved to be a miscalculation. Such claims were of course not automatically accepted; the attempted lynchings of certain politicians during the political turmoils of the Late Republic – for example, of Metellus in 100 (Plut. *Mar.* 29.7) or Piso in 67 (Dio Cass. 36.39.3) – were likely to have been accepted, if at all, only from a partisan point of view.

Nevertheless, the violent forms of popular justice were understood not as expressing any legal principle distinct from the established order but as anticipating or executing the law by way of self-help. This was the case in certain incidents during the Late Republic[47] and increasingly during the Principate. The official sanctions against convicted 'traitors' included destroying their

---

[44] In 67 senatorial opposition to Pompey was expressed in the announcement that he would not escape the fate of Romulus (Plut. *Pomp.* 25.4).

[45] Rabirius is said to have held up Saturninus' head for mockery at banquets (*De viris illustribus* 73.12).

[46] See especially the tradition on the killing of M. Marius Gratidianus (Hinard 1984: 303–7; Marshall 1985b).

[47] E.g., the abuse of the corpse of Cn. Pompeius Strabo at his funeral, which, however, was stopped by tribunes and other senators (Licin. 22–3; Vell. Pat. 2.21.4; Plut. *Pomp.* 1.2); the smashing of statues of Pompey in 55 (Plut. *Cat. Min.* 43.4) and of Antony and Octavian in 40 (Dio Cass. 48.31.5), and the attacks on houses undertaken by the Clodians.

statues and throwing their corpses into the Tiber from the Gemonian steps, ritual punishments which were especially appropriate for the participation of crowds.[48] In a number of incidents, crowds, soldiers[49] and even senators[50] demanded such sanctions against officials or defunct emperors ('Tiberius to the Tiber'; Suet. *Tib.* 75), anticipated official decisions by smashing statues,[51] and participated in the mistreatment of corpses.[52] Sometimes it was even demanded that a culprit be handed over to the crowd to be torn to pieces. An emperor in dire straits would be tempted to acquiesce in such a demand and sacrifice a scapegoat; sources comment on such incidents as a manifestation of the people's judgement.[53] The same mechanism appears in contexts in which the central or local authorities declined to prevent pogroms against ethnic and religious minorities or tacitly or even openly welcomed them.[54] And, of course, any manifestation of popular justice in a political context could be manipulated in such a way as

[48] S.H.A. *Commodus* 17.4; 18–20 depicts the Senate's debate on the treatment of the dead Commodus as similar to a riotous popular demonstration.

[49] Even Nerva was forced to comply with the praetorians' demand for the liquidation of Domitian's murderers ((Aur. Vict.), *Epitome de Caesaribus* 12.6, 8; Dio Cass. 68.3.3–4).

[50] It was senators, not the apathetic *plebs*, who were reported to have demolished Domitian's statues even before passing the formal *damnatio memoriae* (Suet. *Domitianus* 23.1; Pliny, *Pan.* 52.4).

[51] In connection with the trials of Piso, the alleged murderer of Germanicus (Tac. *Ann.* 3.14; Dio Cass. 58.11.3), or of Sejanus during Tiberius' reign (below p. 88) or in reaction to the news of the death of the emperor Maximinus Thrax in AD 238 (S.H.A. *Gord.* 13.6); see Pekáry (1985: 134–51) for further evidence. On the interplay of mob action and official decrees of local councils for the removing of statues of Verres in Sicily, see Cic. *2 Verr.* 2.159–65 and Wallace-Hadrill (1990: 156).

[52] E.g., after the violent deaths of the emperors Vitellius (Tac. *Hist.* 3.85; Suet. *Vitellius* 17; Orosius 7.8.8) and Heliogabalus (S.H.A. *Heliogabalus 17*), or in the case of Commodus' praetorian prefect Cleander and his sons (Herodianus 1.13.6). The lynching of bishop George in Alexandria in AD 361 was followed by the bearing of his corpse on a camel to the shore, where it was burned and the ashes scattered in the sea (Amm. Marc. 22.11.8–11). Indecent invectives were hurled by the (non-Jewish) inhabitants of Caesarea after the death of King Agrippa I in AD 44 (Joseph. *AJ* 19.356–9).

[53] The *plebs* demanding the death of Flavius Sabinus claimed 'righteous killing' (*ius caedis*; Tac. *Hist.* 3.74.2); Commodus, who had handed over his praetorian prefect Perennis for lynching by soldiers (Dio Cass. 72(73).9.4; S.H.A. *Comm.* 6.2), later delivered the successor Cleander's corpse to the *plebs* for punishment (S.H.A. *Comm.* 7.1; Dio Cass. 72(73).13); the Senate's decision on executions in AD 238 was supplemented by the 'people's judgement' (*iudicium populi*) to inflict posthumous sanctions (S.H.A. *Gord.* 13.8).

[54] See, e.g., Diod. 14.45–6 on a pogrom against Carthaginians in Sicily provoked by the tyrant Dionysius in 398 BC, and Joseph. *Bellum Judaicum* 7.46–53 on an anti-Jewish pogrom in Antioch during Vespasian's governorship (cf. Downey 1961: 198–201).

to allow the emperor to pretend that it was only the execution of the will of the people.[55]

Popular justice cannot be properly understood as representing a relic of primitive times which is expected to fade out with the development of the state. That recourse to self-help and popular justice may coexist with institutionalized legal procedures is well known from a great number of ancient and more recent societies (Humphreys 1984–5: 252). It is not peculiar to Rome, and it does not reveal any particular Roman affinity for violence. It was simply one aspect of the public character of Republican juridical and political decision-making and later of acclamation as part of the emperor's legitimation. It was crises of the political system that led to violence, not violence that created crises.

---

[55] Caligula sought to have a senator torn to pieces as a public enemy (*hostis publicus*; Suet. *Caligula* 28); Titus, then praetorian prefect, organized public denunciations of persons he wanted to get rid of (Suet. *Titus* 6.1). With respect to popular demonstrations in favour of Nero's divorced wife Octavia in the form of the smashing of statues of the new empress, Poppaea, the latter claimed that those who pretended to be the *plebs* were simply the clients and slaves of her rival (Tac. *Ann.* 14.61).

CHAPTER 2

Late Republican political violence

RIOTS AND RIOT CONTROL

Breaches of public order, though always exceptional, became a more significant feature of politics over time. Apart from the conflicts associated with the Struggle of the Orders, disturbances intended to influence decisions of the assembly were recorded in some instances during the Middle Republic: the violent obstruction of a trial by tax-farmers (*publicani*) in 212 (Livy 25.3.12–19) and the besieging of the houses of the tribunes by a crowd including even respectable married women (*matronae*), to press them to reverse their veto of the abrogation of a sumptuary law in 195 (Livy 34.1.5, 8.1–3). Turbulence at elections is recorded for 185 (Livy 39.32.10–13).

In the Late Republic disturbances occurred more often (see catalogue of cases from 78 to 49 in Vanderbroeck 1987: 218–67), generally as concomitants of the regular processes of decision-making at times when tendencies to sociopolitical disintegration contributed to a disregard for fundamental constitutional conventions. In particular, the emergence of a new type of popular politics led again and again to clashes within the assembly and made informal meetings (*contiones*) of the *plebs* the starting-point for riotous rallies (Cic. *Clu.* 93). The composition of the assembly was different every time; the supporters of a particular proposal were likely to appear in numbers, with the result that the tribune taking the initiative had a very good chance of obtaining the majority of the tribes' votes. There are apparently only a very few cases in which a bill was defeated by a vote of the assembly, as happened with an agrarian law in 104 (Cic. *De officiis* 2.73).

The more the capacities of the tribunate were employed to pursue aims unsupported or even opposed by the Senate, the more obstructionist the tactics that were used on behalf of the latter. Legislation was impeded by means of *intercessio* (tribunician veto) (Thommen 1989: 216–22; De Libero 1992: 37–49), *obnuntiatio* (reporting thunder or lightning which made assembly proceedings void for reasons of sacral law; Bergemann 1992: 97–113; De Libero 1992: 53–68), and filibuster, a technique which the Younger Cato employed not only in Senate meetings but also in a *contio* (Dio Cass. 39.34.3–4; Groebe 1905; De Libero 1992: 15–22). The opposing official, in several cases a tribune of the People like the proponent, had to appear personally and veto the proceedings in front of the crowd assembled to support the proposal. Such a confrontation could easily lead to rioting (Cic. *Sest.* 77) unless both sides, and especially the presiding tribune, were careful to avoid it. Interference by another magistrate during a meeting arranged by a tribune could, however, be construed as a violation of tribunician rights (Dion. Hal. *Ant. Rom.* 7.17.5 and Livy 43.16.9–16 on a conflict in 169).

Appuleius Saturninus (in 103 and 100) was the first tribune to reject a colleague's veto by violently removing him and dispersing his supporters (Smith 1977; Linderski 1983). Later, others either followed his example or contrived to circumvent *intercessio* – which strictly speaking could be employed only against the technical procedures preliminary to the actual vote, not against the tribune himself – by personally reading out the bill's text (in conflicts in 67 and 62 (Meier 1968; Rilinger 1989)) or, by occupying the voting area beforehand to exclude the opposing party. The latter was a method which could of course be employed by supporters as well as opponents of a particular initiative, most notorious being the cases from 62 (Plut. *Cat. Min.* 27–8) and 57 (Cic. *Sest.* 75; *Att.* 4.3.4–5). Sabotage was also practised by removing the urns required since 131 for secret voting in legislative assemblies (*Rhet. Her.* 1.21, 2.17). Resorting to such means could often be viewed as securing the 'real' public interest against obstructionism or demagogy, but in the long run repeated disruption of procedures undermined the legitimacy of the constitution (Mackie 1992: 60). In some cases, groups who would especially profit from a certain proposal would combine in this way to advance their interests, for example, the Marian veterans who pushed through Saturninus' agrarian law, the knights who with drawn daggers forced through the *lex Varia* in 90 (App. *BCiv.* 1.37.166), and the campaign agents (*divisores*) who in 67 tried to prevent the passage of a bill against electoral bribery (Asc. p. 75, 24–7). In other cases retainers, clients (Sen. *Controv.* 7.4.7) and, sometimes during the last decades of the Republic, even seasoned gladiators (who were regularly needed for privately organized funeral games (Cic. *Sull.* 54, 62; Asc. p. 20, 6–20)), or the slave gangs that were regularly used in conflicts in the countryside (Cic. *Mil.* 26), were employed to terrorize opponents (Nowak 1973). In the time of Pompey's and Caesar's dominance, soldiers and veterans were repeatedly called up to push through legislation or decide elections.

Violence occurred in connection not only with legislation and elections but also with criminal trials, which took place in the Forum (see Cic. *Deiot.* 5–6; Fuhrmann 1991: 102–4; David 1992: 39–45). Jury trials had become a favourite form of elimination contest within the aristocracy (see Cic. *Cael.* 47; Alexander 1993), and this could lead to the threatening of juries, advocates and witnesses and attempts to break up the proceedings (David 1992: 241–59). Well-known cases include trials in 66 and 65 (Asc. pp. 59–60) and the trial of Clodius in 61 (Cic. *Att.* 1.16.3–5).

Even grain riots were connected as a rule with other political disputes, as in the cases of Saturninus and Clodius. It seems likely that in most cases they were not a response to actual starvation but demands for the improvement of supply and distribution in anticipation of problems (Garnsey 1988: 30–1). In any case, the targets were the politicians responsible, and this means that Rome at least from the Middle Republic onward did not see the type of riot known from early modern times as *taxation populaire* – demands that corn dealers, large landowners, millers and bakers market grain or bread for a 'just price' which often met with the approval of local magistrates (Rudé 1964; Tilly 1971, 1975b; Kaplan 1976; Root 1990; Miller 1992). Riots of this kind may have taken place in early Rome (Livy 4.12.10; Dion. Hal. *Ant. Rom.* 7.18.2; 9.25; Lintott 1988; Garnsey 1988: 29–30, 174–5),[1] and they did apparently occur in several communities within the Empire. Cicero refers to a man in Cyme who had been flogged for exporting grain during a famine (*Pro Flacco* 17). Moreover, he boasts that during a famine in

---

[1] Readiness of well-to-do citizens and magistrates in Hellenistic times to subsidize food prices may have been fostered by anticipation of the populace's angry reaction (Veyne 1976: 220–3).

Cilicia he, as the governor (51/50), had been able to make speculators deliver their grain to the populace, on the basis of his authority alone, without having recourse to force or legal measures (*Att.*
5.21.8); the remark suggests that Roman governors were prepared
to respond to popular demands in a food crisis by taking measures
against landowners, traders and bakers. From the time of Caesar or
Augustus onwards there were legal provisions against speculation
(*Lex Iulia de annona*; *Dig.* 48.12.2 pr.) which were also adopted in
municipal charters.

    Riots of the *taxation populaire* type were not to be expected in the
city of Rome during the Middle and Late Republic, the issues there
being strictly political in nature: the amount of subsidy for public
distributions, on the one hand, and the organizational structure
that would ensure an ample food supply on the other. Thus violent
attacks on the consuls during a shortage in 75 (Sall. *Historiae* 2.45
M) contributed to the re-establishment of subsidized public distributions (Vanderbroeck 1987: 220–1). The riots of 57 were in part
directed against Cicero as the alleged instigator of supply delays, in
part over who should be responsible for the organization of the corn
supply (*cura annonae*) and the distributions (*frumentationes*) (below p.
76); the disturbances of 22 required Augustus to assume this task
(below p. 85).

Methods of control

Violent breaches of public order revealed the limitations of the
traditional display of magisterial authority. One could no longer
expect to silence a crowd by declaring that one knew better than
the People what the state's interest was – as the consul Scipio
Nasica in 138 is reported to have done (Val. Max. 3.7.3) – even
though the assumption that a man of dignity and gravity should be
able to quell a riot is still echoed by Virgil (*Aen.* 1.148–53). Just as
rhetoric was of the utmost importance for tribunes who presented
themselves as champions of the People, so other magistrates had to
accommodate themselves to the mood of the crowd. Thus Cicero
during his consulate in 63 quelled threatened disturbances in the
theatre with a well-balanced speech (Plut. *Cic.* 13; Pliny, *HN*
7.117). Sometimes physical courage and strength were also called
for, as in the case of a consul who (probably in 50) personally
destroyed an Isis shrine in the Forum when (public?) workmen

refused to do so (Val. Max. 1.3.4). When the Senate in 54 praised the praetor Cato, who had energetically stopped riotous proceedings in the assembly, he reproached the senators for not having assisted him (Plut. *Cat. Min.* 44.3).

A magistrate who could not control a turbulent meeting was obliged to dissolve it or be held responsible for the consequences; so the Senate formally ruled in 92 (Cic. *Leg.* 3.42–3), establishing a precedent for defining proper conduct for a magistrate (cf. Livy 25.3.19). Since in many cases the presiding magistrates were themselves responsible for or at least accessory to the disturbances, every magistrate and for that matter every good citizen was supposed to assume responsibility if need be. Thus, the quaestor L. Domitius Ahenobarbus, who in 67 with a posse of retainers had put an end to the occupation of the Capitol by the tribune Manilius, was officially praised by the Senate (Asc. p. 45, 11–19). In 61 Q. Caecilius Metellus Celer enforced the Senate's prohibition, issued in 64, of the Compitalian games. As consul-designate he was technically a private person at the time; thus he acted in virtue of his *auctoritas* and not of a magistrate's *potestas* (Cic. *Pis.* 8).

When preventive measures were deemed necessary to ensure undisturbed trials, legislation or elections, ad hoc bodyguards for the higher magistrates might be appointed (Meier 1964: 44–8). This measure was available, however, only for proceedings for which they themselves were responsible; one could not legitimately interfere in assemblies that were called by tribunes of the People. Juries forced to operate under considerable pressure from organized agitators could petition Senate and magistrates to grant them a *praesidium* (bodyguard), as happened in 61 (Cic. *Att.* 1.16.5; *Scholia Bobiensia* p. 85, 27 (Stangl); Sen. *Ep.* 97.6) and in 52 (Asc. p. 40, 4–11). That in the latter case soldiers were used was due to exceptional circumstances; otherwise such bodyguards were probably recruited from among clients and personal followers of the magistrates, but magistrates could also appeal for assistance to citizen volunteers (e.g., in 67, Asc. p. 75, 22). The Senate thus authorized the use of an armed posse, which otherwise would have been considered illegal or at least problematic. The decision was taken only after serious disturbances had already occurred and a repetition of them was to be expected. Furthermore, it was a demonstration of the Senate's resolve, which again could only be displayed in situations in which the necessity for a decisive reaction

was beyond any doubt. This is why during the confused circumstances of most of the year 63 the consul Cicero did not apply for an
authorized *praesidium* but relied, even for undisturbed Senate proceedings and for the arrest of conspirators, on a private bodyguard
consisting of certain knights and of clients from the community of
Reate (Cic. *Cat.* 1.11, 3.5; Sall. *Cat.* 26.4). The crisis meeting of 5
December was guarded by a body of Roman knights (Cic. *Att.*
2.1.7); that they afterwards massively assaulted the senator Caesar,
who had argued against the execution of the arrested conspirators
(Suet. *Iul.* 14.2; Plut. *Caes.* 8.2), illustrates the problem that such a
posse might feel entitled to take the law into its own hands (see Cic.
Cat. 1.21).

Furthermore, the authorities could rely on private means, in that
individual magistrates, senators or other reputable citizens were
prepared to hold suspects under a sort of house arrest (*libera
custodia*) whereby the house-owner in a sense stood bail. There were
public jails which could accommodate a certain number of prisoners (Le Gall 1939), but imprisonment was not a regular penalty,
pre-trial detention had been replaced by bail, and apprehension as
a coercive measure was always subject to intervention by tribunes
(see Mommsen 1899: 299–305, 326–9; Arbandt and Macheiner
1976). Thus there was no practical need for any substantial prison
apparatus, and a loose form of custody seemed reasonable especially when persons of rank were concerned and formal criminal
proceedings had not yet been instituted. This was the case with the
suspected Catilinarians in December 63 (Sall. *Cat.* 47.3–4); it presupposed a sort of gentlemen's agreement, however, and would
have demanded considerable further precautions if a serious
attempt at liberation by an armed gang had been expected (Sall.
Cat. 50.1–2).[2] An ad hoc *praesidium* would probably have been
able to deal with the situation, but long-term strict custody would
best have been achieved by distributing the prisoners over several
municipalities as Caesar proposed (Sall. *Cat.* 51.43) and as
precedent with respect to state prisoners and hostages suggested
(Galsterer 1976: 108–9).

Senate and magistrates were not, then, in as weak a position as is
sometimes assumed. The defects that nevertheless remained could

---

[2] Compare Clodius' success in liberating the Armenian prince Tigranes from a praetor's
house by cunning and then by force (Asc. p. 47, 10–26).

not, however, be overcome by technical means alone. They were consequences of the principles of civil rights and constitutional structures fundamental to the law-making process. Even those who were very critical of the tribunate's role were forced to admit that it fulfilled an indispensable function in integrating and pacifying the mass of citizens (Cic. *Leg.* 3.23–6). Therefore, and since in most cases magistrates would head opposing parties, it would have been almost impossible to solve the problems of public order by establishing a permanent police force, even if a solution could have been found for the delicate problem of which magistrate should be entrusted with command over it. The use of such a force to police public assemblies would have called for detailed regulations on the tribunes' proceedings with the People and on *intercessio* and *obnuntiatio* as well – indeed, an almost total reconstruction of the constitution (Meier 1966: 157).

Issues of law

Many decisions made with disregard of the rules and even by violence were accepted de facto. During the first century the Senate repeatedly proclaimed that laws passed in this way should be considered void (Lintott 1968: 132–48; Bleicken 1975: 463–73; De Libero 1992: 87–103), but apparently the fact that the passage of law was accompanied by violence was insufficient in itself to justify an annulment. That again would have involved almost insoluble problems of definition. It was another matter if the Senate, on the basis of the augurs' opinion (Cic. *Leg.* 2.31), could declare that in addition the sacral law or the regulations for the promulgation of laws (as contained in the *lex Caecilia Didia* of 98) had been violated (Bleicken 1975: 468–9; Smith 1977: 150, 158; Linderski 1986: 2165–8). This is why *obnuntiatio* was so important as a mechanism to be used against magistrates who ignored the will of the Senate. It goes without saying that in any particular case it depended on the constellation of powers in question whether the legislation could actually be annulled for this reason. Thus the Senate was not prepared to provoke further violence by following Bibulus' proposal to annul Caesar's agrarian law in 59 (Dio Cass. 38.6.4); the invalidity of his legislation remained, however, a subject for a possible future arrangement with Caesar (Meier 1975).

It was easier to prosecute the person responsible for a breach of the rules. Trials on the basis of the treason laws from the late second century (Bauman 1967; Ferrary 1983a), which probably already included provisions against the occupation of public places by armed men, were especially susceptible to disputes as to whether a violent procedure had really violated the majesty of the Roman People. Thus the former quaestor Caepio, who had tried to sabotage the passing of Saturninus' corn law, later argued that he had merely been acting in accordance with the Senate's statement that the bill was contrary to the public interest, and therefore could not be charged with a diminution of the *maiestas populi* (*Rhet. Her.* 2.17; Bauman 1980: 125–6; Ferrary 1983a: 568–71).

The post-Sullan laws on violence (*lex Lutatia de vi* of 78 and a *lex Plautia* passed before 63)[3] theoretically improved the chances of successful prosecution, first, because they allowed for speedy proceedings – courts would even sit on holidays (Cic. *Cael.* 1) – and second because they defined certain offences which could not be argued away with reference to the intentions of the actors or the political will of the People. Unfortunately, we cannot be sure of the scope of the laws in comparison with the great number of offences which later could be prosecuted under the *lex Iulia de vi publica* and the *lex Iulia de vi privata* (*Dig.* 48.6–7).[4] In any case, offences such as attacks on the magistrates or the occupation of public places with armed gangs (Cic. *Cael.* 1; Asc. p. 55, 12) were already punishable under Late Republican laws. Furthermore, by declaring that certain actions had threatened the security of the state (*contra rem publicam*), the Senate could allow prosecutions under this law even if political violence did not immediately affect magistrates or public property (see Cic. *Har. Resp.* 15–16). The laws' provisions were especially directed against the identifiable organizers of such violent actions, not only politicians but also the organizers of gangs (*duces operarum*), whom one would not have charged with treason.

It may be that certain clauses, especially the prohibition on carrying arms with offensive intent, could be applied to any identi-

---

[3] On the vexed question of the relationship between the two laws, see Vitzthum (1966), Lintott (1968: 107–24) and Bauman (1978b).

[4] The law texts present problems as to authorship (Caesar and/or Augustus?), identity (one or two laws?), and the criteria for the distinction between 'public' and 'private' violence (see most recently Rilinger 1988: 232–4; Cloud 1988 and 1989). The trial of Caelius in 56 (Cic. *Cael.* 23) suggests that inciting a riot in an Italian city (Naples in this case) and/or attacks on foreign ambassadors could already in Republican times be prosecuted as criminal *vis*.

fied participant in such an event. Such a clause was part of the Sullan law on murderers and poisoners (*lex Cornelia de sicariis et veneficis*) and surely goes back to pre-Sullan times (see Plaut. *Aul.* 415–17; Cic. *Inv. Rhet.* 59–60). Making criminal intent rather than just the completed act a criminal offence, it seems to have been aimed especially at a sort of urban gangsterism (Kunkel 1962: 64–70; Cloud 1969, 1994: 522–3; Nörr 1986: 86–115; Ferrary 1991). It seems probable, however, that the carrying of weapons under certain circumstances could also be prosecuted under the laws against *vis* (Asc. p. 55, 12–13). In some extremely critical situations magistrates, such as Pompey in 52, Antony in 47 and the consuls after Caesar's murder (Pliny, *HN* 34.139; Dio Cass. 42.29.2, 44.51.1), banned any carrying of weapons within the city. This would have guaranteed the possibility of prosecutions for violence, since any excuse for carrying weapons was precluded. It did not extend to an attempt to search houses and sequester all privately owned weapons,[5] though in a situation of proclaimed public danger magistrates would have felt justified in proceeding in this way against individual suspects. In December 63 a praetor backed by the consul's authority took action against the Catilinarian Cethegus, who thereupon tried to declare his weapons collector's items (Cic. *Cat.* 3.8, 10). Eventually the (Caesarian or Augustan) *lex Iulia de vi publica* forbade the assembling of weapons in city and country houses except those customary for hunting or for journeys by land and sea (*Dig.* 48.6.1; cf. Dion. Hal. *Ant. Rom.* 4.48.1).

The Republican laws against violence were apparently not designed particularly as a deterrent to bystanders. In this they differed from legislation known from other periods which was especially intended to criminalize under certain conditions anyone present during a riot. The English Riot Act of 1715, for example (abolished only in 1967), made rioters guilty of a felony if they did not disperse within an hour of the reading of a proclamation by the responsible magistrate (Nippel 1984/5; below pp. 117–8). The use of criminal law as a deterrent to anonymous rioters presupposes that the authorities were capable of arresting them on the spot, and

---

[5] Enforcement by way of house searching – as the fourth-century mercenary general Charidemos ordered in certain towns of Aiolis (Ps. Arist. *Oeconomica* 1351b19–35) – would have been not only practically impossible but also politically scarcely acceptable. The searching of the houses of Alexandrian Jews in AD 38 was part of the Egyptian prefect's extremely partisan handling of the disturbances (Philo, *In Flaccum* 86–94).

this would imply that the magistrates regularly had effective forces to hand.

The recorded trials for political violence (see Alexander 1990) involve either politicians or, notably under the extraordinary circumstances of 52, notorious organizers of mobs. The few convictions which were achieved in the aftermath of the Catilinarian conspiracy and the events of 52 cannot obscure the fact that these laws proved only partly efficacious. As always with the jury trials of the Late Republic (Cloud 1994: 528–30), which we know only from conflicts within the élite, these trials were essentially political manœuvres. The rhetorical contest between the counsels for the prosecution and for the defence concentrated more on the characters and political allegiances of the parties involved than on the issues of law and fact; juries were very reluctant to return a verdict of guilty. The Roman jury trial lacked the judicial instruction and control exercised by the presiding judge in England; there were no rules of evidence, the presiding magistrate did not sum up for the jury and the jurors tended to make their decision on the basis of the parties' character references, emotional appeals and often purely political argumentation (see Cic. *Att.* 4.15.4).

The justification of violence

There was, furthermore, a line of reasoning which justified political violence, at least to a certain degree, if it could be construed as expressing the legitimate will of the People. This was, as we have seen, the message conveyed by acts of popular justice, but the same idea could also be conceived with respect to the Roman past. So ran the argument of the orator M. Antonius (grandfather of the future triumvir) when he defended the former tribune C. Norbanus on a charge of having violently expelled a vetoing tribune from the Forum. In 103 Norbanus had thereby secured the conviction of the former proconsul Q. Servilius Caepio who was held responsible for the defeat of a Roman army by the Cimbri in 105; his own trial took place *c.* 95. Antonius argued that Norbanus had only followed the expressed will of the People. He added that one could learn from the history of the Republic that resort to sedition had proved necessary in order to achieve such healthy results as the expulsion of the kings, the establishment of the tribunate, and the institution of *provocatio*; therefore one could not infringe the People's right to sedition as a last resort (Cic. *De Or.* 2.124, 198–200; *Partitiones oratoriae* 105). Antonius, though notorious as a defender of the Senate's authority, in this particular instance was clearly adopting a line of argument typical of the *populares*, whose practice was to appeal to the tradition of the Struggle of the Orders, when the People had fought hard for and finally gained their fundamental political rights (Plut. *C. Gracch.* 3.2–3; Cic. *Academicae quaestiones* 2.13–14; Sall. *H.* 1.11, 3.48.15). Invoking this tradition did not, however, mean legitimizing political violence without concern for intentions, means and results. That singular breaches of public order led not to large-scale bloodshed comparable to the consequences of civil strife in numerous Greek cities (Lintott 1982; Gehrke 1985), but to political compromises, was the significant lesson of early Roman history. Thus, this line of argument might be acceptable to all parties with respect either to the heroic past or to a temporary breach of order that had no lasting consequences. It was, however, quite a different matter when the authority of magistrates and the Senate was seriously challenged.

CRUSHING INSURRECTIONS

During the great crises which ended in the violent deaths of Tiberius Gracchus, Gaius Gracchus and Saturninus in 133, 121 and 100 respectively, the Senate developed a pattern of crisis management. Its effectiveness was derived straightforwardly from the assertion that the political order as a whole, meaning especially the Senate's key position, was in jeopardy. This can be established as the common feature of these events despite the differences among them and the partisan character of our sources – which either denounced the great *populares* as subverters of the constitution or sought to exculpate them from that charge.

It was not open to the Senate and the chief magistrates simply to order massive repression. Only if the authorities could count on a substantial number of followers among the citizenry would repression be a possible solution, and this meant that the situation had to be clearly perceived as an emergency. Measures against the Gracchi and Saturninus were taken only when they had been driven to open rebellion. In 133 the Senate took no immediate counter measures against Gracchus' having deposed a vetoing tribune to force through an agrarian law fervently supported by great numbers of peasants. Later the climate changed; peasants and day labourers had to return to the countryside to bring in the harvest, and other parts of the populace demonstrated their sympathy with the argument that Gracchus himself, by deposing his colleague Octavius, had shaken the very foundation of the tribunate as an institution (Ungern-Sternberg 1984). The situation came to a head when Gracchus tried to win re-election to the tribunate (which in itself was of doubtful legality) by filling the voting area with his – apparently unarmed – followers. During the Senate meeting which took place simultaneously, the presiding consul declined to proceed against Gracchus at this stage. Thus the former consul and *pontifex maximus* Scipio Nasica (who had girded his toga in the manner usual for sacrificial ritual; Badian 1972: 725–6; Rawson 1974: 194–5; Dubourdieu 1986) took the initiative and led a group of senators and their retainers armed with clubs, staves and broken benches. The tradition stressing that no one was slain by the sword (Plut. *Ti. Gracch.* 19.5–6) may reflect controversies between later jurists over whether the laws which forbade the use of offensive weapons had been violated or not (Bauman 1989: 45, n. 108). In the actual confrontation the Gracchans, standing in awe of the senators, shrank from physically assaulting them (App. *BCiv.* 1.16.69; *Rhet. Her.* 4.68). Although outnumbered, the senators were therefore able to maintain the upper hand, and Tiberius Gracchus, though still a tribune and therefore supposedly sacrosanct, was slain.

The situation in 121 was quite different in that both parties deliberately resorted to armed violence (App. *BCiv.* 1.25–6; Plut. *C. Gracch.* 13–18). That political support for Gaius Gracchus was already waning had been revealed in 122 by his defeat for re-election. The consul Opimius and some of the new tribunes of 121 set out to repeal his legislation. Gracchus resolved to employ a hard core of followers to prevent this, and eventually he occupied the Aventine with a body of armed men. This move was designed to evoke the memory of a *secessio plebis* for the defence of the people's liberty at the time of the Struggle of the Orders (see Dio Cass. 44.25.3–5), and it was an attempt to win him a bargaining position in negotiations with the Senate for the preservation of at least parts of his legislation. The consul, understandably, was not prepared to enter into negotiations and demanded instead the unconditional surrender of the Gracchans. An unprecedented 'final decree of the Senate' (*senatus consultum ultimum*) was passed to authorize a forcible solution of the crisis. The consul appealed to senators and knights to arm both themselves and two servants each (Plut. *C. Gracch.* 14.4). In addition, he employed a body of Cretan archers who happened to be available, and these archers had a devastating effect on the Gracchans (Plut. *C. Gracch.* 16.3; Oros. 5.12.7). The use of such auxiliary troops was also without precedent. One might wonder whether the fact that the Aventine was beyond the *pomerium* (Gell. *NA* 13.14.4–7) was relevant in this respect. The sources, however, give no hint of any debate over the political and legal implications of the employment of troops of this kind. Gracchus was forsaken by most of his followers, to whom the consul had guaranteed impunity if they surrendered in time. In addition, Opimius offered blood-money for the heads of Gracchus and his companion Fulvius Flaccus, the consul of 125 and tribune of 122 (Oros. 5.12.9; August. *De civ. Dei* 3.24). The sources embellish the point that an equal weight of gold was promised in exchange for the heads and that the deliverer of Gracchus' head had taken out the brain and poured melted lead in its place (Plut. *C. Gracch.* 17.3–4; Pliny, *HN* 33.48; Val. Max. 9.4.3), thus underlining the monstrosity of the consul's procedure (see Vell. Pat. 2.6.5).

During his tribunates in 103 and 100 and the interval between them, Saturninus had unscrupulously used force to achieve his political goals, mostly in cooperation with Marius, who from 104 to 100 had been annually re-elected to the consulate (Schneider 1982–3). It was only after the murder of candidates for the tribunate and consulate in late 100 that Marius took sides against Saturninus in order to forestall self-help actions by senators. The volte-face of the popular hero Marius must have decisively diminished the urban *plebs*'s willingness to support Saturninus (Badian 1984). Marius called the citizens to arms. In addition to the senators and knights, who could arm themselves and employ their retainers and clients, some of whom were apparently brought in from Picenum (Cic. *Rab. Perd.* 22), volunteers from the lower classes were employed and supplied with arms from the public arsenals (Cic. *Rab. Perd.* 20). Marius was anxious to organize a disciplined military force (Oros. 5.17.7; Florus 2.4.5) to besiege the Capitol, where Saturninus and his armed followers had entrenched themselves. Saturninus realized that his situation was hopeless and delivered himself to the consul, who had guaranteed him safety – pledging to arrange for a pardon. A body of senators and knights, however, broke into the

Senate House where Saturninus had been brought and lynched him (Oros. 5.17.9; *De Vir. Ill.* 73.10–12).

The pattern of crisis management apparent in the events of 133, 121 and 100 involved a crucial consensus within the ruling élite. Although they had been favoured by Gaius Gracchus and by Saturninus, the knights joined the senators at the critical moments (though not without exacting a political price each time). Access to weapons, military experience, prestige and command of slaves, freedmen and clients guaranteed the élite's success. It is impossible to tell how many plebeians were under such strong social control that they would not have been affected by the *populares*' 'pernicious advances' (see Vell. Pat. 2.3.2). Whatever the size of the 'loyalist' element it was sufficient to overcome the tribunes' hard-core supporters. Whereas the authorities could play a waiting game, the *populares* always had to mobilize support from below. The *plebs rustica* was unable to give such support continuously, and the *plebs urbana* was likely to be impressed by counter-propaganda and material offers from the opposing side, and in the end was unprepared to follow a tribune who had been driven to open illegality. Thus consensus within the ruling class on the necessity of armed repression would be accepted at least passively by the bulk of the citizenry. To stabilize this consensus, the magistrates took additional measures to demonstrate the legitimacy of the actions which had been taken.

LEGITIMIZING THE STATE OF EMERGENCY

The demand for legitimation of emergency measures resulted especially from the fact that they implied a collision with the right of *provocatio* that safeguarded citizens from capital coercion and summary jurisdiction, entitling them to be tried only by a lawfully constituted court. This contradiction between the demands of a crisis and the citizens' constitutional rights, never definitively resolved, emerged again and again in crisis situations until the end of the Republic.

In the Senate meeting of 133 that led to the crushing of the Gracchans, Scipio Nasica urged the presiding consul to save the *res publica* by employing armed force against Tiberius Gracchus (Ungern-Sternberg 1970: 3–20; Bauman 1983: 272–90). The consul P. Mucius Scaevola, a distinguished jurist, replied that he

would not treat a *civis indemnatus* (an untried citizen) in this way –
acknowledging the citizen's inalienable right to formal juridical
proceedings (Plut. *Ti. Gracch.* 19.3). Scipio Nasica responded, however, that in so doing the consul was endangering the very fabric of
law and order, and, since the highest magistrate was not prepared
to save the Republic, he himself, as a private citizen, would take the
initiative and appeal to his fellow-citizens to follow his lead. The
formula he used for this appeal read, *Qui rem publicam salvam esse
volunt me sequantur* ('Let those who wish for the salvation of the state
follow my lead'; Val. Max. 3.2.17). This was the formula which in
earlier times had been used to summon citizens to arms when the
enemy was at the gate and it was too late for an ordinary levy. Late
Roman antiquarian tradition calls it *evocatio* (Serv. *Aen.* 7.614, 8.1;
Linderski 1984a: 76–7), and we may use this term even though it
may be anachronistic.

It was apparently understood that under extreme circumstances
even a private citizen could make such an appeal. Scipio Nasica
had presumably informed himself about this legal tradition before
making his own appeal (Bauman 1978a: 234, n. 61). The striking
thing is that he employed it not in a situation in which no com-
petent magistrate was available but against the expressed will of
the chief authority. No less remarkable was the implication that
those who were responsible for sedition should be treated like
foreign enemies. After the events even the consul Scaevola agreed,
for whatever reason, that Scipio Nasica had acted rightfully (Cic.
Dom. 91). Thus a highly problematic precedent had been created.

A second argument that was employed against Tiberius
Gracchus concerned his alleged attempt to establish a monarchy.
The rejection of monarchy was an essential part of Roman political
culture, one which had indeed been reinforced by the condemnation of tyranny transmitted in Greek literature and rhetorical instruction (Dunkle 1967, 1971; Erskine 1991). It was assumed
that anyone was entitled to kill a would-be tyrant,[6] provided that
he could produce reasonable evidence for his suspicion (Plut. *Publ.*
12.1). With respect to Gracchus' alleged aims, the rumour had
been systematically spread by his opponents and 'confirmed' by

---

[6] As in the Athenian law against tyranny of 337/36 (text in Schwenk 1985: 33–41; compare
Ostwald 1955). In 200 the Athenians decided that anyone could be lawfully killed who
obstructed the symbolic punishments (removing the honorary statues and inscriptions)
aimed at Philip V of Macedon (Livy 31.44.2–9).

later accounts that he had been slain beneath the statues of the Roman kings (see Biliński 1961; Coarelli 1969; cf. Eitrem 1923). The sending of a delegation of priests to the temple of Ceres at Henna in Sicily (Cic. *2 Verr.* 4.108) will have served the same purpose, since the goddess had been associated with sanctions against the violator of the tribunate's *sacrosanctitas* and the would-be tyrant respectively (Dion. Hal. *Ant. Rom.* 6.89.3, 8.79.3; Livy 2.41.10; Pliny, *HN* 34.15; Spaeth 1990). Scipio Aemilianus in 131 formulated his conviction that Gracchus had been lawfully killed (*iure caesus*) in the style of a *responsum*, a legal opinion (Vell. Pat. 2.4.4; Briscoe 1974: 129, n. 45; Bauman 1980: 110, n. 24). His friend Laelius is said to have demanded a memorial to Scipio Nasica as tyrannicide (Cic. *Rep.* 6.8).

The murder of a tribune in office did not, however, fail to elicit an angry reaction on the part of the populace. Tribunes made an effort to identify those responsible for his death and summoned senators before the People. While the majority of them were evasive, Scipio Nasica openly admitted his responsibility, declaring that he and the Senate had recognized Gracchus' tyrannical aspirations but the People had not (Diod. 34/35.33.6–7). The sustained popular anger against him induced the Senate to commission him with an embassy for Pergamum so that he could leave the city.

The following year the Senate set about substantiating its claims concerning Gracchus' true intentions. The consuls conducted special trials (*quaestiones extraordinariae*) against some friends of Gracchus who – like the philosopher Blossius of Cumae and the rhetorician Diophanes – were probably men of a certain prominence. We know only some details of Blossius' case. It is not clear whether he had directly participated in Gracchus' final act of desperation. He was in the end either acquitted or not prevented from going into exile. The famous story of his interrogation – specifically the question whether he would have followed an order of Gracchus to set fire to the Capitol (Cic. *Amic.* 37) – suggests that the real purpose of the trial was to demonstrate the tribune's treacherous intentions; the fear of incendiarism on the Capitol is a standard feature of all accounts of conspiracies in the Early and Middle Republic. This objective having been achieved, there was apparently no need to make an example of the individual defendant.

The proceedings in 121 had a quite different function. Instituted by the consul Opimius immediately after Gaius Gracchus had been crushed, they were aimed at those who had actually formed the body with which Gracchus had occupied the Aventine. Reportedly, more than three thousand men, who, for the most part, must have been arrested on the spot, were executed (Oros. 5.12.10). Their execution without any kind of trial was intended to intimidate the People (see Sall. *Iug.* 31.7). In 121 (as we have seen) for the first time the Senate passed a formal declaration of the kind which in the modern scholarly literature (not in the sources) is usually designated as *senatus consultum ultimum* (Ungern-Sternberg 1970: 55–71), exhorting the responsible magistrates to undertake all appropriate measures to preserve the integrity of the state (Plut. *C. Gracch.* 14.3; Cic. *Cat.* 1.4; *Phil.* 8.14). Senatorial decrees did not have the force of law, and this particular one identified neither the additional powers at the magistrate's disposal nor the citizen rights which might be overridden for reasons of state. Although the Senate's right to issue such a declaration could not reasonably be disputed, in any particular instance the presupposition of sufficient conditions as well as the legal adequacy of the magistrates' measures could be doubted and even made the subject of legal proceedings (Bleicken 1975: 473–86).

In addition, the *senatus consultum ultimum* did not necessarily affect the alleged right of any citizen, asserted by Scipio Nasica, to defend the safety of the Republic on his own initiative (Behrends 1980: 106–13). Cicero later insisted on this point in particular and repeatedly referred to the righteous action of Scipio Nasica the *privatus* (e.g., *Tusculanae Disputationes* 4.51). The *senatus consultum ultimum* of 100 (Cic. *Rab. Perd.* 20) probably narrowly anticipated self-help action on the part of senators and knights which was about to be initiated by the *princeps senatus* Aemilius Scaurus (Val. Max. 3.2.18). Similarly, the posse of senators and knights felt entitled to ignore the consul Marius' pledge of security to Saturninus and take the law into its own hands.

In 121 and 100, the magistrates tried to render permanent the temporary consensus as to the legitimacy of their proceedings by imposing posthumous sanctions on the leaders of the sedition. The goods of Gaius Gracchus and Fulvius Flaccus and later of Saturninus and his comrades were confiscated (Plut. *C. Gracch.* 17.5; Oros. 5.17.10). Gaius Gracchus' widow was not allowed to recover her dowry (Plut. *C. Gracch.* 17.5), despite good legal opinion that she was entitled to it (*Dig.* 24.3.66 pr.; Waldstein

1972). The houses of the seditions' leaders were razed (Val. Max. 6.3.1c; Cic. *Dom.* 102). The bodies of Gaius Gracchus and his companions were thrown into the river, and their widows were forbidden to go into mourning (Plut. *C. Gracch.* 17.5). To mourn Saturninus publicly and to keep his portrait was deemed actionable (though perhaps not directly relevant to the cases in question) in 99 and 98 (Cic. *Rab. Perd.* 24–5; Val. Max. 8.1 damn. 2, 3). All these measures were intended to destroy the continuity of the culprits' family traditions by obliterating the places where their family gods and the portraits of their ancestors were kept, and preventing their relatives from fulfilling their religious duties towards them and displaying their familial traditions in funeral processions.

The purpose of these measures was clearly indicated by precedents involving the alleged would-be tyrants of the Early Republic, Sp. Cassius, Sp. Maelius and M. Manlius Capitolinus (Salerno 1990). The annalistic accounts of their cases no doubt contain later embellishments, but the information on the destruction of their houses is corroborated by good antiquarian tradition (Varro, *De lingua Latina* 5. 157; Cic. *Dom.* 101; Val. Max. 6.3.1b; Livy 6.20.13; Mommsen 1871). Similar measures in various combinations were imposed with respect to persons formally declared public enemies (*hostes*) in the eighties, the victims of the proscriptions under Sulla and under the Triumvirate of 43 (App. *BCiv.* 4.32.139; Dio Cass. 47.13.2), and, finally, the culprits in cases of lese-majesty during the Imperial period[7] and of course those fallen emperors who became subjects of a *damnatio memoriae* (Vittinghoff 1936). There are many parallels from, for example, Greek antiquity,[8] Carthage (against Hannibal after his flight; Nep. *Hann.* 7.7), the Middle Ages (Fischer 1957), the Renaissance (Wolfgang 1954) and the early modern period[9] for the imposition of such posthumous sanctions, especially in cases of high treason. It

---

[7] Dio. Cass. 7.26.1; Tac. *Ann.* 6.29.1; *Dig.* 48.24.1; Grassl (1975); Levick (1976: 282, no. 50). See Eck (1993) for (not yet published) epigraphical evidence on the detailed posthumous sanctions imposed on Cn. Calpurnius Piso, the putative murderer of Germanicus. In his private capacity as heir Augustus had the house of the cruel Vedius Pollio razed to the ground (Dio. Cass. 54.23.1–6).

[8] Hdt. 6.72; Thuc. 5.63.2 (in connection with the deposition of Spartan kings); see Latte (1968: 269–70), Berneker (1971), Connor (1985) and Bauman (1990b: 68–9) for further evidence.

[9] E.g., the very cruel executions and posthumous sanctions applied against regicides and other 'traitors' in the English Restoration in 1660–2 (Adamson and Folland 1973: 427–50).

may be sufficient here to refer to the plot of Sophocles' *Antigone*, according to which the ruler's order that the public enemy must not be buried stood in direct conflict with the religious obligation of his relatives to have him properly buried, and to the measures taken by the Athenians against traitors, namely, house destruction and prohibition of burial (Xen. *Hellenica* 1.7.23), for instance, against members of the oligarchical government of 411 (Plut. *Mor.* 834A–B; Lycurg. *Leocr.* 113; Scholiast on Ar. *Lysistrata* 313) and the general Phocion in 318 (Diod. 18.67.6; Plut. *Phoc.* 37.2).

These attempts at legitimizing the suppression of sedition by killing its leaders were, however, consistently met by agitation asserting the inviolable right of the Roman citizen that a death sentence could be inflicted on him only after a formal trial. A law of Gaius Gracchus had emphasized that special courts (*quaestiones extraordinariae*) instituted by decree of the Senate rather than by plebiscite were to be considered a violation of that principle (Cic. *Rab. Perd.* 12; Plut. *C. Gracch.* 4.2–3). Accordingly, one of the consuls of 132, P. Popillius Laenas, was indicted on this basis. He chose not to stand trial and went into exile, from which he was later, however, recalled (Ungern-Sternberg 1970: 48–54). Opimius, the consul of 121, was prosecuted on the same charge in 120. His acquittal was a clear victory for the champions of the Senate's authority, but did not unequivocally and definitely establish the legitimacy of suspending an individual's civil rights for reason of state. The arguments of prosecution and defence entered the rhetorical text books, as we know from Cicero's rhetorical tracts. They refer not to the mass executions which Opimius had ordered, but to the legitimacy of killing Gaius Gracchus (who in fact had asked his own slave to kill him). As to the question of principle, it was claimed by one side that even the worst criminal was entitled to his rights as a citizen, and by the other side that this principle did not apply to someone who was about to destroy the commonwealth (Cic. *Partitiones oratoriae* 106). One party claimed that the potential tyrant should be killed without trial, the other that denying him due process of law was itself tyrannical (see Cic. *Leg.* 1.42). Hence Scipio Nasica (Plut. *Ti. Gracch.* 21.5), probably Opimius (see Oros. 5.12.10), and, of course, later Cicero were paradoxically denounced as tyrants by their opponents.

In the first decades of the first century BC, Roman politics was dominated by the Allied question, culminating in the Social War, and the struggle for power of generals such as Sulla and Marius. The pattern of senatorial crisis management which had been developed in the conflicts with the great *populares* of the late second century could not simply be repeated. The overlapping of conflicts between magistrates, magistrates and Senate, senators and knights, and old and new citizens precluded the mobilization of, say, all loyal citizens against insurgents. Accordingly, the character of the *senatus consultum ultimum* changed. In some cases it authorized military precautions against a possible attack on the city by the opposing army in a civil war, as in 83, 77 and 63 with respect to Sulla, Lepidus and Catiline. Later, in 62, 53, 52, 49 and 48, it was used in particular to suspend magistrates and to prevent the use of the tribunician veto (Plaumann 1913). In any case, the Senate's decision to levy troops and identify public enemies became more important than the declaration of emergency.

The struggles for power were resolved by military force. Sulla's move in 88 to crush the tribune Sulpicius Rufus by leading an army on Rome set a precedent, openly breaking with the Republican tradition. He and the other potentates of the following years, Octavius, Cinna and Marius, who employed conscripted soldiers as well as newly organized volunteers, gave little attention to strategies for legitimation in assembling their forces. They were, however, anxious to demonstrate that in liquidating their enemies they were acting not merely out of revenge but in the public interest.

This is why a separate *hostis* declaration was invented (Bauman 1973 and, on possible Macedonian precedents, 1990b: 164; Cloud 1994: 496). By decree of the Senate or by a legislative act the leading opponents were declared public enemies, meaning that they could be killed with impunity (App. *BCiv.* 1.60.271). The promise of blood-money and of liberty for slaves prepared to deliver their masters served as an incentive to do so. The property of the *hostes* was confiscated and their houses razed (App. *Mithr.* 51.204; *BCiv.* 1.73.340). In one case, the populace's alleged refusal of the invitation to plunder was understood as a tacit expression of protest (Val. Max. 4.3.14). The proscriptions issued by Sulla in 82 and later by the Triumvirate of 43 further formalized the procedure with particular regard to the confiscation of the property of those declared public enemies (Hinard 1985). The potentates inflicted posthumous sanctions in spectacular ways. The heads of the executed men were publicly displayed in the Forum, and their bodies were dragged through the Forum on the executioner's hook and thrown into the Tiber (see, e.g., Vell. Pat. 2.19.1; Florus 2.9.14; Luc. 2.160–73; Oros. 5.19.23, 20.4). On Sulla's orders the corpse of Marius was exhumed (four years after his death) and the remains scattered (Cic. *Leg.* 2.56); the trophies commemorating his great victories were removed (Suet. *Iul.* 11). These measures were, as we have seen, based on precedent. The extent and the intensity of their application were, however, entirely new, especially as they were used against citizens not killed in open sedition but simply put on a blacklist on the initiative of a particular potentate. One of the unintended consequences of the cruelty of the Sullan period was revived public awareness of the inalienable civil rights which a Roman citizen ought indisputably to enjoy.

This was the matter at issue in the eventual suppression of the Catilinarian conspiracy in 63. The events are all too familiar from the speeches of Cicero and the monograph of Sallust, but it is worth stressing, against the standard view, that they did not indicate the structural weakness of a state lacking adequate standing police and military forces. To be sure, the consul Cicero's warnings over several months of an impending *coup d'état* were not taken seriously by most senators. There was no proof, and the leading circles of the nobility may have thought that the 'new man' Cicero was over-reacting. In any case, they were not prepared to decide precipitately on emergency measures.

However, the various measures which had been taken since October 63, when the crisis had become evident, proved generally successful, except that the offer of impunity and rewards for informers elicited no response (Sall. *Cat.* 30.6, 36.5). Night-watches under the minor magistrates prevented arson (Sall. *Cat.* 30.7, 32.1), citizens assumed responsibility for the safety of their own houses, and the consul's bodyguard (above p. 52), now openly employed as an armed posse (Plut. *Cic.* 16.1), guaranteed his personal safety as well as the undisturbed proceedings of the Senate. Finally, the conspirators within the city were arrested by the concerted action of several magistrates and kept in custody in the houses of reliable magistrates and senators. Military precautions were taken to defend the city against an attack by the Catilinarian 'army'. On 3 December the crisis seemed to have been overcome, but the next day the situation changed dramatically when rumours spread of an imminent liberation by force of the arrested conspirators and a general uprising of the urban *plebs*. On 5 December the Senate was convened for an emergency meeting, and a posse of Roman knights was employed to guarantee its security. In a dramatic session the senators finally agreed that the arrested conspirators should be executed immediately, and the decision was carried out the same day.

The situation was certainly extremely confused. No one could know how much sympathy with the Catilinarians there was among the urban populace, or worse, whether other members of the élite were part of the conspiracy. The determination of the knights to perform security duties (Cic. *Sest.* 28; *Att.* 2.1.7) and the readiness of citizens to appear at an emergency levy of volunteers for the defence of the city (Cic. *Cat.* 4.14–16; *Phil.* 2.16; Dio Cass. 37.35.4) suggest, however, that the Senate's eventual decision to authorize the immediate execution of the leading conspirators was not – or at least not primarily – a question of there not being sufficient means to keep them in secure custody. The motive for this action was surely to make an example of them, with a view to demoralizing Catiline's armed force and putting an end to insinuations and suspicions concerning the involvement of prominent politicians. To hold the arrested men for an ordinary trial would have jeopardized the newly achieved unity of the ruling classes, and risked the acquittal of the accused despite their apparent guilt.

The decision to execute obviously implied ignoring the citizen's right to an ordinary trial, and Caesar, in particular, made a point of reminding the senators of this. As far as we know, the hard-liners made no reference to the *senatus consultum ultimum* of late October. Instead it may have been argued that the Catilinarians should be considered *hostes* who could not claim the protection of the *lex Sempronia* of 123 (Cic. *Cat.* 4.10). This would, however, have been a dubious approach, since they had not been apprehended in open and armed rebellion, and the *hostis* declaration of November had applied only to Catiline and his companions in arms outside Rome.

An alternative legal basis for the execution order was apparently the assumption that criminals who had been caught in the act and confessed were, in accordance with a general rule of criminal law, no longer entitled to be formally tried. According to Sallust (*Cat.* 52.36; compare App. *BCiv.* 2.6.21) this was the essence of the Younger Cato's *sententia*, which carried the day. Whether there had ever been such an unequivocal rule with respect to manifest guilt (beyond the cases of theft and adultery, neither of which, however, was part of criminal law), as at least Sallust supposed, is a matter of scholarly controversy (Crook 1987). In any case, the rule that a confession immediately led to a conviction applied only in the context of proper judicial proceedings, and where the defendant not only confessed the facts but also pleaded guilty in a technical juridical sense (Cic. *Inv. Rhet.* 1.15; *Mil.* 7, 15; *Rhet. Her.* 1.24; 2. 23–4). The latter procedure seems to have been employed in at least some of the extraordinary trials of the Middle Republic, later gained importance in treason trials under the Principate (Hennig 1973: 251; Bauman 1974a; but cf. Crook 1976; Brunt 1984: 475), and finally became the basis for the conviction of Christians (Mayer-Maly 1956).

As for the Catilinarians, even if one might construe their statements and their abandonment of defence in a previous meeting of the Senate (Cic. *Cat.* 3.10–13) as implying confessions (as Cicero did later; *Cat.* 4.4; *Sest.* 145), it is beyond doubt that the Senate had not sat as a court and therefore any so-called confession could not be legally decisive. Moreover, Caesar had declared unequivocally that no exception to the right of a formal trial should be allowed (Plut. *Cat. Min.* 22.4). Consequently, one of the incoming tribunes (who began their term of office, as usual, on 10 December) charged the consul Cicero with being responsible for the execution of *cives indemnati*. The dubious legality of Cicero's action was to constitute a main subject of agitation by *populares* in the ensuing years.

CHAPTER 3

The collapse of the Republican order

NEW DIMENSIONS OF POPULAR PROTEST

During the sixties and the fifties of the first century BC, Rome saw waves of political violence which could no longer be controlled. This was partly because government was paralysed by power struggles within the nobility; thus in 59, for example, Caesar forced the passage of his agrarian law against the opposition of his consular colleague Bibulus. In addition, however, the post-Sullan era witnessed the development of new methods of organizing the *plebs* and articulating social protest. In the end, the Republican system of maintaining law and order collapsed.

Clodius and the plebs urbana

These developments are especially associated with the role played by P. Clodius Pulcher, who obviously profited from the repeated deadlocks in the power struggle between Pompey, Caesar and Crassus and the Senate. He was surely neither the first nor the only person to mobilize parts of the urban populace, but by employing every available means in so concentrated and unscrupulous a way over a considerable period of time he opened up new dimensions of politics. What matters is not his personal motives and ultimate aims (if, indeed, he had clearly formulated any) but that he was able to present himself as the People's champion and to represent his personal cause against Cicero as an issue of the People's liberty. Here we might compare his role to the one played by John Wilkes for the London masses during the 1760s and 1770s (Brewer 1976: 163–200, 1980). Though the following discussion focuses on Clodius, it is to be understood as a case-study of the new elements of popular intervention in politics and their implications.

Clodius' success was the result of his taking up simultaneously all the issues in which the interests of the urban masses had been neglected or violated during the preceding years. As tribune of 58, he immediately brought in a package of laws. His *lex frumentaria* established for the first time the free distribution of (a minimum ration of) corn. Ever since Gaius Gracchus had institutionalized monthly public distributions at a fixed and subsidized price to all adult male citizens resident in Rome, the question of the corn dole had repeatedly aroused controversies (Rickman 1980: 26–54; Garnsey 1988: 198–217). Whereas advocates of the institution claimed that the People was entitled to its share of the profits from the Empire and even tried to make the claim to such benefits (*commoda*) a component of *libertas* (Vanderbroeck 1987: 106–7, 171), its critics pointed to the danger of corruption of the People and burdens on the treasury (which should not be taken too seriously; Meijer 1990; Ungern-Sternberg 1991). Changes in the amount of the subsidy and the number of recipients were sporadically made according to the relative strength of political forces. Sulla's abolition of distributions could not last, but the post-Sullan distributions were of modest dimensions until the end of 63, when they were increased in response to the Catilinarian crisis. Clodius tried to gain control over the corn trade itself, and apparently charged the local administration of the city's quarters (*vici*) with the distribution of the corn (Cic. *Dom.* 25–6; Taylor 1960: 76–8; Rickman 1980: 52–3; Nicolet 1980b).

Clodius' second move concerned the re-legalization of the *collegia*, associations that functioned as primitive trade unions, friendly associations and burial societies and met regularly for common meals (Varro, *Rust.* 3.2.16). They had a long tradition, as the reference to them in the Twelve Tables shows (8.27; cf. *Dig.* 47.22.4), but even the Romans of the Late Republic had no precise knowledge as to their origin. Some were supposed to stem from the Regal period as a creation of either King Numa Pompilius or King Servius Tullius (Gabba 1984), and others had been founded during the Middle Republic. Whatever their original legal status, from the Middle Republic onward it was probably considered a right of Roman citizens to unite in such organizations without special permission from the authorities (Behrends 1981). In most cases the membership was made up of petty tradesmen and craftsmen and included a considerable number of freedmen and even slaves, provided that their masters had agreed (*Dig.* 47.22.3.2). Their internal structure, consisting of elected magistrates and assemblies open to all members, resembled that of the Republic as a whole (cf. *Dig.* 3.4.1.1). Participation in the meetings of a *collegium* and in the election of its magistrates would have entailed considerable quasi-political experience, and election as head of a *collegium* would have conferred special dignity upon a person of humble origin or even servile descent which he could not have achieved otherwise (Ausbüttel 1982; Royden 1988; Fellmeth 1990).

The organization of the *collegia* dovetailed with that of the city districts (*vici*) and even smaller neighbourhood units (Cic. *Dom.* 74) and offered opportunities to organize parts of the *plebs* for political purposes. They had apparently been used in this way, at least from time to time, since the Middle Republic, as we know by chance with respect to Scipio Aemilianus' candidacy for the censorship of 142 (Plut. *Aem.* 38.4). They are presumed to have been the organizers of a cult of the dead Gracchi (Plut. *C. Gracch.* 18.2), and are identified as such in the extraordinary honours paid to M. Marius Gratidianus in the mid-eighties (Cic. *Off.* 3.80; Pliny, *HN* 33.132, 34.27; Sen. *De ira* 3.18.1). From at least the sixties onward, the politicization of the *collegia* was obviously promoted for the comprehensive organization of claques and riots and the distribution of bribes in the run-up to an election. In 67 an attempt to stop the distribution of money by agents (*divisores*) who may well have been identical with the semi-official heads of tribes (Varro, *Ling.* 6.86; App. *BCiv.* 3.23.88) met with strong resistance (Asc. p. 75, 20–76, 2). At the turn of the year 67/66 the tribune C. Manilius chose the day of the Compitalian games to force passage of a law (subsequently annulled) distributing the freedmen over all thirty-five tribes (Asc. pp. 45, 65; Dio Cass. 36.42.2–3). Organized groups were responsible for violent disturbances at trials in 65 (Asc. pp. 59–60). The Senate reacted in 64 by banning the *collegia* which were thought to be behind subversive actions (Linderski 1968; Salerno 1984), but the oldest and most reputable associations were probably excluded from the ban. In particular, the performance of the Compitalian Games was prohibited (Asc. pp. 7, 75; Cic. *Pis.* 8). These games implied a symbolic abolition of the status boundary between free and slave. They were organized by the heads of the districts of Rome (*magistri vicorum*), who for the occasion wore the *toga praetexta* (a garment bordered with purple that was usually reserved for the higher magistrates) and were accompanied by lictors (Cic. *Pis.* 8, 23; Livy 34.7.2).

The ban on *collegia* and on the Compitalian games aroused the *plebs*'s indignation. Attempts to re-introduce the games in defiance of the Senate's decree having failed in previous years (Cic. *Pis.* 8; Asc. p. 7), Clodius had them performed again on 1 January 58 (Cic. *Pis.* 8), which was actually some days before the vote on his bill cancelling the ban on *collegia* and allowing the formation of new ones. Performance of the *Compitalia* on 1 January also amounted to a sort of competition with the consuls, who used to make vows for the good of the state when entering office on this very day (Scheid 1985: 130–1).

These reactivated and newly founded *collegia*, apparently based on the administrative structure of the *vici*, became the backbone of Clodius' activities (Lintott 1968: 77–83; Treggiari 1969: 168–77; Flambard 1977, 1981; Perelli 1982: 211–16). They were probably supported by well-organized associations of Isis-worshippers, who at the beginning of the year 58 and on further occasions during the fifties displayed stubborn resistance to various attempts by magistrates to destroy their shrine on the Capitol (Tert. *Ad nationes* 1.10.17–18, quoted from Varro; *Apologeticum* 6.7–8; Dio Cass. 40.47.3; Taylor 1949; Coarelli 1983; Alföldi 1985: 52–74).[1] The *collegia* produced personnel with organizing ability; the most notorious of them, Sex. Cloelius (who headed the *Compitalia* in 58) was a scribe who apparently possessed remarkable administrative skills, acting, for example, as draftsman of Clodius' laws and as supervisor of the corn dole (Cic. *Dom.* 25 and 47). That such persons, mostly freedmen, are mentioned by name in Cicero's speeches (prosopography in Flambard 1977; Benner 1987: 155–76; Vanderbroeck 1987: 199–209) reveals that they must have been figures of a certain, if dubious, reputation. Their followers were denounced by Cicero as gangsters, scum and runaway slaves, but reference to the involvement of slaves is part of the standard repertoire of political denunciation, and hints at the considerable role played by shopkeepers (*tabernarii*; Cic. *Dom.* 13 and 89; Asc. p. 52, 13) suggest that they included also respectable petty tradesmen (Treggiari 1969: 265–6, 1980; Welwei 1988: 113–36). This assumption is

---

[1] Cic. *Flacc.* 66 suggests that the Jewish community at Rome was able to build up considerable pressure on public proceedings.

strengthened by the parallel of early modern mobs, which were often composed of such *menu peuple* (Brunt 1966).

Finally, Clodius took up the question of civil rights, representing the execution of the five Catilinarians in 63 as a fundamental violation of *libertas*. Through a virtuoso combination of legislation, tribunicial measures and street terror, he managed to demonstrate that the people would not tolerate such an infringement of their rights and would themselves punish violators. He promulgated a law which provided for the exiling of anyone who had killed a *civis indemnatus* (Moreau 1987). Although it might have been applied to all the senators who had been involved in the decision of 63 (cf. Dio Cass. 38.14.4–5), Cicero was singled out for public attack to make it obvious that it was he for whom the law was essentially intended.

Apparently, the law did not specify the form of legal prosecution. Clodius would probably have turned the tables on Cicero and argued that the consul of 63, who had always boasted of his decision to execute the conspirators, should be treated like a confessed criminal and therefore a trial was unnecessary (Lintott 1972: 262). Cicero, however, elected to go into exile the day before the law was passed. (Since he had never been indicted, he later claimed that he had remained a *civis indemnatus* despite his decision to leave Rome.) Once the law had come into force, Clodius staged the destruction of Cicero's house on the Palatine, 'in full view of well-nigh the whole city' (Cic. *Dom.* 100; cf. Vell. Pat. 2.14.3)[2] and of his villas. Thus he demonstratively executed the penalty stipulated for a declared public enemy (Dio Cass. 38.17.6), either as an instance of a sort of popular justice or in virtue of his competence as a tribune. In other conflicts Clodius threatened to consecrate to Ceres the goods of the consul Gabinius, who opposed him (Cic. *Dom.* 124), and in 58 and 57 had the fasces of consuls' lictors broken by riotous crowds (Cic. *Pis.* 28; *Red. Sen.* 7; *Post reditum ad Populum* 14) – both actions which may also have conjured up the symbolism of the Struggle of the Orders. In any case, there could be no doubt as to the symbolic meaning associated with the destruction of Cicero's house (Allen 1944). Cicero later claimed (*Dom.* 100–3) that the case of his own house should not be compared to the proceedings against the would-be tyrants of the Early Republic or the leaders of the 121

---

[2] Cf. Wiseman (1987) and Wallace-Hadrill (1988) on the growing importance of houses as status symbol in Late Republican times.

sedition, but in arguing in this way he was tacitly conceding that Clodius had staged a carefully directed imitation of official sanctions.

A subsequent law aimed directly against Cicero declared his voluntary departure a legal exile and his status that of outlaw on the grounds that he was responsible for the execution of *cives indemnati*.[3] It also contained clauses which confirmed the confiscation of Cicero's property, entrusted Clodius with its sale at public auction, and probably also authorized him to erect a shrine of *Libertas* on the site of Cicero's Palatine house. The last move is especially telling, since Cicero was denounced as tyrant and destroyer of liberty (Cic. *Sest.* 109), but, if valid, it would also have barred the site's being restored to private ownership in the future (Picard 1965; Watson 1992: 55–7; Bergemann 1992: 52–7). Furthermore, the law forbade any reconsideration of Cicero's case in Senate or assembly. The validity of the last-mentioned clause could be doubted especially as far as the actions of future tribunes were concerned (Moreau 1989), but Clodius had thereby established some sort of pretended legal basis even for the violent acts he organized after his tribunate had expired.

The symbolism of political violence

Clodius had not needed to employ violence to have his laws passed. They were highly popular, and no serious attempt had been made to interfere with the relevant proceedings of the assembly by way of *intercessio* or *obnuntiatio* (Tatum 1990b). Violence was employed instead to defend his legislation. Clodius tried to prevent Cicero's being recalled, and when he could no longer block that he concentrated on obstructing the restoration of Cicero's property. Senate and *pontifices* repeatedly had to deal with complicated legal questions that arose; a particular difficulty was the validity of the *Libertas* shrine's dedication, which in the end was denied (Tatum 1993). At one stage in this conflict Clodius even exhorted the people present at a *contio* to come to the defence of the 'consecrated' shrine by playing on the formula of *evocatio* (Cic. *Att.* 4.2.3). His

---

[3] As a rule outlawry by *interdictio aquae et ignis* ('interdiction from fire and water') was voted against someone who after an indictment (Livy 25.4.9) or even a conviction had gone into exile.

repeated attempts to prevent the reconstruction of Cicero's city
house by driving off the construction workers and setting the building on fire and also the concomitant attacks on the houses of
Cicero's brother, Quintus, and of his chief ally, Milo (Masłowski
1976), all took place in broad daylight under the eyes of the whole
city (Cic. *Att.* 4.3.3; *Cael.* 78).

Besides using to the full or abusing the sanctions that a tribune
had at his disposal and staging high-handed imitations and usurp-
ations of official sanctions, Clodius resorted to rituals of popular
justice against Cicero in 57 and Pompey in 56 as responsible for the
famine of the time. There were nightly processions against Cicero
(Cic. *Dom.* 14; *Att.* 4.1.6), and political attacks on Pompey were
shouted in chorus, their insinuations of Pompey's homosexual incli-
nations being a reply in kind to mock verses on the alleged inces-
tuous relations of Clodius with his sister (Cic. *QFr.* 2.3.2; Plut.
Pomp. 48.7).

None of this is meant to make light of the violence that Clodius
employed or to suggest that he had always been able to command a
large following among the populace. Indeed, in some situations
after the end of his tribunate he was obviously supported only by a
hard core of followers, and in all serious clashes with the gladiators
employed by his opponent Milo the Clodians had to turn tail (e.g.,
Cic. *Att.* 4.3.3–5). Even more important, his attempt in 57 to
strengthen the *vici* and indirectly certain *collegia* as a basis for power
and patronage by making them responsible for the corn dole was
thwarted. Instead, Pompey was commissioned with the *cura
annonae*, a post that carried responsibility both for securing the corn
supply of the city and for organizing its distribution. The decision
to appoint Pompey was precipitated by a shortage brought about
or at least aggravated by the manipulations of the great corn mer-
chants (Łoposzko 1979). The crisis had led to angry reactions on
the part of the masses which compelled the senators to place
Pompey in command. Those who were thus articulating the will of
the People had obviously on this occasion pushed aside the close
followers of Clodius (Cic. *Dom.* 6–7, 15), but it was not simply a
question of political manœuvres. The crucial problem was supply,
and the great majority surely had confidence in Pompey's military
and organizational genius. (Indeed, in 67 the *plebs* had supported
Pompey's special command to fight the pirates.) But a stable
supply had to be paid for by means of strict control of the qualifi-

cations for participation in the distributions. Pompey started by drawing up new lists, an operation which the Clodians apparently tried to sabotage by setting fire to the Temple of the Nymphs which housed the relevant archive (Nicolet 1976c). One reason was that Pompey's revision of the dole lists would especially have affected those persons who in consequence of the Clodian corn law had only been informally manumitted and were therefore not yet officially acknowledged as citizens (Dio Cass. 39.24.1; Dion. Hal. *Ant. Rom.* 4.24.5; Scholiast on Persius 5.73).

Nevertheless, Clodius had been able to create a stable alignment with the *plebs urbana* that outlasted the year of his tribunate. This loyalty found especially forceful expression after his murder by Milo during a (chance?) clash on the Via Appia in January 52. The two had already fought during the campaign for the elections for that year. Since other competitors for office had also engaged in street fighting, the elections could not be held, with the result that the year opened without major magistrates in office. The violent reaction of the *plebs* to the murder of its champion[4] culminated in the burning down of the Senate House. Sex. Cloelius, Clodius' former henchman, took the lead in cooperation with three tribunes. The burning of the Senate House was embedded in rituals which amounted to honouring Clodius with the popular version of a state funeral (cf. Dio Cass. 40.49.2–3; Achard 1975). The house of the *interrex* Lepidus, who had been installed by the Senate immediately after the destruction of the *curia*, was besieged in order to compel him to hold the elections immediately (and thus destroy Milo's prospects). When he refused to do this – on the grounds of precedent, which forbade the first *interrex* to organize elections – his house was broken into and the portraits of his ancestors in the atrium were smashed. The destruction of the symbolic marriage bed placed there was apparently a crude form of charivari inflicted on Lepidus' wife, whose immaculate reputation Asconius (p. 43, 6–18) therefore felt obliged to stress.

Later (in April), during the special trials held chiefly for Milo but also for ringleaders of the Clodian party, the Clodians showed up as organized claques and tried to influence the courts' decisions by intimidation. As Clodius himself had done in 57, the tribunes

---

[4] The repercussions throughout Italy are apparent in the inscription published by Solin (1981); cf. Tatum (1990c).

who supported his cause ordered that the *tabernae* be closed; the shopkeepers responded to their appeal to express the People's determination to have Milo convicted (Asc. p. 52, 11–15). That the new Clodian leaders were able to channel the spontaneous anger of the populace as well as deliberately mobilize parts of the *plebs* for organized demonstrations clearly shows the lasting effects of Clodius' policy of organizing and, so to speak, training the *plebs urbana*. Leaders from the political class now needed the cooperation of the intermediate leaders who headed the *collegia* and the *vici* (Vanderbroeck 1987: 52–66), and they had to convince the masses that they were acting on their behalf.

The methods of crisis management which had been developed in the late second century no longer worked. The ruling classes were unable to agree on emergency measures; the urban masses could not be kept in check merely by means of patronage and social control, since they no longer showed the deference to their social superiors which had once (as in 133) restrained them from actual confrontation (see Badian 1972: 725). In extreme situations of popular unrest, public order could be restored only by sacrificing fundamental principles of the Republican constitution.

CALLING IN THE TROOPS

The violent disturbances of the fifties, and especially the anarchy of 53/52, resulted in departures from the constitutional conventions which had thus far governed the conduct of the authorities. On the one hand, there was a resort to self-help no longer legitimized by declarations of the Senate and an underlying consensus of élite and 'loyal citizens'; on the other hand, for the first time regularly conscripted soldiers were used for police functions within the city.

The responsible magistrates were not prepared to take action against Clodius even after his tribunate had expired. In the years 57 and 56 it was Milo, tribune in 57, who became his chief opponent, engaging himself especially in the cause of Cicero before pursuing his own career in 53/52. In carrying out the occupation of public places in order to impede decisions of the assembly (Cic. *Att.* 4.3.4), the defence of Cicero's city house (and of his own), and the associated street fighting with the Clodians (Cic. *Att.* 4.3.2–5; *Mil.* 41), Milo, assisted by Sestius, a colleague in office in 57, and others had from the very beginning relied on a body of their own freedmen, house slaves and especially hired gladiators (Cic. *QFr.* 2.5.3; Dio Cass. 39.8.1; Asc. p. 32, 1–2); the latter proved remarkably successful.

For obvious reasons Cicero always defended Milo's actions, but his line of argument in this context is particularly revealing inasmuch as it demonstrates a crisis of legitimacy. He regularly labelled Milo's and Sestius' gangs legitimate *praesidia* (*Sest.* 90), thus implying that they were acting in the public interest, and even assumed that in certain situations they were entitled to act contrary to the decisions of the Senate and the responsible magistrates (*Sest.* 89, 95; Bleicken 1975: 486–91). In the published (and improved) version of his defence speech for Milo in 52, Cicero, in addition to claiming that Milo had acted in self-defence, argued that as a *privatus* he had defended the *res publica* at a time when its very existence had been at stake and the responsible authorities had refused to take appropriate action. The killing of Clodius was, therefore, comparable to the killing of Sp. Maelius or Tiberius Gracchus (Cic. *Mil.* 72, 83), and far from being accused of murder Milo ought to be honoured as a tyrannicide (*Mil.* 80).

We have already seen that Scipio Nasica's argument, that under extreme circumstances citizens were entitled to defend the commonwealth on their own initiative, had not been completely superseded by the invention of the *senatus consultum ultimum*. It had always been assumed, however, that this *ultima ratio* could be employed only on the basis of the broad consensus that would provide it with retroactive legitimation and defence. With respect to the inherent tension between the legal priority of the magistrate's initiative and the immanent right of citizens to intervene, Cicero in 52 not only took an extreme position in favour of private initiative but also implied that it did not require such retroactive confirmation. Thus he claimed that Milo had acted in the public interest even though the Senate had officially and unequivocally asserted the contrary (Asc. p. 36, 5–9). Cicero's position was not officially accepted in 52, but one should not dismiss it simply as pettifoggery; he was to use the same arguments again in 44, when, speaking now as the recognized leader of the Republican cause, he pleaded for the official acknowledgement of Octavian's private military activities (*Phil.* 3.3). Indeed, Octavian/Augustus himself was later to base his claim of legitimacy for his *coup d'état* on the same line of argument (*Res gestae* 1; Béranger 1958).

The immediate reaction to the anarchy of early 52 led, however, to unprecedented measures of quite a different sort. After the burning down of the *curia* the Senate proclaimed a *senatus consultum ultimum* and authorized Pompey to levy troops in Italy (Asc. p. 34, 2–6). Having completed this levy, Pompey returned to Rome but was anxious not to cross the *pomerium*, which would have entailed the loss of his proconsular powers. Instead he waited in his 'gardens' on the west of the Pincian Hill, outside the *pomerium*, until the Senate was prepared to have him appointed sole consul (Marshall 1985a: 180). The presiding *interrex*, Ser. Sulpicius Rufus, was a distinguished jurist who would have been able to legitimize such a constitutional innovation (Bauman 1985: 27–32). Pompey as consul immediately brought in a bill establishing special courts to deal with the events on the Via Appia, the burning of the *curia*, and the siege of the *interrex* Lepidus' house. Additionally he had a law passed which authorized trials in cases of *ambitus* (electoral corruption) retroactively as far back as the year of his first consulship in 70. The procedure for these trials was streamlined and the jury members were chosen from a panel that Pompey himself had carefully selected (Asc. pp. 36, 9–13; 38, 14–19; Vell. Pat. 2.76.1), but in principle the courts were set up in accordance with constitutional rules and the rule of trial by jury was upheld. Milo and several Clodian activists were thus finally convicted (Alexander 1990: 151–65). In a way, major disturbances were for the first time effectively punished by due process of law.

These 'successes' were achieved, however, in extraordinary circumstances. Pompey had employed his troops to ensure undisturbed proceedings of Senate meetings and trials as well (Asc. pp. 41, 1–3; 50, 25). On some occasions, especially on the final day of Milo's trial, when the presiding judge had formally asked for protection (Asc. p. 40, 7–11), the troops took drastic action against rioting crowds which ended in bloodshed even though they had apparently been instructed to conduct themselves with moderation (Dio Cass. 40.53.3). It might be argued that this use of troops did not differ in principle from the employment of *praesidia*, but this would be a one-sided version of events. The use of formally levied soldiers within the city and over a considerable period was without precedent, if one can except the practice of the potentates during the civil war period of the eighties. The soldiers, who were levied in Italy, were subject to military discipline, and their readiness to follow the instructions of their commander was as a rule not impeded by personal links or a feeling of political solidarity with the urban crowds they confronted. Thus the legal and psychological implications of the use of conscripted troops differed fundamentally from those connected with an emergency appeal to volunteers resident in the city. It therefore ought not to be considered as merely an extraordinary yet perfectly proper measure for restoring law and order. Moreover, this assessment of the events of 52 holds true whatever view one takes of Pompey's constitutional position after he had been elected sole consul – whether or not he doubled as consul and proconsul, thus anticipating for a short time the constitutional position of the Triumvirate and Principate (see Bleicken 1990: 59–60 with comments on Ridley 1983).

In any case, Pompey's extraordinary position (at least until the election of a second consul in August 52) differed only slightly from the dictatorship at which he had been rumoured to be aiming for some years. Furthermore, he had never left any doubt as to his determination to have Milo (and others) convicted (Vell. Pat. 2.47.4). In this and other cases he did not succeed in dispelling the impression that he had unduly influenced the juries' decisions. This is why he could be blamed for having used his soldiers to intimidate the courts; this reproach was issued not only by Cicero in (the published version of) his defence speech on behalf of Milo (*Mil.* 2, 71), but also by the convicts who had to go into exile and had joined Caesar. As tensions increased on the eve of the civil war, the Caesarian side began arguing that the trials conducted in the presence of Pompeian legions had shown that Pompey was a threat to Republican liberty (Caes. *Bellum civile* 3.1.4; Sall. *Ep.* 2.3.2–3; Luc. 1.315–26). Even had Pompey not personally given cause to suspect the impartiality of the trials which he had instituted, the fact that they took place under circumstances incompatible with Republican traditions would have been reason enough for doubt about their legitimacy.

During the ensuing period of civil war from 49 until the establishment of a new order by Augustus in 27, soldiers were regularly employed to quell riots. This should not, however, be understood as a direct consequence of the measures of 52, which after all were temporary and restricted. It was due especially to the dependence of the particular men in power on military might and their willingness to disregard constitutional rules. Violent demonstrations by the urban *plebs* do, however, reveal the persistence of structures developed during the preceding decades. The combination of autonomous organization and spontaneous articulation of the masses' material and cultural interests with cynical manipulation of their wishes in the power struggle between the Senate and certain politicians again constituted an often explosive mixture.

The behaviour of the masses at Caesar's funeral in 44, for example, followed the pattern of 52 (Plut. *Brut.* 20.5). They forced his cremation to take place in the Forum and tried to set the rebuilt *curia* and the houses of Caesar's murderers on fire and to avenge their hero with lynchings (Alföldi 1953: 39–82). During the following weeks they repeatedly tried to erect a shrine to him in the Forum. These efforts, which led to various clashes with the authorities, were organized by a certain Amatius or Herophilus, who pretended to be the grandson of the great Marius. His popularity with the urban masses had already embarrassed Caesar, who had once had him removed from the city. Antony imprisoned Amatius and had him executed (App. *BCiv.* 3.3.6; Yavetz 1969: 58–77). During the continued disturbances the other consul, Dolabella, ordered the arrest of rioters and public punishment by throwing them from the Tarpeian Rock or, if they were slaves, crucifixion (Cic. *Att.* 14.15.2).

Amatius' success after his return in 44 is said to have been based on his role as a patron of the majority of *collegia* (Val. Max. 9.15.1). It was the practice of the *collegia* to elect patrons, in most cases members of the senatorial and equestrian ranks, but however the connection between the Pseudo-Marius and a great number of *collegia* is to be understood, there is at least a hint here that certain *collegia* were still organizations that could mobilize the *plebs*. This was despite the restrictions which had been imposed on them by Caesar in 46, when he had again prohibited the ones recently founded (Suet. *Iul.* 42.3) and decreed that the establishment of a new *collegium* required authorization by the Senate (*CIL* VI, 2193; Yavetz 1983: 85–96). Later, funerary *collegia* were generally allowed and no longer had to obtain special authorization. In the civil-war period following Caesar's death, *collegia nova* are said to have been formed as cover organizations for robbers and criminals (Suet. *Aug.* 32.1).

The events of 44 also display the pattern of loyalty to a popular hero on the part of the *plebs* and attempts to establish a religious cult in his honour (Rini 1983; Alföldi 1985). Here again we observe the cultural and political aspirations of the urban masses which called for new methods of social integration. During the forties and thirties the *plebs urbana* resorted to demonstrations and riots to articulate complaints arising from their material problems. During Caesar's dictatorship but in his absence, ambitious magistrates in 48 and 47 raised the question not only of a general reduction or even cancellation of debts (which was especially desired by certain members of the aristocracy) but also of a reduction in rents (Bruhns 1978: 122–37; Piazza 1980: 54–75; Simélon 1985). Ordinary people always lived on the brink of indebtedness and the ensuing homelessness as a consequence of the rents they had to pay for their lodgings (Frier 1977). Accordingly, this suggestion struck a responsive chord with elements of the *plebs urbana*, and they expressed their demands by rioting and in 47 barricaded the Forum to force the passage of Dolabella's debt-relief measure (Dio Cass. 42.32.3). The uprising was, however, brutally crushed by military force, with an outcome of eight hundred dead (Livy, *Per.* 113), and Caesar agreed to only a moderate reduction or moratorium. The long-term problem of the city's corn supply was aggravated during the civil war by Sex. Pompeius' sea blockade from 41 to 39. Antony and Octavian were physically attacked in the Forum by a starving populace seeking a settlement with Sex. Pompeius, and again the disturbances were crushed by brutal military force (App. *BCiv.* 5.68.287–9; Dio Cass. 48.31.6). Popular pressure did, however, contribute to a temporary agreement between these potentates in 39 (Vell. Pat. 2.77.1).

The common feature of these (and other) events during the domination of Caesar and of the Triumvirate was that those in power, whatever their response to the actual demands of the people, did not hesitate to employ troops when they needed to put down riots. This could lead to the killing of hundreds of people. In other cases, as at Caesar's funeral, the soldiers were apparently instructed to allow a popular outburst but prevent it from being carried to extremes. Sometimes, too, they were employed (for example, by Dolabella in 44) to arrest ringleaders on the spot, for spectacular executions intended to intimidate the masses.

The decision in each case depended on the calculation by those in power of the usefulness of riots in relation to the danger they might involve for their own positions. The powerful were bound by no scruples as to civil rights; the executions of the Pseudo-Marius and of rioters in 44 were carried out by virtue of magisterial *coercitio* without any pretence to judicial justification (App. *BCiv.* 3.3.6, 3.16.57). That such actions were viewed by senators and especially by Cicero as necessary to maintain the state's authority (App. *BCiv.* 3.3.6; Cic. *Att.* 14.15.2; *Phil.* 1.5 and 30) demonstrates the collapse of the Republic's constitutional principles. The occasional acceptance of such actions for opportunistic motives notwithstanding, the use of soldiers in the capital during the civil-war period could not be considered a legitimate method of maintaining public order. This was partly because the soldiers were sometimes undisciplined, as during the famine of 41–39, when they broke into houses and took to robbery and plundering (App. *BCiv.* 5.18.72–3, 5.34.138), and partly because, especially during the proscriptions of 43, they were simply instruments of the political will of their leaders (App. *BCiv.* 4.12.48).

CHAPTER 4

Features of the new Imperial order

THE CITY OF ROME

For Augustus, restoring political and social order meant integrating the relevant social groups. Whereas the senators were won over by the so-called restoration of the Republic, the *plebs urbana* had to be approached in ways which demonstrated the emperor's concern for both their material and their cultural demands.

The emperor and his people

The most important issue was, of course, the capital's corn supply. The people's demand for a stable supply guaranteed by the ruler himself could not be ignored, and in 22 BC Augustus took the opportunity of a famine both to accept the *cura annonae*, which in 43 had been abolished as unconstitutional (Dio Cass. 46.39.3), and to reject the dictatorship that the people were pressing on him (Dio Cass. 54.1.1–5; Suet. *Aug.* 52; Vell. Pat. 2.89.5; *Res gestae* 5). Thereafter the corn supply remained the responsibility of the emperor (see Tac. *Ann.* 3.54.4–5), symbolizing his role as the great patron of the *plebs frumentaria*. Those registered for the corn distribution were also entitled to receive occasional gifts of money; not necessarily the very poor, they tended to represent a relatively well-off segment (Van Berchem 1939; Nicolet 1985: 828–33; Virlouvet 1991). The living conditions of the urban population were, furthermore, considerably improved by measures regulating the water supply, sewers, maintenance of the banks of the Tiber, public works, etc., for which services a number of boards headed by senior senators were established (Ramage 1983; Scobie 1986; Schneider 1986;

Bruun 1991; Robinson 1992).[1] These improvements of public administration were not the result of systematic planning but responses to actual crises; the eventual regulation was often achieved only after a certain amount of experimentation (Eck 1986).

Emperors were also concerned to incorporate the organizations of the *plebs urbana* into the new system. On the one hand, control over the *collegia* was revived; on the other, the Compitalia festival was combined with the cult of the Imperial dynasty – the *lares* and the *genius Augusti*. The *vici* formed the backbone of the new organizational structure of the city. The *vicomagistri* were granted official status and entrusted with the supervision of their districts, and their number was increased (Bleicken 1958). *Vici* may also have been employed as units in organizing the distribution of corn (Rickman 1980: 190). The *plebs*'s functionaries, often freedmen, were thus made part of the cultural and administrative infrastructure of the new order, just as the municipal *Augustales*, who performed the cult of the emperor, were primarily recruited among the *magistri* of *collegia* there. This was probably of more practical importance than the procedure established at the same time, by which for each of the now fourteen regions of the city one praetor, aedile or tribune of the people was appointed by lot as nominal head (Suet. *Aug.* 30.1; Dio Cass. 55.8.7).

Emperors' attempts at integrating and pacifying the *plebs urbana* did not prevent popular protest, but as a rule such demonstrations as occurred were intended not to undermine an emperor's position but to strengthen the affective ties between ruler and ruled. Fluctuations in the price of corn and difficulties with the supply remained major problems despite the efforts of the Imperial administration (Virlouvet 1985; Pavis d'Escurac 1976; Herz 1988a: 55–105; Galsterer 1990; Sirks 1991). Various measures for improvement (including some aimed at the supply of the free market) were undertaken under the stimulus of popular demonstrations. The emperor's presence in the capital was seen as a guarantee against shortages (Tac. *Ann.* 15.36.4). It was he who was held directly responsible and expected to resolve crises and introduce lasting improvements; see, for example, Claudius' reaction to his being reminded of his task by hissing from the *plebs* during a corn short-

---

[1] On the archaeological evidence, see the survey of recent scholarship by Patterson (1992: 210–14).

age in 51 (Tac. *Ann.* 12.43; Suet. *Divus Claudius* 18–19; Gai. *Inst.* 1.32c). Such exchanges were one aspect of an almost symbiotic relationship between the ruler and the capital's citizenry (Veyne 1976: 539–791; Flaig 1992: 38–93),[2] a phenomenon for which there are parallels from other periods and places (Hobsbawm 1971: 108–25).

In Rome, theatre and circus were the arenas in which *princeps* and *plebs* met (Cameron 1974, 1976; Tengström 1977; Millar 1977: 368–75; Fraschetti 1990). There the People could legitimize the *princeps*'s extraordinary position, as they did in 2 BC when the Senate's proclamation of Augustus as *pater patriae* followed popular acclamations during the games (Suet. *Aug.* 58). Official recognition that the games (now including gladiatorial contests and combats of wild beasts) were the occasions on which the people expressed their will was underlined by Augustus' regulation of the seating order to reflect the hierarchical order of society (Suet. *Aug.* 44; *Dom.* 8.3; Tac. *Ann.* 13.54.3; Rawson 1987; Frei-Stolba 1988). The games now also performed the safety-valve function of the Republic's popular assemblies. The ruler could use them to test his popularity, to respond to demands from the people, and, depending on the situation and his mood, to display either paternal affability or imperatorial severity; an emperor who knew how to handle the *plebs urbana* would take care to explain a negative reply (Suet. *Aug.* 42) rather than arrogantly demanding silence (Suet. *Dom.* 13.1). During the games, too, he could obtain the people's endorsement of the administration of justice by parading informers or executing criminals before them (Suet. *Tit.* 8.5; Martial, *Spectacula* 4; Pliny, *Pan.* 34.1–4; Coleman 1990). His confronting his people face-to-face could sometimes be more important than the substance of his response; this was a lesson that, for example, Tiberius had difficulty in learning (Tac. *Ann.* 6.13; Wallace-Hadrill 1982). In the majority of cases, popular demonstrations expressed the people's confidence in their emperor and their loyalty to the dynasty. They might sometimes, however, involve an implied affront to the ruler,

---

[2] A quite different attitude would prevail if an organized ethnic group such as the Jews took to demonstrations. This may have been the background of expulsion orders issued during the reigns of Tiberius and Nero (Williams 1989). The recurrent banishment of philosophers and magicians during the second half of the first century A D (Kneppe 1988) may also have been partly motivated by suspicion of organized groups (see Philostr. *Vita Apollonii* 4.41).

as in the case of the *plebs*'s exaggerated mourning over the death of Germanicus in AD 19, which eventually annoyed Tiberius (Suet. *Calig.* 5–6; Tac. *Ann.* 3.6; Versnel 1980).[3]

The special communication between emperor and people could also lead to the singling out of an Imperial minister as a scapegoat. Thus in AD 31 a mob anticipated the formal condemnation of Sejanus by demolishing his statues on the Gemonian steps (where the bodies of those found guilty of high treason were displayed) and afterwards abused his corpse there (Dio Cass. 58.11.3–4; Juv. 10.58–67). The emperor Galba rejected the popular demand for the sacrifice of Nero's praetorian prefect Tigellinus, but in doing so, undermined his standing; his successor Otho pursued popularity by proceeding against Tigellinus, who then committed suicide (Plut. *Galba* 17–8; Suet. *Galba* 15.2; Tac. *Hist.* 1.72; Plut. *Otho* 2).[4] In AD 69 Vitellius actually handed the former city prefect Flavius Sabinus over to a mob for lynching (Tac. *Hist.* 3.74.2) in a context, as Tacitus (*Hist.* 1.32.1) puts it in connection with another such event, that was similar to the addressing of acclamations and demands to the emperor at the public games (Alföldi 1970: 79–88).

It was only very exceptionally that the People's complaints directly addressed fundamental elements of the social order. This was the case in AD 61, when the masses violently protested against the Senate's decision to have the four hundred urban slaves of the city prefect Pedanius Secundus executed as responsible for his murder under his own roof (Bellen 1982; Yavetz 1986). Any slave who had been present in the house at the time of the murder was according to law presumed guilty of not giving sufficient aid to his master, and was therefore subject to torture and execution. Such collective punishment also carried with it an implied deterrent, in that a murderer even if unidentified would be caught by the collective sanction. The principle had been formally established by the *senatus consultum Silanianum* (*Dig.* 29.5), dating from AD 10, but was probably based on Republican precedents (Nörr 1982; Wolf 1988; Bau-

---

[3] The extent of the official honours which were established for the memory of Germanicus (in addition to the provisions known from the *Tabula Hebana*, which was discovered in 1947) is revealed by the recently published *Tabula Siarensis* (González 1984; see Lebek 1990b, 1992).

[4] Tigellinus' colleague Nymphidius Sabinus, who had removed Tigellinus from office when he tried to seize power after Nero's death, sought to gain popularity by allowing lynchings of some of Nero's intimates (Plut. *Galba* 8.5). On later cases see above p. 45.

man 1989: 92–5). Its application to an impressive number of undoubtedly innocent persons clashed with the people's conception of elementary justice, one shared by a considerable minority of senators.[5] The crowd was apparently well informed of the Senate's proceedings, but it would be too speculative to propose an immediate connection between the opposing senators and the rioting crowd. At the instigation of the famous jurist Gaius Cassius Longinus, who sternly refuted the arguments for a pardon, the decision to have all four hundred slaves executed was upheld. During the Senate's meeting the *plebs urbana*, incensed by rumours of a harsh decision, rioted in front of the Senate House and threatened to set it afire. This caused the emperor to intervene, issuing an edict and ordering soldiers to line the route along which the slaves were led to the place of execution (Tac. *Ann.* 14.42–5).

This seems to be an instance in which the people's sense of outrage led to a more or less spontaneous reaction. In a comparable case of AD 105 no such reaction occurred (Pliny, *Ep.* 8.14.12–26), but we do not know whether this was because of precautionary security measures and the more moderate decision of the Senate, or because of the populace's ignorance of the Senate's proceedings, or of even a generally different political atmosphere (Yavetz 1986: 153–7). In other cases a certain amount of organization beforehand can be assumed, but by whom the sources usually do not say (Whittaker 1964; Kohns 1993). There will have been situations in which manipulation from above directed popular anger against an Imperial minister; the *praefectus annonae* (grain commissioner) in particular ran the risk of being made a scapegoat in a food crisis (Sen. *Brev. vit.* 18.6).[6] It is unclear whether, in spite of renewed official control and integration into the official structures, the *collegia* and their leaders continued to play a role in mobilizing people and organizing protest. With respect to disturbances in cities outside the capital, at any rate, the authorities were inclined to see these groups as instigators of riots. One may cite Tacitus' account (*Ann.* 14.17) of the famous incident in AD 59 when the

---

[5] That there could be doubts as to the appropriateness of the measure in a particular case is best illustrated by the example of Augustus, who had once argued that a certain victim did not deserve to be avenged (Sen. *Quaestiones naturales* 1.16.1).

[6] In AD 189 the grain commissioner was successful in casting blame on the praetorian prefect Cleander, and the emperor Commodus, after manipulated protests in the theatre, had him executed (see above p. 45 at n. 53).

inhabitants of Pompeii and Nuceria violently clashed during gladiatorial games in Pompeii, and a great number of people were wounded and killed (Moeller 1970; Castrén 1975: 111–3; Galsterer 1980). The emperor had delegated the case to the Senate and the Senate to the consuls, who referred it back to the Senate, but in the end the Roman authorities found the Pompeians guilty of a preme-ditated attack. They suspended the games for ten years and dis-solved the *collegia* which had been illegally founded there.[7]

Whether their behaviour was spontaneous (though following established patterns as to form and subject) or organized, the spec-tators present at the public games were undoubtedly regarded as expressing the will of the Roman People. This means that under the conditions of the Principate it could not simply be argued by the authorities (as it tends to be in other political systems) that rioters were merely an unrepresentative minority or a mob. It was in any case left to the emperor's discretion whether a massive response by the government was appropriate. He had available to him special-ized forces for ensuring public order. Employing them, however, was an option that a 'good' ruler would exercise only in exceptional cases, and the behaviour of a potentate such as Caligula, who ordered the massacre of a protesting crowd (Dio Cass. 59.28.11; Joseph. *Antiquitates Judaicae* 19.24–26), was unpredictable. The alternative is nicely expressed in a later anecdote ascribed to Constantine the Great. On being hissed in the Roman theatre, he asked his brothers how to react: the one answered that he should cut the spectators down with armed force, the other that he should demonstrate his majesty by ignoring the crowd's behaviour – and, of course, Constantine followed the latter advice (Libanius, *Orationes* 19.19).

The new forces of order

In comparison with the Republic, the constitutional constellations had changed. Already with the Triumvirate, a new combination of the powers of regular magistrates and promagistrates had been established. This was continued under Augustus, for whom the

---

[7] On *collegia* in Pompeii, see Ausbüttel (1982: 93–5); in numerous other cities, see MacMullen (1974: 68–80). On the association of *collegia* with conspiracies, see *lex Irnitana* 74; Pliny, *Ep.* 10.33–4; on the link between illegal associations and armed violence, see *Dig.* 47.22.2.

constitutional limitations that the *pomerium* had implied for the use of tribunician power, on the one hand, and military command, on the other, were gradually abolished (Dio Cass. 51.19.6, 53.17.4–6, 53.32.5). The permanent military escort of those in power became a sign that Republic had given way to Principate (see Tac. *Ann.* 1.7.5; *Hist.* 4.11.1). With the establishment and consolidation of the new political system, the military forces which the emperor had at hand in the capital (Keppie 1984: 153–4) had to be remoulded to suit the requirements of a régime that promised order, peace and prosperity. As with other aspects of the new order, the process was a gradual one.

Praetorian and 'urban' cohorts made up the new military apparatus for maintaining law and order in Rome and Italy. The praetorians evolved out of the élite units of bodyguards that the *triumviri* had employed during the civil wars (Millar 1977: 61; Bleicken 1990: 42). Octavian retained these units after his final victory in 31 BC and even after the so-called restoration of the Republic in 27 BC. In 2 BC command over them was entrusted to two equestrian praetorian prefects (Dio Cass. 55.10.10) to ensure that one commander would always be present in the capital even when some of the praetorians had to be sent elsewhere (Brunt 1983: 59–60). The praetorians were the only troops regularly stationed in Italy, and in comparison with ordinary legionaries they received better pay, higher donatives, and shorter terms of service (Durry 1938; Watson 1971; Campbell 1984: 110–11). This might be expected to have guaranteed civilized behaviour on the part of soldiers with respect to the city population, but in emergencies such as the great fire of AD 64 they too took to looting (Dio Cass. 62.17.1; Tac. *Ann.* 15.38.7; cf. Joseph. *AJ* 19.160). An emperor might also use them as a sort of task force. Tiberius, for example, sent out praetorian units to suppress a slave insurrection in Calabria (Tac. *Ann.* 4.27), and Tiberius and Nero commissioned them to quell riots in the Italian towns of Pollentia and Puteoli respectively (Suet. *Tib.* 37.3; Tac. *Ann.* 13.48; D'Arms 1975).

The praetorians' main function was to control the capital. As a rule, though, they appeared in public with weapons concealed and clothed in togas (Tac. *Hist.* 1.38.2; *Ann.* 16.27.1). Augustus himself had only some of them stationed in the city itself, the rest being distributed among neighbouring towns (Suet. *Aug.* 49.1). Under Tiberius, however, the praetorians were stationed in the capital;

first dispersed, they were finally concentrated and accommodated in a single camp on the initiative of the praetorian prefect Sejanus (Tac. *Ann.* 4.2; Suet. *Tib.* 37.1; Juv. 10.94–5). Emperors made it quite clear that the praetorians were 'their' troops and that they would accept no interference from the Senate (Tac. *Ann.* 6.3).

The nine praetorian cohorts were supplemented by three urban cohorts (Tac. *Ann.* 4.5.3), intermediate in pay and terms of service between praetorians and legionaries (Freis 1967; Lieb 1986). The size of a cohort is uncertain, but five hundred seems probable. A cohort became a thousand strong temporarily in AD 69 (Tac. *Hist.* 2.93.2), then permanently after the reorganization of Septimius Severus in 193 (on the occasion of his dissolving the existing praetorian guard and establishing an entirely new one). The urban cohorts were probably under the command of the city prefect (*praefectus urbi*). After certain experiments which met with senatorial opposition (Della Corte 1980), this office (filled by a senator of consular rank) was made a permanent institution as late as the last years of Augustus or the early years of Tiberius (Tac. *Ann.* 6.10.3). Granting the city prefect command over three separate cohorts was probably not just a political gesture towards the Senate and the nobility, but an effort to supply the magistrate responsible for the security of the city (Vell. Pat. 2.98.1; cf. Statius, *Silvae* 1.4) with effective means of control ready to hand, especially when the emperor was not present.[8] Whether the emperor closely supervised the city prefects' activities (see Dio Cass. 52.21.6–7) or allowed them latitude (see Tac. *Hist.* 3.75.1; Juv. 4.75–81; Stat. *Silvae* 1.4) varied from time to time.

Charged in particular with protecting the emperor's life, the praetorians were assisted during the Julio-Claudian period by a force of Germanic bodyguards. Separate bodies were attached to princes of the Imperial dynasty, and even the family of Augustus' general Statilius Taurus kept such a bodyguard (Bellen 1981; Speidel 1984). The praetorians manned the palace guard (Tac. *Ann.* 1.13.6, 12.69.1) and accompanied the emperor on all his journeys and military campaigns.[9] From Tiberius onwards, emperors attended the Senate's meetings (with its official per-

---

[8] During the crises of AD 41 and December 68, however, this command structure sometimes led to confrontation between urban and praetorian cohorts (Flaig 1992: 224–8, 393–8).

[9] On the presumably military functions of the urban cohorts in the time of Domitian and Trajan, see Bérard (1988), but also the objections by Roxan and Eck (1993).

mission) only in the company of praetorian officers (Tac. *Ann.*
6.15.2). An emperor who visited a private residence without an
escort was thereby demonstrating trust in his host (Tac. *Ann.*
15.52.1). Because of their proximity to the emperor, the praetorian
prefects occupied key positions in the Imperial government. At the
same time, they were often involved or notoriously suspected of
involvement in court intrigues and conspiracies. The loyalty of the
praetorian guard as a whole was especially at issue when the suc-
cession to the throne was disputed. Their crucial role in the
accessions of Claudius and Nero and in AD 68/69 (and later in 193)
is well known (Grant 1974: 130–66; Campbell 1984: 118–20; Flaig
1992). The concern that a palace revolt might coincide with unrest
among the urban *plebs*, allowing a pretender to the throne to
present himself as champion of the masses (Tac. *Ann.* 14.61), never
materialized, however. Only on a few occasions was it considered
necessary to display a massive military presence within the city and
have public places occupied by troops. For example, this was
ordered by Augustus after the disastrous defeat of Varus in the
Teutoburg Forest in AD 9 (Suet. *Aug.* 23.1) and by Nero on the
occasion of the 'Pisonian conspiracy' in AD 65 (Tac. *Ann.* 15.58). In
cases of an alleged conspiracy against the emperor, units or individual officers of the praetorian guard were employed to make arrests
(Tac. *Ann.* 11.1.3), to force suspects to commit suicide (Tac. *Ann.*
15.60–4; Juv. 10.15–18 on Seneca's death), or to kill them (Tac.
Ann. 1.53.5).

It is difficult to determine what regular police functions the
praetorians and the urban cohorts assumed. In the first place,
inferring general rules from extraordinary incidents is problematic;
secondly, the literary sources, especially Tacitus, often simply mention the use of soldiers without specifying to which body they
belonged. One cohort (either praetorian or urban) was regularly on
hand at the public games in the theatre and the circus; the first
recorded instance is in AD 15 (Tac. *Ann.* 1.77.1; Rich 1991: 194).
Their job was to exercise reasonable control over potential out-
bursts, whether political or the result of hooliganism on the part of
the organized supporters of rival actors (Suet. *Tib.* 37.2; Tac. *Ann.*
1.16.3). Perhaps surprisingly, pantomimes, with their strong element of competition between actors, more often incited rioting
than chariot races, whereas the blood sports of the circus (for which
the audience was much larger) provoked none at all (Jory 1984;

Scobie 1988).[10] In response to such disorders, actors were subjected to corporal punishment (see Suet. *Aug.* 45.3–4) and even
banished from the capital and from Italy (see, e.g., Tac. *Ann.*
4.14.3, 13.25.4; Suet. *Tib.* 37.2; *Dom.* 7.1; Pliny, *Pan.* 46.2; Leppin
1992: 64–7. On the Senate's role in such cases, see Talbert 1984:
383–6). In some cases spectators were arrested as well and perhaps
also prohibited from attending the spectacles, or even banished
from the city by the praetors who, from 22 BC (Dio Cass. 54.2.3),
were responsible for the conduct of the public games (Tac. *Ann.*
1.77, 13.28.1–2; cf. *Dig.* 1.12.1.13 on the later competences of the
praefectus urbi). Courting popular approval, Nero once removed the
cohort from the games, but the resulting disorder led him to restore
the previous arrangements (Tac. *Ann.* 13.24–5; cf. 14.15.4). This
shows that, the praetors' responsibility notwithstanding, the
emperors could obviously intervene at their discretion. More or less
psychopathic rulers such as Caligula (Suet. *Calig.* 30.2), Nero (Tac.
Ann. 16.5.3), Vitellius (Suet. *Vit.* 14.3), Domitian (Suet. *Dom.* 10.1),
and later Commodus (S.H.A., *Comm.* 15.6) and Caracalla (Hdn.
4.6.4–5) would also employ soldiers to observe the behaviour of the
public and punish spectators who did not respond appropriately to
the emperor's favourite drivers or actors, or even (in Nero's case) to
the performance of the emperor himself.[11]

As to the regular police functions of the urban cohorts, the literary sources, though of course mentioning their extraordinary role
in the power struggle of AD 41 and the civil war of 68/69, provide
little substantive information. That they had such functions is an
inference from the responsibilities of the city prefect, who gradually
absorbed more and more of the duties traditionally attributed to
praetors, aediles and minor magistrates. Ulpian's catalogue of his
duties (*Dig.* 1.12.1) reflects an increase in his responsibilities
during the first and second centuries culminating in the Severan
reorganization, but we cannot precisely date his assumption of
particular tasks. To his task of ensuring order at public games and

---

[10] See Wistrand (1992) on the attitudes of contemporary Roman writers who associated
theatrical performances with licentiousness and sedition, but praised the morally edifying
effects of the bloody games. On the hooliganism of circus factions in Antioch and Constantinople, see Cameron (1976), Fotiou (1978), and Roueché (1993: 152–6).

[11] In addition to the soldiers, Nero employed allegedly five thousand young knights and
plebeians called *Augustani*, who as an organized claque forced others to join them in
hailing the emperor (Suet. *Ner.* 20.3; Tac. *Ann.* 14.15.5; Dio Cass. 61.20.3–4).

banishing riotous spectators from the games or from the city was added the general charge of keeping the public peace and gathering information about disturbances through guards distributed across the city. In addition to preventing riots the city prefect was expected to prosecute illegal associations, but here it was assumed that he would respond to indictments rather than necessarily undertake preventive surveillance. (The same probably holds true for investigations of Christians, at least before the beginning of systematic prosecution.)[12] Supervision of markets and control of weights and measures may again mean not regular inspections but response to the initiatives of private persons seeking redress. A further rationale for the prefect's office was, according to Tacitus, (*Ann.* 6.11.2) the need to discipline the slave masses that could no longer be controlled by means of ordinary justice. Yet Ulpian's catalogue of duties deals especially with his competence to hear complaints of slaves against their masters, especially when a slave had sought asylum at an emperor's statue (Bellen 1971: 64–78; Bradley 1984: 123–4; Pekáry 1985: 130–1).

The development of the city prefect's criminal jurisdiction, which eventually superseded that of the jury courts, is a complicated matter and involves much more than the prosecution of lower-class criminality (Schiller 1949; Kunkel 1974: 99–102; Garnsey 1970: 90–100). As to the latter, the increase in efficacy may be seen in the fact that after an initial indictment the prefect could proceed *ex officio*. Furthermore, theft could now be prosecuted as a criminal offence, carrying as a penalty corporal punishment or, in cases of aggravated larceny, deportation, forced labour or even death. This may have been an attractive alternative, where the defendant was without means, to a private suit for a penalty assessed as a multiple of the damage (Crook 1967: 168–9). Trials of thieves, burglars, robbers, concealers and arsonists (MacCormack 1972) were after a certain time delegated to the *praefectus vigilum*, who could, however, remit cases involving dangerous criminals to the city prefect (*Dig.* 1.15). All this does not mean that the *praefectus urbi* and the *praefectus vigilum* and their staffs engaged in the systematic pursuit and *ex officio* prosecution of ordinary criminals. Rather,

---

[12] For later evidence on the city prefect's actions against Christians, see Freis (1967: 23–7). The general policy of first- and second-century authorities of simply responding to indictments can be assumed from Trajan's answer to the Bithynian governor Pliny's request (Pliny, *Ep.* 10.96–7).

in the majority of cases brought before them the initiative probably still lay with private persons seeking redress for damages who had collected evidence and identified suspects. At any rate, there were no detective police.

Finally, the *vigiles* formed a permanent fire brigade that considerably improved the situation in a city constantly endangered by fires in the urban slums (Hirschfeld 1905: 252–7; Baillie-Reynolds 1926; Robinson 1977; 1992: 106–10, 184–8). The *vigiles* started out as a body of six hundred state slaves which Augustus had set up in 22 BC and placed under the command first of the aediles and later of the *vicomagistri* (Dio Cass. 54.2.4, 55.8.6–8). Augustus' initiative may have been a reaction to the activities of the ambitious aedile Egnatius Rufus, who had achieved particular popularity by employing a privately recruited fire-fighting squad (Dio Cass. 53.24.4–6). The *vigiles* achieved their final form after a devastating conflagration in AD 6 with the establishment of a paramilitary corps of seven cohorts so distributed that each cohort was responsible for two of the regions of the city (Dio Cass. 55.26.4; *Dig.* 1.15.3 pr.; Nicolet 1988: 210–13). These were now recruited among freedmen (who qualified for Roman citizenship after six and later three years of service; Gai. *Inst.* 1.32b), their command being entrusted to an equestrian *praefectus vigilum.*

Augustus may have thought of employing the *vigiles* as a sort of riot police if necessary (Suet. *Aug.* 25.2), but we have no evidence that they were really used in this way. In the crisis of AD 31 they were ordered to secure the Senate's proceedings against Tiberius' praetorian prefect Sejanus, apparently because of lack of confidence in the urban cohorts' readiness to oppose the praetorians (Dio Cass. 58.9.2–6, 58.12.2; Visscher 1966).[13]

The *vigiles* went on regular nightly patrols. In addition to fire-prevention they supervised building regulations and obligatory protective measures (Strabo 5.3.7 = C 235; Tac. *Ann.* 15.43.4; *Dig.* 1.15.3.4). Their capacity to pursue thieves and runaway slaves should not be overestimated; their numbers do not necessarily indicate that they performed such functions to any significant degree. In an overcrowded city with a low technological standard of fire-fighting (which precluded the effective use of water) they

---

[13] On the involvement of the *vigiles* in the fights of AD 69 see Tac. *Hist.* 3.64.1, 69.1; Joseph. *BJ* 4.645.

would have been busy enough with their tasks as a fire brigade (Rainbird 1986), even assuming that there were seven thousand (and not just thirty-five hundred) of them; the size of their cohorts is disputed. In any case, the experience of later times argues against the assumption that street patrolling would have been effective against, for example, burglary or assault.

The idea that the *vigiles* performed ordinary police functions is based on the juridical competences of their commanding officer. The *praefectus vigilum* was surely authorized to arrest runaway slaves as had been the Republican *tresviri capitales*, but it is again an open question whether the *vigiles* on their patrols were able to undertake effective searches. A duty to pursue *fugitivi* was assigned to the *praefectus vigilum* by the emperor Septimius Severus (*Dig.* 1.15.4), but we should be sceptical of any long-term effective implementation of this measure (Bellen 1971: 13–15, 121).

As in the previous discussion on the functions of the *tresviri capitales*, I have deliberately stressed the limits of our knowledge here. There may have been additional precautions, for example, during the public games; Augustus stationed guards (*custodes*) in various parts of the city to prevent burglary during times when only a few people were at home (Suet. *Aug.* 43.1). Because of the character of our sources, in particular Juvenal (3.268–304; 13.145–6), Tibullus (1.2.25–6) and Propertius (2.29; 3.16) and the stories of Nero's nightly escapades (Tac. *Ann.* 13.25.1–3, 13.47.2; Suet. *Nero* 26),[14] we know more about the insecurity of the city streets at night during the presumably much better-policed Imperial era than during Republican times. It of course remains likely that life and property in the metropolis were considerably safer under the Empire (though Pliny, *HN* 19.59 points in passing to burglary as a persistent problem). We should not forget, however, that it remained primarily the task of the individual to take care of himself, that the well-to-do not only employed a considerable staff for the protection of their property but also used them to harass their social inferiors (Juv. 14.305 and 6.413–18) and, finally, that the presence of soldiers could also be a nuisance, especially since individuals would find it difficult to defend themselves physically or legally against mistreatment by them (Juv. 16.7–12; Campbell 1984: 246–54). Again, the new enforcement agencies may have had

---

[14] On later emperors, see S.H.A., *Ver.* 4.6 and Amm. Marc. 14.1.9.

more comprehensive duties and executed them more efficiently than our sources reveal, but we must avoid the tendency to assume that the gaps would necessarily have been filled or filled exclusively or primarily by the new governmental agencies themselves. In comparison with the Republican period, a dramatic change had no doubt occurred with respect to the government's capacity to quell riots with a permanently available force of militarily trained and disciplined men. Whether in practice it did so as a rule depended, however, not on the level of disturbance of the public peace but on the emperor's perception of the situation. An emperor concerned about his popularity with the masses would be reluctant to resort to repression unless he considered his own position to be in jeopardy.

Public order in late Rome

The situation with regard to public order during the Principate is further illuminated by contrast with conditions in later times. From the time of Constantine onward the city prefect assumed responsibility for the city administration as a whole, though the lack of clear-cut demarcations of competence in relation to other offices was a constant cause of friction (Jones 1964: 690–1). He was at the same time representative head of the Senate and delegate of the emperor; individual prefects occupied the office as the summit of their career for an average term of only about one year (Chastagnol 1960; Matthews 1975: 12–23). The prefect kept the emperor informed (see, e.g., Symmachus' forty-nine reports in AD 384; Barrow 1973) and received instructions, but it was he who confronted the citizens at the public games and had to find the means to manage any crisis.

With Constantinople's establishment as the new capital, Rome lost its absolute priority with respect to the grain supply (Tengström 1974; Rickman 1980: 198–209; Herz 1988a: 220–77), and food crises, including shortages of wine (Amm. Marc. 14.6.1, 15.7.3), frequently led to disturbances. In such cases the city prefect became the specific object of popular ill will (Kohns 1961; Kneppe 1979; Graeber 1984). He could enjoy peace and order only if there were no 'seditions out of justified complaints' (Amm. Marc. 29.6.19). Satisfying popular demands for the expulsion of non-residents (Amm. Marc. 28.4.32; Kohns 1961: 73–7, 169–81; Faure 1965) would not in any case have sufficed to prevent serious unrest.

No longer did the city prefect have considerable forces of order at his disposal, because during the fourth century A D the praetorians, urban cohorts and *vigiles* were one after another dissolved, and fire-fighting became the task of certain *collegia* (Waltzing 1896: II, 127–30; Sinnigen 1957: 88–100; Chastagnol 1960: 254–72). What role was played by the heads of the city's districts and quarters is impossible to say (Kohns 1961: 107; Jones 1964: 694). The remaining staff of the prefect's office apparently did not form an effective riot squad. During troubles in A D 356 (which started as a protest against the punishment of a popular chariot driver and then took in the cost of wine), a prefect had ringleaders arrested by his *apparitores* and then had them physically punished and expelled from the city. In a second serious confrontation with an angry crowd he was deserted by some of his staff, but nevertheless drove his carriage into the midst of it. That he was able to control the situation was due to the courage and firmness he showed at this moment (Amm. Marc. 15.7.1–5). The individual prefect's performance must have been very important (Matthews 1987).

Ammianus' picture of the prefects' (and the aristocracy's) policy towards the *plebs* suggests that it oscillated between displays of generosity and provocative arrogance (e.g., 27.3.5–7, 10; Matthews 1989: 414–20), but popular anger sometimes led to attempts to set the prefect's house on fire or even to lynch him.[15] In one case, in which a grain shortage was anticipated but not yet critical, the prefect was able to calm the crowd by offering to deliver his little sons to it, thus demonstrating his readiness to assume the responsibility for the situation (Amm. Marc. 19.10; Gregory 1984: 141). In another context, the destruction of a prefect's house was prevented by his retainers and neighbours (Amm. Marc. 27.3.8), but this assistance would not always be sufficient. Milan's Bishop Ambrose (*Ep.* 40.13) had special reasons for claiming that the burning of the Roman prefect's house had happened quite regularly without producing any response from the Imperial government (see below p. 111), but there must have been a kernel of truth in his statement. Sometimes prefects reacted to a crisis simply by leaving the city. This happened in A D 366, when violent clashes between factions on the occasion of a disputed papal election led to more than a

---

[15] Lynching in the Forum in A D 409 is reported by the *Vita S. Melaniae Iun.* (= Analecta Bollandiana 8, 1889, 42).

hundred deaths (Amm. Marc. 27.4.13; *Collectio Avellana* (*CSEL* XXXV, 1) 1.7; Green 1971),[16] and in other cases as well (Amm. Marc. 27.3.9).

In contrast to the situation during the Republic, the city prefect could not rely on the support of the aristocracy and its personnel, though aristocrats apparently liked to boast of their numbers of retainers (cf. Ammianus' caricature: 14.6.16–17, 28.4.8–9). Members of the nobility were likely to be attacked during situations of unrest,[17] and although they tried to prevent food riots by helping to purchase and subsidize the distribution of grain, during actual crises they preferred to leave the city (Kohns 1961: 71–2, 89–90, 97, 109).

Broadly speaking, even in the new capital Constantinople, the general structure was not very different from that of fourth- and fifth-century Rome. Fire-fighting was entrusted to certain *collegia*. The *praefectus urbi* and *praefectus vigilum*, whose offices had been established after the mid-fourth century, never had special cohorts at their disposal, and the magistrates were repeatedly subjected to violent attacks (Jones 1964: 692–5; Dagron 1974: 233–4; Patlagean 1977: 215–25; Tinnefeld 1977: 178). The emperor's palace guards were apparently incapable of suppressing public disturbances, as is especially suggested by the fact that the famous Nika Riot of 532 was put down only by bringing (Gothic) mercenary troops in from the battlefield (Bury 1958: II, 39–48; Frank 1969: 206–19; Gizewski 1988: 149–63, 172).

OUTSIDE THE CAPITAL

The Imperial government's relatively impressive military and administrative apparatus was only partly designed to address problems of law and order in the Empire's cities and provinces. The internal policing functions performed by the army were guided by the central government's interests, and were only indirectly intended to secure law and order on behalf of the citizens. Special units such as the *frumentarii* (primarily responsible for the army's

---

[16] During the schism of AD 419, the city prefect and his deputy, who had tried to quell the factional conflict, only narrowly escaped violence (Chastagnol 1960: 176).

[17] The house of the former city prefect Symmachus was set on fire when the rumour was spread that he had refused to lower the price of wine (Amm. Marc. 27.3.4; Symm. *Ep.* 1.44.1).

corn supply) and, after Diocletian's reorganization, the *agentes in rebus* (primarily engaged in carrying the emperor's letters throughout the Empire) were not the gigantic surveillance apparatus terrorizing the population that has sometimes been inferred from the alleged analogy with modern systems of state police and secret services. Certainly, besides their main tasks they served as intelligence gatherers for the Imperial government, brought evidence against suspects, appeared as witnesses for the prosecution in trials, carried out arrests and even undertook 'special tasks' such as liquidating persons on the government's order. Complaints of abuse and corruption were common. The objects of their surveillance being especially higher-ranking bureaucrats and notables, the *agentes in rebus* served as the central government's control organ over its branches and local aristocracies.[18] In this sense comparison to modern security services, which in authoritarian and totalitarian systems are also engaged in the control of the state apparatus itself, may be to some degree justified (Frank 1982).

Attention was also directed towards the suppression of banditry, which was no longer left exclusively to the self-help of local communities, such as that attributed to Minturnae in 43 BC by Appian (*BCiv.* 4.28.120). Augustus and Tiberius initiated appropriate action by military forces in Italy, and other emperors followed their example (Strabo 4.6.6 = c 204; App. *BCiv.* 5.132.547; Suet. *Aug.* 32.1; *Tib.* 8 and 37);[19] praetorians were from time to time engaged in fighting robbers, as in the case of the famous bandit chief Bulla Felix in the early third century AD (Dio Cass. 76.10). In the provinces governors were especially alert if banditry overlapped with massive desertion from the army and slave flight (Bellen 1971: 104–6, 143–7; Alföldy 1971) or expressed stubborn native resistance to Roman rule.[20] At least in the eastern frontier provinces, the main concern was the safety of the army's supply and communication

[18] On the *frumentarii*, see Clauss (1973: 82–109) and Mann (1988); on *agentes in rebus*, see Clauss (1980: 23–45) and Schuller (1975), with references to the problematic comparisons in previous works; on control over the bureaucracy, see Blockley (1969) and Rosen (1990); on the *saiones* as successors to the *agentes in rebus* in Ostrogothic times, see Morosi (1981).

[19] Juv. 3.305–8 suggests that the suppression of banditry in Italy led robbers to make for the capital.

[20] See Shaw (1990) on Isauria and Cilicia in the first centuries BC and AD, Hellenkemper (1986) on the same province in the fourth century AD, Herz (1988b) on problems with nomads in various regions, and Dyson (1975) on native revolts and banditry in western provinces.

lines, and thus stability of Roman rule, and this could lead to
punitive action against communities suspected of supporting
bandits and rebels (Brunt 1977; Horsley 1977; Isaac 1984, 1990:
77–80).[21] That the population as a whole gained more security
from the suppression of banditry was the more likely when the
stability of Roman authority was beyond doubt: Quinctilius Varus'
disaster in Germania is ascribed to his incorrect assumption that
the province was pacified and that therefore he could distribute his
troops according to the demands of communities for assistance in
guarding places, arresting robbers or protecting supply trains (Dio
Cass. 56.19). But in fully pacified provinces the governor had insufficient forces at hand (apart from some auxiliary units), and
whether legions were sent to suppress banditry often depended on
the success of an appeal to the emperor by an influential person
(Millar 1981: 67). Security was surely improved by *stationarii*, military posts on the public roads (Tert. *Apol.* 2.8; Hirschfeld 1913:
591–612; Domaszewski 1902; Davies 1974: 321–4; and Herrmann
1990 on complaints of villagers about trespasses by such soldiers),
but this would not have eliminated the need for self-protection on
journeys (see, for example, Epictetus 4.1.91). Local militias took on
robber bands in the hinterland. In the eastern provinces they were
headed by *eirenarchai*, peace officers performing a compulsory
public service (liturgy) who were appointed by the governor from a
list of notables submitted by the local authorities (Aristides, *Or.*
50.72–4).[22] Large private estates were guarded by bodies of slaves
and those belonging to the emperor by soldiers (Rostovtzeff 1905).
Exhortation of citizens themselves to pursue robbers was underlined by the granting of indemnity if a robber happened to be killed
(*Codex Iustinianus* 9.16.3; *Codex Theodosianus* 9.14.2, 7.18.14). Apprehended robbers were made the subject of at best summary judgement and of cruel punishments which were supposed to serve as a
general deterrent; they were either crucified or thrown to the beasts
at the public games (Hengel 1977: 46–50; Kuhn 1982: 724–32;

[21] See Shaw (1979) on the concern of Roman authorities that rural markets in a North
African area of tribal unrest be kept under reasonable control.
[22] Jones (1940: 212–13; 1972: 116), Magie (1950: 647) on *eirenarchai*; Robert (1937: 90–110),
Jones (1987) on local militias in Asia Minor; Hopwood (1983) on militias in Cilicia–
Isauria from the second to the fourth century AD, with the qualification by Shaw (1990:
232–3) that the examples refer to the 'civilized' coastal area. A western equivalent, called
praefectus arcendis latrociniis, is known from an inscription from Swiss Nyon, but the date
and circumstances are far from clear (Flam-Zuckerman 1970; van Berchem 1982).

Shaw 1984: 20–1; Liebs 1985: 90–1; MacMullen 1986; Lanata 1987; Coleman 1990: 48–9). Such spectacular executions and a general trend to judicial savagery do not, however, indicate an increase in law enforcement but instead are typical of a system of criminal law which depended on the exemplary effects of erratic acts (Garnsey 1968b: 157–8; Wiedemann 1992: 68–97). Indeed, these efforts were effective only within limits; banditry remained widespread in much of the Empire, partly because landowners tended to cooperate with robber bands who in turn served as their private security forces (MacMullen 1966: 255–68; Ste Croix 1981: 474–88; Shaw 1984, 1991; van Hooff 1988; Hopwood 1989: 181–5).[23] The more local potentates monopolized the available forces of order, the more they were likely to misuse their positions.[24] (A similar context gave rise to the Sicilian Mafia during the nineteenth century.[25]) In any case, large landowners in their capacity as patrons played a considerable part in resolving everyday conflicts (Krause 1987: 34–49).[26]

Preserving order in the cities was generally left to the local authorities. Tiberius sought to curb the Greek cities' habit of offering asylum in their temples to debtors, fugitive slaves and criminals, but instead of abolishing the institution (as Suetonius, *Tib.* 37.3, reports) ordered that the cities' titles be scrutinized by the Senate; in the end several cities that could prove ancient rights or claim special services to Rome had their privileges approved (Tac. *Ann.* 3.60–3, 4.14.1–2; Herrmann 1989: 127–30).[27] Italy was not treated as a province, administrative intervention from the Imperial government remained on a comparatively low level, and with the exception of the garrisons at Rome there were no regular army units stationed there during the first two centuries (Eck 1979; Millar 1986). Praetorians were sent into Italian towns during the first century AD only under exceptional circumstances (see above p. 91). The standing units (counted as urban cohorts) which the Imperial government posted at Puteoli and Ostia had fire-

---

[23] The same may be applied at least partly to the Bagaudae of Late Roman Gaul (van Dam 1985; Drinkwater 1989).
[24] Cf. Veyne (1987: 151) and Krause (1987: 126–44) on the private forces called *buccellarii*.
[25] Blok (1972), with further comparative material on cooperation between bandits and established power-holders in various modern societies.
[26] Krause, however, concentrates more on their role with respect to trials than to extrajuridical arbitration.
[27] On the function of slave asylum in general, see Christensen (1984).

prevention and other security functions with respect to the grain imports, which in the second century A D were taken over by units of the Roman *vigiles* sent there in rotation (Meiggs 1973: 75, 81, 305–8).[28] Septimius Severus entrusted civil and criminal jurisdiction in Italy to the city prefect (within a hundred miles of Rome) and the praetorian prefect (outside that zone), but it is far from clear what implications this had for the maintenance of public order within the communities (Millar 1986: 312–4).

For communal problems, responsibilities varied with the type of municipal constitution, with, roughly speaking, *duoviri* and aediles in the west, *strategoi* and *agoranomoi* in the east. Local magistrates in the west had staffs made up of lictors, *scribae*, *viatores* and public slaves comparable to the auxiliaries of Roman Republican magistrates (*lex Ursonensis* 62 and cf. Petronius 97; Apul. *Met.* 9.41.7). In addition, they were apparently entitled to require citizens to stand watch if necessary (*lex Irnitana* 19 on *vigiliae*). Municipal charters seem to have had no provision for appealing to the governor for troops (Galsterer 1988: 85). As a legacy from the former Hellenistic régimes the cities of the east had security officers, especially as heads of a night-watch; these magistrates were probably performing a liturgy, whereas their watchmen were paid (Jones 1940: 212).[29] In Egypt, compulsion to perform police functions extended to the village level: in addition to (paid) local beadles, a certain number of village dwellers were appointed who were obliged to assist as 'thief-catchers' (Hirschfeld 1913: 614–15; Hohlwein 1905; Oertel 1917: 263–86; Bagnall 1977). That fire prevention was entrusted to *collegia* of craftsmen who in return were granted exemption from other municipal duties is known from the western parts of the Empire (Waltzing 1896: II, 193–208; Hirschfeld 1913: 96–111; Rostovtzeff 1957: 409–10; 637, n. 57; Millar 1983: 82–3; Kneissl 1994). With respect to the more unruly cities of the east the central government objected that this solution could foster politically dangerous associations: Pliny's proposal to establish such a *collegium* in Nicomedia was for that reason rejected by Trajan, who advised Pliny simply to provide equipment which could be used by

[28] There were two cohorts outside Italy: one in Lugdunum protected the Imperial mint, and another in Carthage was used especially for military actions against rebellious natives (Freis 1967: 10–16, 28–35).

[29] On the *phylakitai* of Ptolemaic times, see Kool (1954); as is so often the case, the evidence allows no exact knowledge of the functions actually fulfilled.

house-owners and volunteer helpers (Pliny, *Ep.* 10.33-4). In a few cases known from cities in Asia in the second century A D, governors threatened to prosecute bakers and workers involved in some sort of strike action as illegal associations after the local authorities had proved unable or unwilling to cope with them (Buckler 1923; Magie 1950: 635).

It is, of course, almost impossible to make a general assessment of the efficiency of local magistrates and their various sorts of underlings[30] in guaranteeing the safety of the streets and enforcing public order regulations (Reynolds 1988: 32-4).[31] As a rule, self-organization of citizens – employment of slaves and appeal for neighbourly help in private quarrels (see Petron. 21),[32] the offering of rewards for the arrest of thieves and runaways (Petron. 97; Dio Chrys. 7.123), and various means of social control in cases of public interest – played a decisive part. This seems to have been true also for Roman Egypt, with its special conditions. The great number of petitions to civil and military authorities in cases of theft, burglary and assault is probably no evidence of official prosecution of crime; these petitions aimed at the restitution of a victim's property and dignity, and were submitted only if self-regulation within a village did not work as usual (Bagnall 1989; Hobson 1993).[33] In general, reliance on local means meant that certain violations of public order, for example, by upper-class youth, were likely to remain rather unrestricted (Apul. *Met.* 2.18; Millar 1981: 69; *Dig.* 48.19.28.3; Vanzetti 1975; Eyben 1993: 98–127), whereas outsiders were considered suspect (Apul. *Met.* 3.1–11).

[30] Trajan's above-mentioned reply to Pliny's concern about the employment of criminals in public services suggests that petty criminals could be required to work in the public baths, clean out drains or build streets (Millar 1984: 134-5).

[31] Sperber (1970) claims that public night-watchmen in Palestinian cities of the third and fourth century A D were rather efficient and especially enforced rules as to licensing hours, which were intended to reduce the incidence of drunken brawls.

[32] In one case from Cnidos, a person who had taken part in the siege of a house was killed when a slave defending the house dropped a chamber-pot on him, and the local authorities sought to prosecute the house-owners and managed to present their accusation to Augustus (surely an extraordinary case; Millar 1977: 443). After an investigation by a high-ranking senator, however, the emperor decided that it had been a case of legitimate self-defence (English translation of the inscription in Braund 1985, no. 545). On neighbourly help as protection against rebellious slaves and criminals, see also Xen. *Hiero* 4.3.

[33] *Contra* Davies (1973). For evidence on such petitions, see further Łukaszewicz (1983) and Drexhage (1988); for complaints of police brutality, see Caulfield, Estner and Stephen (1989). Orders to local magistrates to produce certain persons before a higher court were presumably issued in fiscal cases (Drexhage 1989).

As for disturbances involving considerable parts of the citizenry, local magistrates had to rely on the acceptance of their authority. In some situations a courageous person who was not a magistrate was able to quell disturbances by virtue of his personal appearance and rhetoric. At Athens the philosopher Demonax was successful in stopping a quarrel, on an issue unknown to us (Lucian, *Demonax* 64). In contrast, the rhetorician Lollianus, as the magistrate responsible for the food supply and the provision market, barely escaped being stoned during a food crisis, but was then rescued by the witty remark of a Cynic philosopher that diverted the crowd (Philostr. *Vitae Sophistarum* 1.23). The well-known Ephesus riot on the occasion of St Paul's mission was stopped by a magistrate's persuasiveness (Acts 19.23–40), in particular his convincing argument that persistence would bring a response from the provincial governor. But local authorities who called for intervention might undermine their own standing (Plut. *Mor.* 815), and took the risk that the governor might blame them for the crisis. Moreover, the appearance of (often undisciplined) soldiers could be a threat, especially to the well-to-do (MacMullen 1963: 77–98). Thus, local magistrates had to choose the lesser of two evils.

Governors would only under specific circumstances intervene in local affairs. They exercised the criminal jurisdiction which was beyond the competence of local authorities. Appeal to the emperor was available from capital sentences on Roman citizens. But governors, who had to preside over capital criminal proceedings in person (being unable to delegate this particular competence), in practice had the means to sabotage those citizen rights, from outright defiance of the law (Suet. *Galba* 9) to simply delaying a decision (Garnsey 1966; 1968a; Liebs 1981). St Paul, who had a mixed experience with regard to respect for a Roman citizen's legal protection against scourging (Acts 16.37, 22.25–9), had been imprisoned for two years by the governor Felix; the case was left undecided for the succeeding governor Festus, who finally acknowledged St Paul's appeal to Caesar (Acts 24–5 – incidentally, the first recorded case; Sherwin-White 1963; Tajra 1989). Luke accuses Felix of intending to extort money from St Paul (Acts 24.26), a practice which is attributed to other governors as well. Legally, imprisonment was only for pre-trial detention, but governors tended to turn it into a sort of penalty, even though this was repeatedly forbidden by Imperial edicts (Millar 1984: 130–2). The habit of governors of being quick to order detention but very slow to come to a decision is still and again a subject of complaint by Libanius (*Or.* 45).

That proconsuls went on assize tours throughout their provinces offered them opportunities to become involved in local affairs, but at the same time this involvement could be only sporadic and discontinuous with respect to particular communities (Burton 1975). Involvement in cases relative to communal public order was especially likely in a province's capital. Here a governor might dismiss charges as irrelevant in the eyes of the law, as happened in Corinth with respect to St Paul (Acts 18.12–17), or be inclined to act in line with the wishes of local élites and public opinion.

The tendency to base decisions on more or less formal demands by the People sometimes seems to be an attempt to shift the responsibility onto them; the most famous case is, of course, Pilate's treatment of Christ (Tert. *Apol.* 21.18).[34] This seems especially the case with the persecution of Christians before the beginning of systematic and comprehensive suppression in the mid-third century – which brought more active participation by the military forces as well (Lopuszanski 1951). The theme had already been the subject of a famous exchange of letters between Trajan and the Bithynian governor Pliny, who asked how he should deal with the charges brought before him (Pliny, *Ep.* 10.96–7). At Lyons in AD 177, prosecutions had started with proceedings before the local authorities in response to mob action; the governor, who had then taken over the investigation, disregarded the emperor's legal instruction, which he himself had duly requested, in order to please the crowd (Euseb. *Historia ecclesiastica* 5.1.44–51; Keresztes 1967). Tertullian's assertion (*Apol.* 37.2) that the authorities undertook the persecution of Christians in reaction to popular pressure, or were inclined to acquiesce in lynchings, is supported by several incidents (Ste Croix 1974: 225–7; Keresztes 1979; Schäfke 1979;

---

[34] Evidence on governors' and local authorities' tendency in the eastern cities of the Empire to act in accordance with the articulations of the people's will (especially in the theatre) is collected by Colin (1965); however, his thesis that such acclamations constituted legally binding decisions cannot be accepted. We have reviewed comparable cases in Rome itself; a further one is the case of AD 398 in which Stilicho paraded African officials (who were made responsible for stopping the ships destined for Rome during Gildo's insurrection) in the Forum and decided on their individual fates according to their reception by the people (Claud. *De consulatu Stilichonis* 3.99–119).

Vittinghoff 1984; Molthagen 1991),[35] and by Hadrian's rescript to
the proconsul of Asia in AD 124/25 (Euseb. *Hist. eccl.* 4.9.1–3);
humiliating execution of Christians at public games, involving
throwing them to the beasts, aimed at popular acclamation as well
(Shaw 1993). The same applies, of course, to the many cases from
the Christian period in which Christians persecuted pagans, Jews
and 'heretics', or Christian factions clashed over the election or
removal of a bishop (Ste Croix 1981: 448–52; Gregory 1984;
MacMullen 1984: 86–101). In AD 38 the Greek community in
Alexandria systematically, through the organized action of the
collegia including a mock parade of the Jewish king Agrippa (Philo,
In Flacc. 36–41), provoked and attacked the Jewish inhabitants and
finally staged an outright pogrom with executions as part of theatre
performances (Philo, *In Flacc.* 62–96). The prefect of Egypt, who
throughout the disturbances had taken a partisan stance, did not
employ his troops, though he had enough at hand to have restored
order quickly (Philo, *Legatio ad Gaium* 132; Barraclough 1974: 429–
36; Smallwood 1976: 235–42; Kasher 1985: 317–18; Bergmann and
Hoffmann 1987; Feldman 1993: 113–17).[36]

When governors became concerned with riots of the *taxation populaire* style, they had to decide whether they should use their means
to discipline the masses or instead apply pressure to the local
magistrates, landowners or traders to fulfil justified demands with
regard to market supply and prices. Dio Chrysostom, in an oration
from the seventies (*Or.* 46), deals with such an occurrence in his
native Prusa. He himself and other members of the local aristocracy had been threatened with arson and stoning for apparently
having hoarded grain to raise prices. Dio tried to threaten the
people with playing the Roman card (46.14; Stahl 1978: 160–72;
Jones 1978: 19–25), but how the governor would have reacted is an
open question. On a later occasion disturbances in Prusa were
answered by a ban on public assemblies, but when the governor
appeared in person Dio was anxious to exhort the people to demonstrate unity; he must have expected that the governor would lend

[35] It should also be mentioned that a principal source on an *eirenarches* and his local militia
reports the pursuit of a Smyrna Christian as if he were a brigand (*Martyrdom of Polycarp* 6–
8).

[36] See Downey (1961: 192–5) on a pogrom against Jews in Antioch in AD 40, and Levine
(1974) on conflicts between Jews and Greeks in Caesarea in which the Jewish inhabitants
initiated the violence.

his ear to the populace's grievances against members of the local
élite (*Or.* 48).

In another case of grain speculation by landowners from the late
first century AD, people in Pamphylian Aspendos directly attacked
the governor, who was even forced to seek asylum beneath an
emperor's statue. The itinerant philosopher Apollonius of Tyana
persuaded the crowd to give him a hearing, and he then named the
speculators and exhorted the people to force them to sell their grain
(Philostr. *Vita Apollonii* 1.15). During a famine in Domitian's time
in Pisidian Antioch, the local authorities petitioned the governor
for assistance; he issued an edict requiring everyone to declare his
stock before the magistrates and then sell all the grain which he did
not need for his personal use at a maximum price twice the ordinary price of former years (*AnnEpigr* 1925, 126; Levick 1985, no.
106; Kohns 1994: 167–73). A considerable number of cases are also
known from fourth-century Syrian Antioch, which in contrast to
Rome and Constantinople could not rely on government supply
(despite certain subsidies for public distributions). The fact that it
was the residence of the emperor's representative (*comes orientis*) and
temporarily of emperors[37] led to the involvement of these authorities; when the people attacked local magistrates, substantial
landowners and bakers (sometimes by arson), the Imperial representatives generally called for fixed low prices and sometimes
undertook the public punishment of bakers, on one occasion
scourging them and parading them with naked backs through the
city streets (Libanius, *Or.* 1.228; Petit 1955: 105–22; Tinnefeld
1972: 151–4).[38]

Governors might themselves become victims of more or less
violent attacks by protesting crowds. During his time in Africa,
Vespasian was once bombarded with turnips (Suet. *Vesp.* 4.3). In
Ephesus a governor was almost stoned by people complaining
about the water temperature in the public baths (Philostr. *VA*
1.16). The Alexandrians, always unruly (see Polyb. 34.14.1), were
notorious for their violent attacks on their prefects from the
early Principate (Strabo 17.1.53 = c 819) through late antiquity

---

[37] Julian's attempts to lower prices during his stay in 362 were apparently sabotaged by the
local élite (Downey 1951).
[38] See Ste Croix (1981: 320) with reference to St John Chrysostom's approval of lynchings
(Migne, *PG* 61.343–4); Liebeschuetz (1972: 126–32 and 208–219) on the communication
between urban population and governors in general.

(Lib. *Or.* 19.14). The fourth-century *Expositio totius mundi et gentium* (37) calls their habit of attacking representatives of the Roman government with firebrands and stones an expression of 'popular justice' (*iustitia populi*). Apart from this there were violent clashes between circus factions (Philostr. *VA* 5.26) even though the games were under the supervision of a military unit (Dio Chrys. *Or.* 32.72; Borthwick 1972; Jones 1978: 36–44; Barry 1993: 102).

In cases of disturbances serious enough to endanger the governors' own authority or even that of the emperor, troops might be called in. Their availability in a technical sense had increased over time, especially since the fourth century AD when military units were apparently more often garrisoned near cities than in earlier times (MacMullen 1988: 209–17). Unrest in Antioch in AD 387 expressed itself in theatre and street demonstrations, but troops were used to suppress the riots only after crowds had begun smashing the Imperial family's statues and setting fire to government buildings; Libanius (though apologetic) stressed the long inactivity of the local commander and the *comes orientis* (*Or.* 19.34–7).[39] Apprehended rioters, even youths, were sentenced to death after summary proceedings, and in addition punishment was inflicted on the whole city. A commission conducted an investigation on behalf of the emperor against the city councillors, who were held responsible for the riots. Many of them, in anticipation of indiscriminate punishment, had attempted to flee the city, but had been prevented from doing so by the armed forces. The commission passed the decision on to the emperor, and meanwhile the councillors were detained. Theodosius in the end accepted a petition in their favour, pardoned them, and restored the city's privileges (Baur 1929: 212–33; Browning 1952; Downey 1961: 426–35; Tinnefeld 1977: 154–63).

Finally, the same pattern can be observed in the direct responses of emperors to major disturbances in the cities. Whether punitive measures[40] were taken and how harsh they were depended on the

---

[39] Libanius clearly differentiates between archers under a local commander and the troops that the *comes* brought in later. The identity of the first-mentioned units is a problem. It is difficult to believe that bowmen under the command of an experienced officer constituted a sort of local police force (Browning 1952: 15, n. 42; Liebeschuetz 1972: 124–5); they were more likely a small military force at the governor's disposal (Petit 1955: 187).

[40] Augustus reacted with financially effective sanctions to an incident in Athens that connoted insult to Rome and himself (Dio Cass. 54.7.2–3; Hoff 1989); Athens, however, was formally a free city. Cyzicus lost its freedom in 20 BC when during a riot (due to causes unknown to us) Roman citizens were killed (Dio Cass. 54.7.6).

ruler's perception of whether his own authority and dignity were at issue. Caracalla engineered a massacre of Alexandrian youths who had derided him with regard to the murders in his family and his emulation of Alexander and Achilles; he did not appreciate that this was intended as a form of comedy (Hdn. 4.9). In contrast, Constantius II did not respond when his statue was smashed at Edessa (Lib. *Or.* 19.48, 20.27–8), and Julian answered the mocking verses and charivaris of the Antiochenes by publicly posting a satirical reply (the *Misopogon*). In both these latter cases the emperors recognized the behaviour as akin to the mock rituals attacking the authorities that were traditionally staged on the occasion of particular festivals, and judged it inappropriate to respond to the people's licentiousness with severity (Gleason 1986). Violent clashes between pagans and Christians in Alexandria finally led in AD 361 to the outrageous lynching by a (pagan) crowd of the (Arian) bishop George. Having at first considered punishment, Julian only rather mildly censured the Alexandrians; though admonishing them not to take the law into their own hands, he acknowledged that the bishop had deserved his death (*Epistulae* 10H = 60B).[41] During a food riot in Antioch in AD 353, the Caesar of the east, Gallus, whose order to lower the price of grain had not been followed, blamed the governor for the continuing crisis, and the governor was consequently 'torn to pieces as if he were delivered to the people by the emperor's judgement' (Amm. Marc. 14.7.6; cf. Lib. *Or.* 1.103). The Antiochenes were, however, shortly afterwards punished, though apparently mildly, by the senior emperor Constantius II (Julian, *Misopogon* 370c; Lib. *Or.* 19.47; Downey 1961: 365–6).[42]

In AD 388/9 Theodosius responded in accordance with his general policy towards the Jews when he ordered that the synagogue in the Euphrates city of Callinicum, which had been burned by a Christian mob headed by the local bishop, be rebuilt at the church's expense. He reconsidered his decision, however, when Milan's Bishop Ambrose protested that a Christian emperor should not be supporting 'blasphemy'. Unauthorized attacks on

---

[41] For details of the events see Amm. Marc. 22.11.3–11; Socr. 3.2–3; Soz. 5.7.8; the church historians' treatment of them seems to suggest that responsibility for the lynching lay directly with a Christian faction (Hunt 1985).

[42] Gallus also had a praetorian prefect and his quaestor lynched by soldiers (Amm. Marc. 14.7.13–17; 15.3.1).

pagan temples under a devoted Christian emperor were quite a different matter; they mostly went unpunished (Noethlichs 1986: 1177–82). In AD 390, when an Illyrian military commander who had arrested a chariot driver at Thessalonike was lynched, the emperor ordered the city's population to be assembled in the circus and cut down by (Gothic) soldiers; the repeal of this order came too late, and between seven thousand and fifteen thousand victims are recorded. In consequence of his excommunication by Ambrose (whose moral indignation was probably due to the fact that Arian soldiers had executed Catholics), Theodosius eventually did penance and established the rule that, in future, death sentences should be carried out only after a waiting period of thirty days (Jones 1964: 166–9; Matthews 1975: 232–7; Kolb 1980).

All this suggests the absence at every level of administration of a clear understanding that violent breaches of public order should be stopped regardless of the motives of the rioters and the outcome of their actions; a variety of political considerations might result in letting things take their course. Local authorities had to consider public opinion (as the magistrates of the Roman Republic had done) because they depended on volunteer support. Both local magistrates and governors had to take into account that higher authorities might intervene in response to appeals or on their own initiative. As long as soldiers were available, governors and emperors could react at their own discretion, and this led to unpredictability of response and sometimes serious overreaction. But all this was not peculiar to the Roman case.

EPILOGUE

Law and order in comparative perspective

The foregoing discussion of public order in the cities and provinces of the Roman Empire suggests that in general governmental intervention was limited. Protection of property and personal security were the responsibility of citizens themselves and involved reliance on the help of kin and neighbours, access to patrons and/or command over social inferiors. Enforcement of general rules of law and order was the business of local authorities, and, dependent as they were on the support of the community, they tended to act in accordance with its expressed or supposed wishes unless the higher authorities were alerted. This meant selectivity of law enforcement, on the one hand, and self-help which under certain circumstances might extend to lynchings and pogroms, on the other. The maintenance of public order concentrated on basic rules. There was apparently (even under Christian emperors) no comprehensive policy for disciplining the lower orders of society.

Uncertainty with respect to a number of questions remains because of the inevitable limitations of our sources. My general approach here has been to avoid assuming modern standards of policing; some comparative considerations may lend support. It is of course extremely hazardous to generalize about the societies of medieval and early modern Western Europe, but it does seem reasonable to argue that state intervention concentrated on cases which were considered a direct threat to the political and social order. In addition to treason and sedition, these included counterfeiting, smuggling and brigandage, as well as particularly shocking crimes such as parricide, serial rape and murder, and sodomy. The majority of everyday conflicts were left to be settled through private initiative and communal arbitration (Lenman and Parker 1980; Soman 1980).

This seems especially to have applied to the Italian city-

republics of late medieval and Renaissance times. The political
order was apparently particularly vulnerable to conspiracies and
sedition, whether arising from feuds within the nobility or from
uprisings of the lower classes. Such political concerns led to the
establishment of various boards with executive as well as judicial
competences superseding an earlier structure based on parish
units. Though they might have considerable numbers of hired
(armed) staff, they remained distinct bodies subordinated to the
various authorities (see Bowsky 1967 on Siena). Putting down
serious disturbances remained the task of militias composed of
propertied citizens whose unconditional loyalty to the city government could not be assumed.[1] For the detection and prevention of
politically dangerous conspiracies, boards of magistrates such as
the Venetian *Dieci* (established after a conspiracy in 1310) and the
Florentine *Otto di Guardia* (created in response to the Ciompi insurrection of 1378) offered rewards for informers, made use of spies
and employed inquisitorial methods with minimal procedural
rights for defendants (Cozzi 1973: 306–9, 318, 336; Brucker 1977:
index s.v. 'Eight on Security'; Cohn 1980: 156–61, 181–4, 199). But
in cases of conflict between citizens such as theft, trespass and
assault magistrates saw their primary function as the official endorsement of agreements between the parties in which the offender
guaranteed his future good behaviour by a money bond (Becker
1976 on Florence; cf. Bowsky 1967: 12–13 on Siena and Blanshei
1982 on Bologna). Public order policy regarding prostitution and
gambling involved a certain amount of regulation but tolerated
both as necessary evils (Brucker 1972: 167 on Florence; Pavan 1980
on Venice). Venice was extraordinarily successful in maintaining
political stability, and is also considered to have been highly effective in suppressing street violence and enforcing public order. If
this aspect of the 'Myth of Venice' proves to stand up to thorough
critical examination, it surely cannot be explained in terms of the
size of the forces that the magistrates had at their disposal. Any
explanation will have to stress the impartial application of the law,

[1] During the 1378 Ciompi disturbances in Florence, the oligarchic government was unable
to depend on such support (Brucker 1977: 43); the transitional popular régime took to
employing a salaried militia drawn from the lower classes, which was on the one hand an
insult to their 'betters', and on the other was a strategy for controlling popular radicalism
by turning potential rioters into forces of order (Brucker 1968: 334; Trexler 1984: 377,
385).

the self-discipline of Venice's governing class, its ability to increase social cohesion through paternalistic policies and the highly ritualized symbolic integration of its citizenry (Chojnacki 1972; Ruggiero 1980; Pullan 1971; Muir 1981).

Professional police forces distinct from ordinary citizens and amateur magistrates, on the one hand, and the military, on the other, whose corporate identity was symbolized by the wearing of uniforms, emerged in most European states during the eighteenth and nineteenth centuries. Broadly speaking, the notion of *police* in French, borrowed by the English, and of *Polizei* in German oscillates between an older, broader sense of provisions for the welfare of the society, and a newer, narrower sense of a specialized apparatus for law enforcement (Radzinowicz 1956: 1–8; Raeff 1975; Boulet-Sautel 1980; Emsley 1983: 2–3; Heidenheimer 1988; Schwartz 1988: 3–4; Pasquino 1991; Knemeyer 1978). Organizational structures, defined competences and actual functions, legal status with respect to citizens, judicial authorities, local and central government, political role, arms and uniforms, internal specialization, recruitment, public esteem, etc., vary considerably from country to country and, of course, from period to period, in response to changing political régimes and societal demands within each country's history (Bayley 1975; Emsley 1983; Mann 1993: 403–12).

Despite all the differences, the existence of a police apparatus as such became a uniform element of modern societies. It was, however, not a perfectly 'natural' solution to objective problems. The development of English police institutions from the mid-eighteenth to the mid-nineteenth century is especially useful for demonstrating this point, in that we have documentation of the controversy over traditional principles and new instruments of social discipline, the prevention and detection of crimes, riot control and evidence of the degree to which the functions of newly established apparatuses diverged from their proclaimed aims (Silver 1967; Philips 1980, 1983; Donajgrodzki 1977; Styles 1987).

Traditionally, maintaining public order in England had been the task of Justices of the Peace drawn from the local gentry and parish constables appointed in rotation from among householders (who, however, could engage substitutes). Law enforcement depended on the mechanisms of patronage and extrajudicial arbitration, made use of the discretionary powers inherent in the summary jurisdiction of the Justice of the Peace, employed vagrancy and poor laws against people on the fringes of a community and turned a blind eye to public order offences committed by the respectable. In general, flexible handling of the law in accordance with public opinion was preferred to comprehensive enforcement of the letter of the law (Beattie 1972; Wrightson 1980; Sharpe 1980, 1984: 73–93; Rock 1983; Landau 1984; Herrup 1987; Oberwittler 1990; Cohen 1991).

Despite some shortcomings (especially in times of growing social tension), the system was considered adequate in that it accommodated the gentry's position as the 'natural rulers' in the counties (Thompson 1974), and any reform was seen as a potential infringement of local autonomy and therefore of liberty itself. Opponents of reform in every political and social camp pointed to the French model (Lévy 1965; Cameron 1977; Williams 1978) as an abhorrent example of political abuse which could not be adopted under a free constitution (Emsley 1983). Although reform proposals related especially to the problems of the overcrowded metropolitan area, which was administered by a diversity of authorities, they aroused the suspicion that they were aimed at nationwide uniformity. Resistance to them did not, however, necessarily mean unwillingness to modify the existing communal structures.

Reform propagandists such as Henry and John Fielding and later Colquhoun, who argued for extensive protective measures, seem to have been obsessed by the idea that in addition to protecting property it was necessary to make the poor useful members of society and therefore to suppress gambling, drinking, prostitution and idleness as the parent of vice (Radzinowicz 1948: 399–415; 1956: 11–28, 211–51; Goldgar 1985; McGowen 1987: 656–64; 1980: 174–80; Terrill 1980). Their ideas coalesced with those of (evangelical) movements for the reformation of manners (Curtis and Speck 1976; Bristow 1977; Roberts 1983; Innes 1990). Opposed to them were local élites resistant to increased tax rates and fearful of the repercussions of reform on their traditional way of life. During the nineteenth century the hostility of the lower classes to the newly established police forces was aroused especially by their role as 'domestic missionaries' who, among other things, suppressed popular entertainments on Sundays (Storch 1975; Miller 1977). Gradual acceptance emerged from the experience that appeal to police and police courts could be beneficial for ordinary people, who, instead of exacting informal retribution, now took to the prosecution of thieves (Philips 1977: 127–40; Jones 1983; Davis 1984; and see Dinges 1992 on Paris).

An alleged increase in the eighteenth century in offences against property had been answered by an increase in the number of offences punishable by death. The system relied on the effects of exemplary punishments; the harshness of the law was mitigated by the discretionary use that victims, magistrates and juries made of it and allowance for various sorts of pardons (Hay *et al.* 1975; Brewer and Styles 1980; Innes and Styles 1986; King 1984). Discontent with the presumed inefficiency of the operation of criminal law arose from the broadcasting of news about crimes made possible by new communication structures, creating the impression of crime waves (Styles 1983). It was fostered by enlightened ideas from Beccaria to Bentham of a criminal law which would match the penalty with the crime and produce sentences designed to improve the delinquent's morals rather than punish his body (Radzinowicz 1948: 277–86, 355–96; 1956: 425–41; Ignatieff 1978; Beattie 1986: 554–9). The first steps towards a more comprehensive prosecution were made, however, not through official intervention but by organizations of citizens set up to share the cost of rewards and of prosecutions (Shubert 1981; Beattie 1986: 48–59; Philips 1989).

The eighteenth century saw a great number of riots. The 1715 Riot Act stressed the responsibility of local magistrates and all loyal citizens. An hour after the public reading of the proclamation of the Riot Act by the magistrate responsible, rioters who had not dispersed were guilty of a felony, and anyone who assisted a magistrate in apprehending them was guaranteed indemnity if one of them happened to be hurt or killed. The reactions of magistrates varied with their assessment of the rioters' motives (which were likely to be approved in cases of food riots and *taxation populaire* (Thompson 1971; Shelton 1973: 95–121; Stevenson 1974)), especially since they depended on the support of their measures by substantial parts of the community. In any case, they had to appear in person at the scene of the disturbance. When as an *ultima ratio* they called for the employment of the militia or of regular troops, the soldiers were legally considered ordinary citizens, and were thus subject to prosecution when conformity to the legal criteria for the use of force was called into question. That is why the military wanted to withdraw from internal security tasks. If rioters were

apprehended on the spot and later indicted, the tendency of the
authorities to make examples of them was to a certain degree
mitigated by the courts' scrupulous interpretation of the law. When
the limitations of the traditional system of riot control were
exposed, as they were in the case of the 1780 Gordon Riots (when
no magistrate took action and the cabinet finally ordered the use of
troops as an emergency measure), the reaction tended not to be a
demand for new enforcement agencies; instead, recourse to the
common-law principle of citizens' collective responsibility led to
the formation of voluntary associations and the calling out of
special constables if necessary (Hayter 1978; Nippel 1984/5; Rogers
1990). The efficacy of such solutions depended on the loyalty of
most of the middle and lower classes as evidently was the case
during the 1790s (Western 1956; Stevenson 1977; Booth 1983;
Dickinson 1990).

Thus late-eighteenth-century responses to real or alleged break-
downs of public order stressed self-help and societal self-regulation.
Eventually, however, in the course of the nineteenth century, a new
police force came to be considered the appropriate instrument for
coping with all problems of law and order, and the model of the
Metropolitan Police of 1829 was gradually adopted nationwide
within the established framework of local government (Emsley
1983; Palmer 1988; Storch 1989; Gatrell 1990). Organized mass
demonstrations were considered more dangerous than traditional
riots, and indicated an increase in class tensions which made it
impossible any longer to count on the loyalty of the working classes
(Stevenson 1979: 245–74). Moreover, the time-schedule of an in-
dustrializing society both demanded a quicker response to disturbances and made ordinary citizens unavailable for duties in
connection with public order. These and other factors contributed
to a reform of the public order system as one aspect of sweeping
changes in the structure of society.

From a broader perspective, experience with modern police
systems has shown that selectivity of law enforcement persists;
discretion becomes associated with the police apparatus as it
employs regular strategies of prevention and prosecution necessarily involving biases with regard to certain offences and certain
groups of offenders, which as self-fulfilling prophecies appear to be
time-tested. A society's perception of public order is filtered
through the police's viewpoint and practice. From the citizens'

point of view, the habit of calling on the police for support is linked
to a feeling of vulnerability when the response is ineffective. The
failure of the modern state to achieve the level of law and order
which it promises may undermine its legitimacy. Thus the establishment of the modern police force, whatever its undeniable
advantages, has its social costs.[2] More comparative work on the
maintenance of public order in pre-modern as well as modern
societies should help to increase our understanding of the merits
and shortcomings of the system of public order in ancient Rome.

[2] All this applies to police forces that closely fit the ideal of an impartial law-enforcement
agency. I have deliberately left out the problems of corruption, brutality, racism, etc., as
well as the part played by police in political surveillance and repression in authoritarian
or totalitarian régimes.

Bibliographical essay

References and bibliography provide information on the scholarly literature dealing with the various topics touched on here. Despite its length, the bibliography is highly selective; I have omitted almost all works dealing with the narrative history (*histoire événementielle*) of the Late Republic and Principate, and concentrated on works on their social and legal aspects; furthermore, the bibliography gives preference to fairly recent publications, which as a rule contain references to earlier works. For a more exhaustive list of works published through the late 1980s readers may consult the bibliography of my *Aufruhr und 'Polizei' in der römischen Republik* (Stuttgart, 1988). Though owing much to this former publication (which deals in greater detail with Late Republican politics), the present book was written specifically for the Key Themes in Ancient History series, covers much more of the Imperial period and pays particular attention to the mechanisms of social control and to comparative aspects.

The following comments draw attention to those works which either have been of importance in the shaping of my views or represent alternative approaches.

'POLICE'

Discussions of public order in Roman society often assume that the absence of a police apparatus jeopardized the stability of the political order. Nineteenth-century German works on Republican constitutional law and history do not necessarily show this tendency; in speaking of means of 'policing' they are referring to the older, comprehensive sense of *Polizei*, which covers the whole spectrum of public welfare and order. It is only in the works from the late nineteenth century that the association with institutionalized forces of order becomes prominent, and there is a tendency to see gross deficiencies in both the Republican and the Late Imperial order in contrast with the alleged efficiency of the Principate. Otto Hirschfeld's pioneer studies on policing in the Empire, collected in his *Kleine Schriften* (Berlin, 1913), best represent this view, and it is to some extent reflected in A. W. Lintott's *Violence in Republican Rome* (Oxford, 1968), which has stimulated the recent debates about political violence in the Late Republic. A concomitant of the concentration on 'police' forces is the tendency, represented by E. Echol's article on the 'Roman city police' in *CJ* 53 (1957/8) 377–85, to take certain temporary measures as indicating the establishment of permanent institutions. The point that a standing police force was inconceivable under the Republican constitution has been forcefully argued by Christian Meier in *Res Publica Amissa* (Wiesbaden, 1966) 157–61.

That the Principate brought a breakthrough in policing is suggested by, for example, R. W. Davies ('Augustus Caesar: a police system in the ancient world', in P. J. Stead, ed., *Pioneers in Policing* (Maidenhead, 1977: 12–32)). Standard works on the praetorians (M. Durry, *Les cohortes prétoriennes*, Paris, 1938), urban cohorts (H. Freis, *Die cohortes urbanae*, Cologne, 1967), and *vigiles* (P. K. Baillie-Reynolds, *The Vigiles of Imperial Rome*, Oxford, 1926) all attempt to remedy the lack of concrete information on the actual security functions of these forces by making assumptions about 'necessary tasks' and by claiming unspecified source references to soldiers as relevant to the particular force they describe. That, for example, the *vigiles* were probably fully occupied with their duties as a fire brigade is, however, clearly brought out in J. S. Rainbird's 'The Fire Stations of Imperial Rome', in *PBSR* 54 (1986) 147–69. All aspects of the administration of the city of Rome are dealt with by O. F. Robinson in *Ancient Rome: City Planning and Administration* (London, 1992), but she tends to take legal rules for actual practice. On the maintenance and use of city streets, the article by R. Frei-Stolba in *Labor omnibus unus: Festschrift G. Walser* (Wiesbaden, 1989: 25–37) is to be recommended. The police functions of the Roman army throughout the Empire are placed in perspective by B. Isaac's *The Limits of Empire* (Oxford, 1990, 2nd edn, 1992); R. W. Davies, 'The daily life of the Roman soldier under the principate', in *ANRW* II, 1 (1974) 229–338 overestimates their use in this way.

REPUBLICAN MAGISTRATES

The distinction between the civil and military capacities of the magistrates and the legal spheres inside and outside the city is a controversial subject. The standard view, formulated by Mommsen, has been seriously challenged by A. Giovannini, *Consulare Imperium* (Basel, 1983: 1–30), but this ambitious attempt to reinterpret the notions of *imperium domi* and *militiae* as relating to Roman citizens in their civil capacity and to conscripted soldiers respectively has not yet provoked the discussion it deserves; see, however, the review by J. Crook (*JRS* 76 (1986) 286–8), which identifies the problems entailed by Giovannini's solution. In any case, the decisive point for my argument – the distinction between soldiers under oath and citizen volunteers – is not affected by that debate. Again, with regard to the nature of Pompey's constitutional position in 52, R. T. Ridley's attempt to deny any cumulation of competences in

RhM 126 (1983) 136–48, is not decisive; in any case, the Triumvirate of 43 and later Octavian on his own combined the competences of regular magistrates and promagistrates, and thus made obsolete the distinction between the spheres within and outside the city; compare J. Bleicken, *Zwischen Republik und Prinzipat* (Göttingen, 1990).

On the emergence of *provocatio* from the *plebs*'s self-help activities, A. Lintott's article in *ANRW* I, 2 (1972) 226–67 is fundamental. The importance of the censorship to the self-discipline of the ruling élite is stressed by A. E. Astin in *JRS* 78 (1988) 14–34, and by E. Baltrusch in a book (Munich, 1989) on *regimen morum*. The primarily symbolic role of the lictors is brought out in a brilliant article by B. Gladigow in *ANRW* I, 2 (1972) 295–314, and the social-historical significance of the *apparitores* is discussed by B. Cohen in C. Nicolet, ed., *Des ordres à Rome* (Paris, 1984: 23–60) and by N. Purcell in *PBSR* 51 (1983) 125–73. C. Meier has drawn attention to the importance of ad hoc *praesidia* in *GGA* 216 (1964) at pp. 44–8. H. Galsterer in *JRS* 78 (1988) 78–90, examining the *lex Irnitana*, discusses the municipal laws and their implications for local government.

SOCIAL CONTROL

Reflections on the social background of the magistracy necessarily include assessment of the importance of patronage. P. A. Brunt (*'Clientela'*, in *The Fall of the Roman Republic* (Oxford, 1988: 382–442)) rightly warns against overestimation of its role, but may go too far in making the decisive criteria explicit mention in the sources of the employment of clients. On the impact of rhetoric on Late Republican politics one should especially consult J.-M. David, ' "Eloquentia popularis" et conduites symboliques des orateurs de la fin de la république' in *QS* 12 (1980) 171–98; on the Roman élite's perception of religion, see J. North on 'religious toleration' and the Bacchanalia in *PCPhS* 205 (n.s. 25) (1979) 85–103, and his review-article on the subject in *JRS* 76 (1986) 251–8. The use of *patria potestas* in political conflicts is analysed by Y. Thomas in his contribution to the conference volume *Du châtiment dans la cité* (Paris 1984: 499–548). On the importance of private initiative and social control for maintaining public order in Athens, compare now V. J. Hunter, *Policing Athens. Social Order in the Attic Lawsuits, 420–320 B.C.* (Princeton, 1994).

My approach to popular justice as a concomitant of official sanctions in Republican as well as Imperial times differs from that of Lintott, *Violence in Republican Rome* (Oxford, 1968: 6–21), and *Violence, Civil Strife, and Revolution in the Classical City* (London, 1982: 24–31)), who, following H. Usener ('Italische Volksjustiz', in *Kleine Schriften*, vol. IV (Leipzig, 1913: 356–82)), perceives the phenomenon as a sort of survival from an archaic, pre-state period. P. Veyne instead stresses the synchronic perspective in 'Le folklore à Rome' in *Latomus* 42 (1983) 3–30.

CRIMINAL LAW

W. Kunkel's theory on the judicial functions of the *tresviri capitales* (*Untersuchungen zur Entwicklung des römischen Kriminalverfahrens in vorsullanischer Zeit*, Munich, 1962) has been discussed at some length. The assumption that already in Republican times criminal law operated with a two-class system has since been shattered by R. Rilinger's proof (*Humiliores-Honestiores*, Munich, 1988) that no such system existed even in Imperial times. That we know almost nothing about the practice of criminal law before Late Republican times is best illustrated by the totally divergent account of A. H. M. Jones, *The Criminal Courts of the Roman Republic and Principate* (Oxford, 1972), which in fact implies a return to Mommsen's position that criminal trials took place before the popular assembly.

As to the judicial significance of manifest guilt and confession, J. Crook, 'Was there a "doctrine of manifest guilt" in the Roman criminal law?' in *PCPhS* 213 (n.s. 33) (1987) 38–52, has shown that ordinary legal proceedings did not include any such regular mechanism of self-condemnation. In my opinion, however, this clarification does not affect my argument that manifest guilt and confession played a significant part in extraordinary proceedings conducted by magistrates and in the justification of the Catilinarians' execution (see J.-M. David, 'La faute et l'abandon', in the conference volume *L'aveu* (Rome 1986: 71–87)). Interrogation of slaves in cases of conspiracy is analysed by L. Schumacher, *Servus Index* (Wiesbaden, 1982).

Evidence on Late Republican criminal trials is collected in M. C. Alexander, *Trials in the Late Roman Republic* (Toronto, 1990). J.-M. David, *Le patronat judiciaire au dernier siècle de la république romaine* (Rome, 1992), exhaustively investigates the social implications of court proceedings as an arena for conflicts between Roman nobles. Legislation against violence as well as murder and the carrying of weapons with offensive intent is analysed in articles by J. D. Cloud in *Athenaeum* 66 (1988) 579–95, 67 (1989) 427–65, and J.-L. Ferrary in *Athenaeum* 69 (1991) 417–34 respectively.

Discussion of the legal implications of the so-called *senatus consultum ultimum* (J. v. Ungern-Sternberg, *Untersuchungen zum spätrepublikanischen Notstandsrecht*, Munich, 1970) has been enriched by O. Behrends' demonstration (in *Das Profil des Juristen in der europäischen Tradition* (Eberbach, 1980: 25–121)) that private citizens' claim to be saving the state in an emergency was not superseded by the establishment of the Senate's formal declaration.

THE *PLEBS URBANA*

Our understanding of demonstrations by the *plebs urbana* has clearly profited from the new view of the 'mob' in the early modern period reflected in the works of G. Rudé (*The Crowd in History*, New York, 1964),

E. Hobsbawm (*Primitive Rebels*, Manchester, 1959, 2nd edn 1971), and E. P. Thompson ('The moral economy of the English crowd', in *P & P* 50 (1971) 76–136); compare my 'Die *plebs urbana* und die Rolle der Gewalt in der späten römischen Republik', in H. Mommsen and W. Schulze, eds., *Vom Elend der Handarbeit* (Stuttgart, 1981: 70–92). As for the Roman case, P. Brunt, 'The Roman Mob', in *P & P* 35 (1966) 3–27 and Z. Yavetz, *Plebs and Princeps* (Oxford, 1969) have been pathbreaking for an approach which has proved fruitful in a number of further studies on the *plebs* from Republican times (e.g., P. J. J. Vanderbroeck, *Popular Leadership and Collective Behavior in the Late Roman Republic*, Amsterdam, 1987) to the Late Empire (A. Cameron, *Circus Factions*, Oxford, 1976). The material and symbolic significance of corn distributions has been explored by P. Veyne, *Le pain et le cirque* (Paris, 1976; abridged Eng. tr. 1990), G. Rickman, *The Corn Supply of Ancient Rome* (Oxford, 1980), and P. Garnsey, *Famine and Food Supply in the Graeco-Roman World* (Cambridge, 1988).

The 'rehabilitation' of Clodius, now viewed not as simply a gangster in politics or a henchman of the *triumviri* of the 50s but as a political figure in his own right, began with articles by E. S. Gruen, 'Clodius: instrument or independent agent?', *Phoenix* 20 (1966) 120–30, and A. W. Lintott, 'P. Clodius Pulcher-Felix Catilina?' *G & R* 14 (1967) 157–69; 'Cicero and Milo' in *JRS* 64 (1974) 62–78. His cooperation with the *collegia* has been analysed by J.-M. Flambard, 'Clodius, les collèges, la plèbe' in *MEFR* 89 (1977) 115–56. That the *collegia* provided 'intermediate leaders' of the *plebs* is also rightly stressed in Vanderbroeck's above-mentioned book. The importance of these unions for offering ordinary people the opportunity to obtain positions of honour is also underlined in H. L. Royden's study on the *collegia* during the Principate (*The Magistrates of the Roman Professional Collegia*, Pisa, 1988). Clodius' banishment of Cicero and the ensuing legal struggles have recently been studied anew in two thorough articles by P. Moreau in *Athenaeum* 65 (1987) 465–92; 67 (1989) 151–78.

On the symbolic interaction between emperors and the *plebs*, see in addition to the already cited works of Yavetz and Veyne the stimulating study by E. Flaig, *Den Kaiser herausfordern* (Frankfurt, 1992).

COMPARATIVE ASPECTS

The impact of studies of riots in early modern times upon ancient historians has already been mentioned. My account also owes a great deal to the many studies of criminal law in pre-police times published during the past two decades. The stance of historians in this field who identified with the aims of the late-eighteenth- and early-nineteenth-century reformers (as did L. Radzinowicz in his monumental *History of English Criminal Law and Its Administration from 1750*, 4 vols., London, 1948–68) has been challenged by a new social history which interpreted the features of the old law as well as the new institutions as changing strategies of social control. The controversial *Albion's Fatal Tree* (London, 1975) of D. Hay and others marked the beginning of a series of 'revisionist' works. The steady stream of historical studies on law and order in various societies has not yet, however, produced comparative studies examining the common elements of pre-modern societies.

Bibliography

ACHARD, G. (1975) ' "Ratio popularis" et funérailles', *LEC* 43: 166–78
   (1981) *Pratique rhétorique et idéologie politique dans les discours "optimates" de Cicéron.* Leiden
ADAMSON, J. H. and FOLLAND, H. F. (1973) *Sir Harry Vane. His Life and Times 1613–1662.* London
ALEXANDER, M. C. (1985) 'Praemia in the quaestiones of the late republic', *CPh* 80: 20–32
   (1990) *Trials in the Late Roman Republic, 149 B.C. to 50 B.C.* Toronto
   (1993) 'How many Roman senators were ever prosecuted? The evidence from the late republic', *Phoenix* 47: 238–55
ALFÖLDI, A. (1953) *Studien über Caesars Monarchie.* Lund
   (1970) *Die monarchische Repräsentation im römischen Kaiserreiche.* Darmstadt
   (1985) *Caesar in 44 v. Chr. Bd. I: Studien zu Caesars Monarchie und ihren Wurzeln.* Bonn
ALFÖLDY, G. (1971) 'Bellum desertorum', *BJ* 171: 367–76
   (1989) 'Cleanders Sturz und die antike Überlieferung', in *Die Krise des Römischen Reiches. Geschichte, Geschichtsschreibung und Geschichtsbetrachtung.* Stuttgart: 81–126
ALFORD, V. (1959) 'Rough music or charivari', *Folklore* 70: 505–18
ALLEN, W. (1944) 'Cicero's house and libertas', *TAPhA* 75: 1–9
ANNEQUIN, J. (1992) 'La "civitas", la violence et la loi', *Index* 20: 1–11
ARBANDT, S. and MACHEINER, W. (1976) ' "Gefangenschaft" ', *RAC* 9: 318–45
ASTIN, A. E. (1988) 'Regimen morum', *JRS* 78: 14–34
AUSBÜTTEL, F. M. (1982) *Untersuchungen zu den Vereinen im Westen des römischen Reiches.* Kallmünz
AUSTIN, M. M. (1981) *The Hellenistic World from Alexander to the Roman Conquest. A Selection of Ancient Sources in Translation.* Cambridge
BADIAN, E. (1972) 'Tiberius Gracchus and the beginning of the Roman revolution', *ANRW* I, 1: 668–731
   (1984) 'The death of Saturninus, studies in chronology and prosopography', *Chiron* 14: 101–47
   (1989) 'The scribae of the Roman Republic', *Klio* 71: 582–603

BAGNALL, R. S. (1977) 'Army and police in Roman Upper Egypt', *JARCE* 14: 67–88
(1989) 'Official and private violence in Roman Egypt', *BASP* 26: 201– 16
BAILLIE-REYNOLDS, P. K. (1926) *The Vigiles of Imperial Rome*. Oxford
BAIN, D. (1981) 'Menander, Samia 580 and 'Not- und Hilferufe' in Ptolemaic Egypt', *ZPE* 44: 169–71
BALTRUSCH, E. (1989) *Regimen Morum. Die Reglementierung des Privatlebens der Senatoren und Ritter in der römischen Republik und frühen Kaiserzeit.* Munich
BARRACLOUGH, R. (1974) 'Philo's politics. Roman rule and hellenistic Judaism', *ANRW* II, 21/1: 417–553
BARROW, R. H. (1973) *Prefect and Emperor: The Relationes of Symmachus AD 384.* Oxford
BARRY, W. D. (1993) 'Aristocrats, orators and the "mob". Dio Chrysostom and the world of the Alexandrinians', *Historia* 42: 82–103
BARTON, C. A. (1989) 'The scandal of the arena', *Representations* 27: 1–36
BAUMAN, R. A. (1967) *The Crimen Maiestatis in the Roman Republic and Augustan Principate.* Johannesburg
(1972) 'Review of Labruna (1971)', *Antichthon* 6: 63–73
(1973) 'The hostis declarations of 88 and 87 B.C.', *Athenaeum* 51: 270–93
(1974a) *Impietas in principem. A Study of Treason against the Roman Emperor with Special Reference to the First Century A.D.* Munich
(1974b) 'Criminal prosecutions by the aediles', *Latomus* 33: 245–64
(1978a) 'Five pronouncements by P. Mucius Scaevola', *RIDA* 25: 223– 45
(1978b) 'Il "sovversivismo" di Emilio Lepido', *Labeo* 24: 60–74
(1980) 'The "leges iudiciorum publicorum" and their interpretation in the Republic, Principate and later Empire', *ANRW* II, 13: 103–233
(1983) *Lawyers in Roman Republican Politics. A Study of the Roman Jurists in their Political Setting 316–82 BC.* Munich
(1984) 'Family law and Roman politics', in *Sodalitas. Scritti in onore di A. Guarino.* Naples: 1283–1300
(1985) *Lawyers in Roman Transitional Politics. A Study of the Roman Jurists in their Political Setting in the Late Republic and Triumvirate.* Munich
(1989) *Lawyers and Politics in the Early Roman Empire. A Study of Relations between the Roman Jurists and the Emperors from Augustus to Hadrian.* Munich
(1990a) 'The suppression of the Bacchanals. Five questions', *Historia* 39: 334–348
(1990b) *Political Trials in Ancient Greece.* London
BAUR, C. (1929), *Der heilige Johannes Chrysostomos und seine Zeit.* Vol. I: *Antiochien.* Munich
BAYLEY, D. H. (1975) 'The police and political development in Europe', in Tilly, ed., (1975a): 328–79

BEARD, M. (1980) 'The sexual status of Vestal Virgins', *JRS* 70: 12–27

BEATTIE, J. M. (1972) 'Towards a study of crime in 18th Century England: A note on indictments', in P. Fritz and D. Williams, eds., *The Triumph of Culture. 18th Century Perspectives.* Toronto: 299–314

(1986) *Crime and the Courts in England 1660–1800.* Oxford

BECKER, M. B. (1976) 'Changing patterns of violence and justice in fourteenth- and fifteenth-century Florence', *CSSH* 18: 281–96

BEHRENDS, O. (1978) 'Grabraub und Grabfrevel im römischen Recht', *Abhandlungen der Akademie der Wissenschaften Göttingen*, ser. III, 113: 85–106

(1980) 'Tiberius Gracchus und die Juristen seiner Zeit – die römische Jurisprudenz gegenüber der Staatskrise des Jahres 133 v. Chr.', in *Das Profil des Juristen in der europäischen Tradition. Symposium aus Anlaß des 70. Geburtstages von F. Wieacker.* Eberbach: 25–121

(1981) 'Die Rechtsformen des römischen Handwerks', in H. Jankuhn *et al.*, eds., *Das Handwerk in vor- und frühgeschichtlicher Zeit*, vol. I. Göttingen: 141–203

BELLEN, H. (1971) *Studien zur Sklavenflucht im römischen Kaiserreich.* Wiesbaden

(1981) *Die germanische Leibwache der römischen Kaiser des julisch-claudischen Hauses.* Wiesbaden

(1982) 'Antike Staatsräson. Die Hinrichtung der 400 Sklaven des römischen Stadtpräfekten L. Pedanius Secundus im Jahre 61 n. Chr.', *Gymnasium* 89: 449–67

BENNER, H. (1987) *Die Politik des P. Clodius Pulcher. Untersuchungen zur Denaturierung des Clientelwesens in der ausgehenden römischen Republik.* Stuttgart

BÉRANGER, J. (1973) 'L'accession du Auguste et l'idéologie du "privatus"', in *Principatus. Études de notions et d'histoire politiques dans l'antiquité gréco-romaine.* Geneva: 243–58

BÉRARD, F. (1988) 'Le rôle militaire des cohortes urbaines', *MEFR* 100: 159–82

BERCÉ, Y. M. (1974) *Histoire des Croquants. Etude des soulèvements populaires au XVIIe siècle dans le sud-ouest de la France.* Geneva

BERESFORD, M. W. (1957/58) 'The common informer, the penal statutes and economic regulations', *Economic History Review* 10: 221–37

BERGEMANN, C. (1992) *Politik und Religion im spätrepublikanischen Rom.* Stuttgart

BERGMANN, W. and HOFFMANN, C. (1987) 'Kalkül oder "Massenwahn"?. Eine soziologische Interpretation der antijüdischen Unruhen in Alexandria 38 n. Chr.', in R. Erb and M. Schmidt, eds., *Antisemitismus und Jüdische Geschichte.* Berlin: 15–46

BERNEKER, E. (1971) 'Der Felssturz im alten griechischen Recht', in *Studi in onore di E. Volterra*, vol. I. Milan: 87–97

BICKERMAN, E. J. (1946/47) 'The warning inscriptions of Herod's temple', *Jewish Quarterly Review* 37: 387–405

BILIŃSKI, B. (1961) 'Fornix Calpurnius e la morte di Tiberio Graccho. Un contributo alla topografia del Colle Capitolino', *Helikon* 1: 264–82

BLANSHEI, S. R. (1982), 'Crime and law enforcement in medieval Bologna', *Journal of Social History* 16, no. 1: 121–38

BLEICKEN, J. (1958) ' "Vici magister" ', *RE* 8A: 2480–3

(1968) *Das Volkstribunat der klassischen Republik*. 2nd edn. Munich

(1975) *Lex Publica. Gesetz und Recht in der römischen Republik*. Berlin

(1990) *Zwischen Republik und Prinzipat. Zum Charakter des Zweiten Triumvirats*. Göttingen

BLOCKLEY, R. C. (1969) 'Internal self-policing in the late Roman administration. Some evidence from Ammianus Marcellinus', *C&M* 30: 403–19

BLOK, A. (1972) 'The peasant and the brigand: social banditry reconsidered', *CSSH* 14: 494–503

BOOTH, A. (1983) 'Popular loyalism and public violence in the north-west of England, 1790–1800', *Social History* 8, no 3: 295–313

BORTHWICK, E. K. (1972) 'Dio Chrysostom on the mob at Alexandria', *CR* 22: 1–3

BOULET-SAUTEL, M. (1980) 'Police et administration en France à la fin de l'ancien régime. Observations terminologiques', in W. Paravicini and K. F. Werner, eds., *Histoire comparée de l'administration (IVe–XVIIIe siècles)*, Zürich (*Beihefte der Francia* 9): 47–51

BOVE, L. (1967) 'Due iscrizioni da Pozzuoli e Cuma', *Labeo* 13: 23–48

BOWSKY, W. M. (1967) 'The medieval commune and internal violence: police power and public safety in Siena, 1287–1355', *AHR* 73: 1–17

BRADLEY, K. R. (1984) *Slaves and Masters in the Roman Empire: A Study in Social Control*. Brussels

(1989) *Slavery and Rebellion in the Roman World, 140 B.C.–70 B.C.* Bloomington

BRAUND, D. C. (1985) *Augustus to Nero. A Sourcebook on Roman History 31 BC–AD 68*. London

BRECHT, C. H. (1937) ' "occentatio" ', *RE* 17: 1752–63

BREWER, J. (1976) *Party Ideology and Popular Politics at the Accession of George III*. Cambridge

(1980) 'The Wilkites and the law, 1763–74: a study of radical notions of governance', in Brewer and Styles 1980a: 128–71

BREWER, J. and STYLES, J., eds. (1980a) *An Ungovernable People. The English and their Law in the Seventeenth and Eighteenth Centuries*. London

(1980b) 'Introduction', in 1980a: 11–20

BRISCOE, J. (1974) 'Supporters and opponents of Tiberius Gracchus', *JRS* 64: 125–35

BRISTOW, E. J. (1977) *Vice and Vigilance. Purity Movements in Britain since 1700*. Dublin

BROWN, R. M. (1979) 'The American Vigilante Tradition', in H. D. Graham and T. R. Gurr, eds., *Violence in America. Historical & Comparative Perspectives.* Rev. edn. Beverly Hills: 153–85

BROWNING, R. (1952) 'The riot of A.D. 387 in Antioch. The role of the theatrical claques in the later empire', *JRS* 42: 13–20

BRUCKER, G. A. (1968) 'The Ciompi Revolution', in N. Rubinstein, ed., *Florentine Studies. Politics and Society in Renaissance Florence.* London: 314–56

(1972) 'The Florentine popolo minuto and its political role, 1340–1450', in L. Martines, ed., *Violence and Civil Disorder in Italian Cities 1200–1500.* Berkeley: 155–83

(1977) *The Civic World of Early Renaissance Florence.* Princeton

BRUHNS, H. (1978) *Caesar und die römische Oberschicht in den Jahren 49–44 v. Chr. Untersuchungen zur Herrschaftsetablierung im Bürgerkrieg.* Göttingen

BRUNS, C. G. (1882) 'Die römischen Popularklagen', in *Kleinere Schriften,* vol. I. Weimar: 313–75

BRUNT, P. A. (1966) 'The Roman mob', *P&P* 35: 3–27

(1971) *Italian Manpower 225 B.C.–A.D. 14.* Oxford

(1977) 'Josephus on social conflicts in Roman Judaea', *Klio* 59: 149–53

(1983) 'Princeps and equites', *JRS* 73: 42–75

(1984) 'Did emperors ever suspend the law of "maiestas"?', in *Sodalitas* (see Bauman 1984): 469–80

(1988) *The Fall of the Roman Republic and Related Essays.* Oxford

BRUUN, C. (1991) *The Water Supply of Ancient Rome. A Study of Roman Imperial Administration.* Helsinki

BUCKLER, W. H. (1923) 'Labour disputes in the province of Asia', in *Anatolian Studies presented to Sir William M. Ramsay.* Manchester: 27–50

BUGH, G. R. (1992) 'Athenion and Aristion of Athens', *Phoenix* 46: 108–23

BURKE, P. (1978) *Popular Culture in Early Modern Europe.* London

(1983) 'The virgin of the Carmine and the revolt of Masaniello', *P&P* 99: 3–21

BURKERT, W. (1977) *Griechische Religion der archaischen und klassischen Epoche.* Stuttgart [English translation: Oxford, 1985]

BURTON, G. P. (1975) 'Proconsuls, assizes and the administration of justice under the empire', *JRS* 65: 92–106

BURY, J. B. (1958) *History of the Later Roman Empire from the Death of Theodosius I to the Death of Justinian.* 2 vols. Reprint New York

BUSOLT, G. and SWOBODA, H. (1920–26) *Griechische Staatskunde.* 2 vols. Munich

CAMERON, A. (1974) *Bread and Circuses: the Roman Emperor and His People. Inaugural Lecture King's College London.* London

(1976) *Circus Factions. Blues and Greens at Rome and Byzantium.* Oxford

CAMERON, I. A. (1977) 'The police of eighteenth-century France', *European Studies Review* 7: 47–75

CAMPBELL, J. B. (1984) *The Emperor and the Roman Army, 31 BC–AD 235.* Oxford

CARAWAN, E. M. (1984) 'Akriton apokteinai: execution without trial in fourth-century Athens', *GRBS* 25: 40–58

CASTRÉN, P. (1975) *Ordo populusque pompeianus.* Rome

CAULFIELD, T., ESTNER, A. and STEPHEN, S. (1989) 'Complaints of police brutality (P. Mich. inv. 6957, 6961, 6979)', *ZPE* 76: 241–54

CHASTAGNOL, A. (1960) *La préfecture urbaine à Rome sous le Bas-Empire.* Paris

CHOJNACKI, S. (1972) 'Crime, punishment, and the trecento Venetian state', in L. Martines, ed., *Violence and Civil Disorder in Italian Cities, 1200–1500.* Berkeley: 184–227

CHRISTENSEN, K. A. (1984) 'The Theseion. A slave refuge at Athens', *AJAH* 9: 23–32

CLAUSS, M. (1973) 'Untersuchungen zu den principales des römischen Heeres von Augustus bis Diokletian. Cornicularii, speculatores, frumentarii'. Diss. Bochum

(1980) *Der magister officiorum in der Spätantike (4.–6. Jahrhundert). Das Amt und sein Einfluß auf die kaiserliche Politik.* Munich

CLOUD, J. D. (1969) 'The primary purpose of the lex Cornelia de sicariis', *ZRG* 86: 258–86

(1988) 'Lex Iulia de vi. (I)', *Athenaeum* 66: 579–95

(1989) 'Lex Iulia de vi. (II)', *Athenaeum* 67: 427–65

(1994) 'The constitution and public criminal law', in J. A. Crook, A. Lintott and E. Rawson, eds., *The Cambridge Ancient History.* 2nd edn. Vol. IX: *The Last Age of the Roman Republic, 146–43 B.C.* Cambridge: 491–530

COARELLI, F. (1969) 'Le tyrannoctone du Capitole et la mort de Tibérius Gracchus', *MEFR* 81: 137–60

(1983) 'Iside Capitolina, Clodio e i mercanti di schiavi', in *Alessandria e il mondo ellenistico-romano. Studi in onore di A. Adriani,* vol III. Rome: 461–75

COHEN, B. (1984) 'Some neglected ordines: the apparitorial status-groups', in C. Nicolet, ed., *Des ordres à Rome.* Paris: 23–60

COHEN, D. (1983) *Theft in Athenian Law.* Munich

(1991) 'The church courts and the enforcement of morals. Public order in England 1580–1640', *Ius Commune* 18: 17–36

COHN, S. K. (1980) *The Laboring Classes in Renaissance Florence.* New York

COKER, F. W. (1933) ' "Lynching" ', in *Encyclopaedia of the Social Sciences,* vol. IX. New York: 639–43

COLEMAN, K. M. (1990) 'Fatal charades: Roman executions staged as mythological enactments', *JRS* 80: 44–73

COLIN, J. (1965) *Les villes libres de l'Orient gréco-romain et l'envoi au supplice pour acclamations populaires.* Brussels

CONLEY, C. A. (1991) *The Unwritten Law. Criminal Justice in Victorian Kent.* New York

CONNOR, W. R. (1985) 'The razing of the house in Greek society', *TAPhA* 115: 79–102

CORNELL, T. J. (1981) 'Some observations on the "crimen incesti" ', in *Le délit religieux dans la cité antique*. Rome: 27–37

COZZI, G. (1973) 'Authority and law in Renaissance Venice', in J. R. Hale, ed., *Renaissance Venice*. London: 293–345

CROOK, J. A. (1967) *Law and Life of Rome*. London and Ithaca, NY
(1976) 'Rev. of Bauman 1974', *RHD* 44: 167–69
(1986) 'Rev. of Giovannini 1983', *JRS* 76: 286–88
(1987) 'Was there a "Doctrine of manifest guilt" in the Roman criminal law?', *PCPhS* 213 (n.s. 33): 38–52

CURTIS, T. and SPECK, W. A. (1976) 'The Societies for the Reformation of Manners. A case study in the theory and practice of moral reform', *Literature & History* 3: 45–64

CUTLER, J. E. (1905) *Lynch-Law. An Investigation into the History of Lynching in the United States*. London

D'ARMS, J. H. (1975) 'Tacitus, Annals 13, 48 and a new inscription from Puteoli', in *The Ancient Historian and His Materials. Essays in Honour of C. E. Stevens*. Farnborough: 155–66

DAGRON, G. (1974) *Naissance d'une capitale: Constantinople et ses institutions de 350 à 451*. Paris

DANILOVIČ, J. (1974) 'Observations sur les "actiones populares" ', in *Studi in onore di Giuseppe Grosso*, vol. VI. Torino: 15–43

DAUBE, D. (1951) ' "Ne quid infamandi causa fiat". The Roman law of defamation', in *Atti del Congresso Internazionale di Diritto Romano e di Storia del Diritto (Verona 1948)*, vol. III. Milan: 413–50
(1952) 'Slave-Catching', *Juridical Review* 64: 12–28
(1986) 'Fraud No 3', in *The Legal Mind. Essays for Tony Honoré*. Oxford: 1–17

DAVID, J.-M. (1980) ' "Eloquentia popularis" et conduites symboliques des orateurs de la fin de la République: problemes d'efficacité', *QS* 12: 171–98
(1984) 'Du comitium à la Roche Tarpéïenne ... Sur certains rituels d'exécution sous la république, les règnes d'Auguste et de Tibère', in *Du châtiment dans la cité. Supplices corporels et peine de mort dans le monde antique*. (Table ronde ... Rome 9–11 novembre 1982). Rome: 133–76
(1986) 'La faute et l'abandon. Théories et pratiques judiciaires à Rome à la fin de la république', in *L'Aveu. Antiquité et Moyen Age. Actes de la table ronde ... Rome 28–30 mars 1984*. Rome: 71–87
(1992) *Le patronat judiciaire au dernier siècle de la république romaine*. Rome

DAVID, J.-M. and DONDIN, M. (1980) 'Dion Cassius, XXXVI, 41, 1–2. Conduites symboliques et comportements exemplaires de Lucullus, Acilius Glabrio et Papirius Carbo (78 et 67 a.C.)', *MEFR* 92: 199–213

DAVIES, M. (1990) '"Popular justice" and the end of Aristophanes' "Clouds"', *Hermes* 118: 237–42

DAVIES, R. W. (1973) 'The investigation of some crimes in Roman Egypt', *AncSoc* 4: 199–212

(1974) 'The daily life of the Roman soldier under the principate', *ANRW* II, 1: 299–338

(1977) 'Augustus Caesar. A police system in the ancient world', in P. J. Stead, ed., *Pioneers in Policing*. Maidenhead: 12–32

DAVIS, J. (1984) 'A poor man's system of justice: the London police courts in the second half of the nineteenth century', *Historical Journal* 27: 309–35

DAVIS, N. Z. (1971) 'The reasons of misrule. Youth groups and charivari in sixteenth-century France', *P&P* 50: 41–75

DE LIBERO, L. (1992) *Obstruktion. Politische Praktiken im Senat und in der Volksversammlung der ausgehenden Römischen Republik (70–49 v. Chr.)*. Stuttgart

DE MARTINO, F. (1955) 'I "quadruplatores" nel "Persa" di Plauto', *Labeo* 1: 32–48

(1975) 'I "supplicia" dell'iscrizione di Pozzuoli', *Labeo* 21: 211–14

DELLA CORTE, F. (1980) 'La breve praefectura urbis di Messala Corvino', in *Philias charin. Miscellanea di studi classici in onore di E. Manni*. vol. II. Rome: 667–77

DICKINSON, H. T. (1990) 'Popular loyalism in Britain in the 1790s', in E. Hellmuth, ed., 1990: 503–33

DINGES, M. (1992) 'Frühneuzeitliche Justiz. Justizphantasien als Justiznutzung am Beispiel von Klagen bei der Pariser Polizei im 18. Jahrhundert', in H. Mohnhaupt and D. Simon, eds., *Vorträge zur Justizforschung. Geschichte und Theorie 1*, Frankfurt: 269–92

DOMASZEWSKI, A. V. (1902) 'Die Beneficiarierposten und die römischen Straßennetze', *Westdeutsche Zeitschrift* 21: 158–211

DONAJGRODZKI, A. P. (1977) 'Social police and the bureaucratic elite: a vision of order in the age of reform', in *Social Control in Nineteenth Century Britain*. London: 51–76

DOWNEY, G. (1951) 'The economic crisis at Antioch under Julian the Apostate', in *Studies in Economic and Social History in Honor of A. C. Johnson*. Princeton: 312–21

(1961) *A History of Antioch in Syria from Seleucus to the Arab Conquest*. Princeton

DREWS, R. (1972) 'Light from Anatolia on the Roman fasces', *AJPh* 93: 40–51

DREXHAGE, H. J. (1988) 'Einbruch, Diebstahl und Straßenraub im römischen Ägypten unter besonderer Berücksichtigung der Verhältnisse in den ersten beiden Jahrhunderten n. Chr.', in Weiler, ed., 1988: 313–23

(1989) 'Zu den Überstellungsbefehlen aus dem römischen Ägypten

(1.–3. Jahrhundert n. Chr.)', in *Migratio et commutatio . . ., Festschrift Th. Pékary z. 60. Geburtstag.* St Katharinen: 102–18

DRINKWATER, J. (1989) 'Patronage in Roman Gaul and the problem of the Bagaudae', in Wallace-Hadrill, ed., 1989: 189–203

DRUMMOND, A. (1989) 'Rome in the fifth century', in F. W. Walbank *et al.*, eds., *The Cambridge Ancient History.* 2nd edn, vol. VII, 2: *The Rise of Rome to 220 B.C.* Cambridge: 113–242

DUBOURDIEU, A. (1986) 'Cinctus Gabinus', *Latomus* 45: 3–20

DUCOS, M. (1990) 'La condition des acteurs à Rome: données juridiques et sociales', in J. Blaensdorf *et al.*, eds., *Theater und Gesellschaft im Imperium Romanum.* Tübingen: 19–33

DUNKLE, J. R. (1967) 'The Greek tyrant and Roman political invective of the late republic', *TAPhA* 98: 151–71

(1971) 'The rhetorical tyrant in Roman historiography: Sallust, Livy and Tacitus', *CW* 65: 12–20

DURRY, M. (1938) *Les cohortes prétoriennes.* Paris

DYSON, S. L. (1975) 'Native revolt patterns in the Roman Empire', *ANRW* II, 3: 138–75

ECHOLS, E. (1957–8) 'The Roman city-police: origin and development', *CJ* 53: 377–85

ECK, W. (1978) 'Abhängigkeit als ambivalenter Begriff: Zum Verhältnis von Patron und Libertus', *MHA* 2: 41–50

(1979) *Die staatliche Organisation Italiens in der hohen Kaiserzeit.* Munich

(1986) 'Augustus' administrative Reformen: Pragmatismus oder systematisches Planen', *AClass* 29: 105–20

(1993) 'Das s. c. de Cn. Pisone patre und seine Publikation in der Baetica', *Cahiers du Centre G. Glotz* 4: 189–208

EDER, W. (1980) *Servitus Publica. Untersuchungen zur Entstehung, Entwicklung und Funktion der öffentlichen Sklaverei in Rom.* Wiesbaden

EDER, W. ed. (1990) *Staat und Staatlichkeit in der frühen römischen Republik.* Stuttgart

EITREM, S. (1923) 'G. Gracchus und die Furien', *Philologus* 78: 183–7

ELTON, G. R. (1958) 'Informing for profit', in *Star Chamber Stories.* London: 78–113

EMSLEY, C. (1983) *Policing and its Context 1750–1870.* London

EPPERS, M. and HEINEN, H. (1984) 'Zu den "Servi venerii" in Ciceros Verrinen', in *Sodalitas* (see Bauman 1984): 219–32

ERSKINE, A. (1991) 'Hellenistic monarchy and Roman political invective', *CQ* 41: 106–20

EYBEN, E. (1993) *Restless Youth in Ancient Rome.* London

FAURE, E. (1965) 'Saint Ambroise et l'expulsion des pérégrins de Rome', in *Etudes d'histoire du droit canonique dédiées à G. le Bras*, vol. I. Paris: 523–40

FELDMAN, L. H. (1993) *Jew and Gentile in the Ancient World. Attitudes and Interactions from Alexander to Justinian.* Princeton

FELLMETH, U. (1990) 'Politisches Bewußtsein in den Vereinen der städtischen Massen in Rom und Italien zur Zeit der Republik und frühen Kaiserzeit', *Eirene* 27: 49–71

FERRARY, J.-L. (1983) 'Les origines de la loi de majesté à Rome', *CRAI*: 556–72

(1991) 'Lex Cornelia de sicariis et veneficis', *Athenaeum* 69: 417–34

FINLEY, M. I. (1983) *Politics in the Ancient World*. Cambridge

FISCHER, E. (1957) *Die Hauszerstörung als strafrechtliche Maßnahme im deutschen Mittelalter.* Stuttgart

FLAIG, E. (1992) *Den Kaiser herausfordern: die Usurpationen im Römischen Reich.* Frankfurt

(1993) 'Politisierte Lebensführung und ästhetische Kultur. Eine semiotische Untersuchung am römischen Adel', *Historische Anthropologie* 1: 193–217

FLAM-ZUCKERMAN, L. (1970) 'A propos d'une inscription de Suisse (CIL XIII, 5010): étude du phénomène du brigandage dans l'Empire romain', *Latomus* 29: 451–73

FLAMBARD, J.-M. (1977) 'Clodius, les collèges, la plèbe et les esclaves. Recherches sur la politique populaire au milieu du Ier siècle', *MEFR* 89: 115–56

(1981) 'Collegia Compitalicia: phénomène associatif, cadres territoriaux et cadres civiques dans le monde romain à l'époque républicaine', *Ktèma* 6: 143–66

FOTIOU, A. S. (1978) 'Byzantine circus factions and their riots', *JÖByz* 27: 1–10

FRANK, R. I. (1969) *Scholae Palatinae: the Palace Guards of the Later Roman Empire.* Rome

(1982) 'Rev. of Clauss 1980', *Gnomon* 54: 755–63

FRASCHETTI, A. (1988) 'La tabula Hebana, la tabula Siarensis e il iustitium per la morte di Germanico', *MEFR* 100: 867–89

(1990) *Roma e il principe.* Bari

FREI-STOLBA, R. (1988) 'Textschichten in der Lex Coloniae Genetivae Iuliae Ursonensis. Zu den Kapiteln 66, 70, 71, 125–127 über die Spielveranstaltungen', *SDHI* 54: 191–225

(1989) 'Straßenunterhalt und Straßenreinigung in Rom. Zu einigen Paragraphen der Tabula Heracleensis', in *Labor omnibus unus. Festschrift G. Walser.* Wiesbaden: 25–37

FREIS, H. (1967) *Die cohortes urbanae.* Cologne

FRIER, B. W. (1977) 'The rental market in early Imperial Rome', *JRS* 67: 27–37

(1983) 'Urban praetors and rural violence. The legal background of Cicero's Pro Caecina', *TAPhA* 113: 221–41

FUHRMANN, M. (1991) '"Grundrechte" im Strafprozeß der römischen Republik und ihr Widerhall im 18. und 19. Jahrhundert', in *Libertas. Grundrechtliche und rechtsstaatliche Gewährungen in Antike und Gegen-*

wart. Symposion aus Anlaß des 80. Geb. v. F. Wieacker. Ebelsbach: 97–112

GABBA, E. (1984) 'The collegia of Numa: problems of method and political ideas', *JRS* 74: 81–6

GALSTERER, H. (1976) *Herrschaft und Verwaltung im republikanischen Italien. Die Beziehungen Roms zu den italischen Gemeinden vom Latinerfrieden 338 v. Chr. bis zum Bundesgenossenkrieg 91 v. Chr.* Munich

(1977) 'Rev. of Simshäuser 1973', *GGA* 229: 64–81

(1980) 'Politik in römischen Städten: Die "seditio" des Jahres 59 n. Chr. in Pompeii', in *Studien zur antiken Sozialgeschichte. Festschrift F. Vittinghoff*. Cologne: 323–38

(1988) 'Municipium Flavium Irnitanum: a Latin town in Spain', *JRS* 78: 78–90

(1990) 'Plebiculam pascere – Die Versorgung Roms in der Kaiserzeit', *CS* 27: 21–40

GARDNER, J. F. (1993) *Being a Roman Citizen*. London

GARNSEY, P. D. A. (1966) 'The lex Iulia and appeal under the empire', *JRS* 56: 167–89

(1968a) 'The criminal jurisdiction of governors', *JRS* 58: 51–9

(1968b) 'Why penalties become harsher: the Roman case, late republic to fourth century empire', *Natural Law Forum* 13: 141–62

(1970) *Social Status and Legal Privilege in the Roman Empire*. Oxford

(1976) 'Urban property investment', in M. I. Finley, ed., *Studies in Roman Property*. Cambridge: 123–36

(1988) *Famine and Food Supply in the Graeco-Roman World. Responses to Risk and Crisis*. Cambridge

GAROFALO, L. (1989) *Il processo edilizio. Contributo alla studio dei "iudicia publica"*. Padova

GATRELL, V. A. C. (1990) 'Crime, authority and the policeman-state', in F. M. L. Thompson, ed., *The Cambridge Social History of Britain 1750–1950*, vol. III. Cambridge: 243–310

GATRELL, V. A. C., LENMAN, G. and PARKER, G., eds. (1980) *Crime and the Law. A Social History of Crime in Western Europe since 1500*. London

GAUDEMET, J. (1980) 'La répression de la délation au bas-empire', in *Philias charin. Miscellanea E. Manni*, vol. III. Rome: 1065–83

GAUVARD, C. and GOKALP, A. (1979) 'Les conduites de bruit et leur signification à la fin du Moyen Age: le Charivari', *Annales (ESC)* 29: 693–704

GEHRKE, H.-J. (1978) 'Das Verhältnis von Politik und Philosophie im Wirken des Demetrios von Phaleron', *Chiron* 8: 149–93

(1985) *Stasis. Untersuchungen zu den inneren Kriegen in den griechischen Staaten des 5. und 4. Jahrhunderts v. Chr.* Munich

GHIRON-BISTAGNE, P. (1985) 'Le cheval et la jeune fille ou de la virginité chez les anciens grecs', *Pallas* 32: 105–21

GIOVANNINI, A. (1983) *Consulare Imperium*. Basel

(1986) 'Pline et les délateurs de Domitien', in *Opposition et résistances à l'Empire d'Auguste à Trajan*. Geneva (*Entretiens sur l'Antiquité classique* XXXIII): 219–48

(1990) 'Magistratur und Volk. Ein Beitrag zur Entstehungsgeschichte des Staatsrechts', in Eder, ed. (1990): 406–36

GIOVANNINI, A., ed. (1991) *Nourrir la plèbe*. Basel

GIZEWSKI, C. (1988) *Zur Normativität und Struktur der Verfassungsverhältnisse in der späteren römischen Kaiserzeit*. Munich

(1989) 'Mores maiorum, regimen morum, licentia. Zur Koexistenz catonischer und plautinischer Sittlichkeitsvorstellungen', in *Festschrift Robert Werner*. Konstanz: 81–105

GLADIGOW, B. (1972) 'Die sakralen Funktionen der Liktoren. Zum Problem von institutioneller Macht und sakraler Präsentation', *ANRW* I, 2: 295–314

GLEASON, M. W. (1986) 'Festive satire: Julian's Misopogon and the new year at Antioch', *JRS* 76: 106–19

GNILKA, C. (1973) 'Lynchjustiz bei Catull', *RhM* 116: 256–69

GOLDGAR, B. A. (1985) 'Fielding and the whores of London', *Philological Quarterly* 64: 265–73

GONZÁLEZ, J. (1984) 'Tabula Siarensis, Fortunales Siarenses et Municipia Civium Romanorum', *ZPE* 55: 55–100

(1986) 'The Lex Irnitana: a new copy of the Flavian municipial law', *JRS* 76: 147–243

GRAEBER, A. (1984) 'Ein Problem des staatlich gelenkten Handels: Memmius Vitrasius Orfitus, praefectus urbis Romae und die Versorgungskrise in den Jahren 353–359 n. Chr.', *MBAH* 3, no. 2: 59–68

GRANT, M. (1974) *The Army of the Caesars*. New York

GRAS, M. (1984) 'Cité grecque et lapidation', in *Du châtiment dans la cité* (see David 1984): 75–89

GRASSL, H. (1975) 'Tristitia als Herausforderung des Prinzipats', *GB* 4: 89–96

GREEN, M. R. (1971) 'The supporters of the antipope Ursinus', *JThS* 22: 531–8

GREER, A. (1990) 'From folklore to revolution: charivaris and the lower Canadian rebellion of 1837', *Social History* 15, no. 1: 25–43

GREGORY, T. E. (1984) 'Urban violence in late antiquity', in R. T. Marchese, ed., *Aspects of Greco-Roman Urbanism*. Oxford: 138–61

GROEBE, P. (1905) 'Die Obstruktion im römischen Senat', *Klio* 5: 229–35

GRUEN, E. S. (1966) 'P. Clodius: instrument or independent agent?', *Phoenix* 20: 120–30

(1974) *The Last Generation of the Roman Republic*. Berkeley

(1990) *Studies in Greek Culture and Roman Policy*. Leiden

GSCHNITZER, F. (1981) 'Das System der römischen Heeresbildung im Zweiten Punischen Krieg: Polybios, die Annalisten und die geschichtliche Wirklichkeit', *Hermes* 109: 59–85

GUILLAND, S. R. (1966) 'Les spectacles de l'hippodrome', *Byz Slav* 27: 289–307

HALL, E. (1989) 'The archer scene in Aristophanes' Thesmophoriazusae', *Philologus* 133: 38–54

HAMMERICH, L. L. (1941) *Clamor. Eine rechtsgeschichtliche Studie.* Copenhagen

HAMPL, F. (1983) 'Zum Ritus des Lebendigbegrabens von Vestalinnen', in *Festschrift für Robert Muth.* Innsbruck: 165–82

HANSEN, E. V. (1971) *The Attalids of Pergamum.* Ithaca

HANSEN, M. H. (1976) *Apagoge, Endeixis and Ephegesis against Kakourgoi, Atimoi and Pheugontes. A Study in the Athenian Administration of Justice in the Fourth Century B.C.* Odense

(1980) 'Seven hundred archai in classical Athens', *GRBS* 21: 151–73

HARRIS, T. (1986) 'The Bawdy House Riot of 1668', *Historical Journal* 29: 537–86

HARRIS, W. V. (1986) 'The Roman father's power of life and death', in *Studies in Roman Law in Memory of A. A. Schiller.* Leiden: 81–95

HARVEY, D. (1990) 'The sykophant and sykophancy: vexatious redefinition?', in P. Cartledge, P. Millett and S. Todd, eds., *Nomos. Essays in Athenian Law, Politics and Society.* Cambridge: 103–21

HAY, D., LINEBAUGH, P. and THOMPSON, E. P., eds. (1975) *Albion's Fatal Tree. Crime and Society in Eighteenth Century England.* London

HAY, D. and SNYDER, F., eds. (1989a) *Policing and Prosecution in Britain 1750–1850.* Oxford

(1989b) 'Using the criminal law, 1750–1850: policing, private prosecution, and the state', in 1989a: 3–52

HAYTER, T. (1978) *The Army and the Crowd in Mid-Georgian England.* London

HEIDENHEIMER, A. J. (1986) 'Politics, policy and *Polizey* as concepts in English and continental Languages: an attempt to explain divergences', *Review of Politics* 48: 3–30

HELLENKEMPER, H. (1986) 'Legionen im Bandenkrieg – Isaurien im 4. Jh.', in *Studien zu den Militärgrenzen Roms,* vol. III (= 13. Intern. Limeskongreß Aalen 1983). Stuttgart: 625–34

HELLMUTH, E., ed. (1990) *Transformation of Political Culture. England and Germany in the Late Eighteenth Century.* Oxford

HEMELRIJK, E. A. (1987) 'Women's demonstrations in republican Rome', in J. Blok and P. Mason, eds., *Sexual Asymmetry. Studies in Ancient Society.* Amsterdam: 217–40

HENDRICKSON, G. L. (1925) 'Verbal injury, magic, or erotic comus? ("Occentare Ostium" and its Greek counterpart)', *CPh* 20: 289–308

(1926) 'Occentare Ostium bei Plautus', *Hermes* 61: 79–86

HENGEL, M. (1977) *Crucifixion in the Ancient World and the Folly of the Message of the Cross.* London

HENNIG, D. (1973) 'T. Labienus und der erste Majestätsprozeß de famosis libellis', *Chiron* 3: 245–54

HENRICHS, A. (1970) 'Pagan ritual and the alleged crimes of the early Christians: a reconsideration', in *Kyriakon. Festschrift Johannes Quasten*, vol. I. Münster: 18–35

HERRMANN, P. (1989) 'Rom und die Asylie griechischer Heiligtümer: Eine Urkunde des Dictators Caesar aus Sardeis', *Chiron* 19: 127–64

(1990) 'Hilferufe aus römischen Provinzen. Ein Aspekt der Krise des römischen Reiches im 3. Jhdt. n. Chr.', *Berichte aus d. Sitzungen d. J. Jungius-Gesellschaft Hamburg* 8: no. 4

HERRUP, C. B. (1987) *The Common Peace. Participation and the Criminal Law in Seventeenth-Century England.* Cambridge

HERTER, H. (1960) 'Die Soziologie der antiken Prostitution im Lichte des heidnischen und christlichen Schrifttums', *JAC* 3: 70–111

HERZ, P. (1988a) *Studien zur römischen Wirtschaftsgesetzgebung. Die Lebensmittelversorgung.* Stuttgart

(1988b) 'Latrocinium und Viehdiebstahl. Soziale Spannungen und Strafrecht in römischer Zeit', in I. Weiler, ed. (1988) Graz: 221–41

HINARD, F. (1984) 'La male mort. Exécutions et statut du corps au moment de la première proscription', in *Du châtiment dans la cité* (see David 1984): 295–311

(1985) *Les proscriptions de la Rome républicaine.* Rome

(1987) 'Spectacle des exécutions et espace urbain', in *L'urbs. Espace urbaine et histoire (Ier siècle avant J.-C. – IIIe siècle après J.-C.).* Rome: 111–25

HIRSCHFELD, O. (1905) *Die kaiserlichen Verwaltungsbeamten bis auf Diocletian.* Berlin

(1913) *Kleine Schriften.* Berlin

HIRZEL, R. (1900) *Die Strafe der Steinigung* (Abh. Sächs. Akad. Phil-hist. Kl. V, Bd. 27. Nr. 7). Leipzig

HOBEN, W. (1978) *Terminologische Studien zu den Sklavenerhebungen der Römischen Republik.* Wiesbaden

HOBSBAWM, E. (1971) *Primitive Rebels.* 2nd edn. Manchester

HOBSON, D. W. (1993) 'The impact of law on village life in Roman Egypt', in B. Halpern and D. W. Hobson, eds., *Law, Politics and Society in the Ancient Mediterranean World.* Sheffield: 193–219

HOFF, M. C. (1989) 'Civil disobedience and unrest in Augustan Athens', *Hesperia* 58: 267–76

HOHLWEIN, N. (1905) 'La police des villages égyptiens à l'époque romaine', *Musée Belge* 9: 394–9

HOPKINS, K. (1991) 'From violence to blessing: symbols and rituals in ancient Rome', in A. Molho, K. Raaflaub and J. Emlen, eds., *City-States in Classical Antiquity and Medieval Italy.* Stuttgart: 479–98

HOPWOOD, K. (1983) 'Policing the hinterland. Rough Cilicia and Isauria', in *Armies and Frontiers in Roman and Byzantine Anatolia* (Coll. Swansea April 1981) London: 173–87

(1989) 'Bandits, elites and rural order', in Wallace-Hadrill, ed. (1989): 171–87

HORAK, F. (1963) ' "quaestio lance et licio" ', *RE* 24: 788–801

HORSLEY, R. A. (1979) 'Josephus and the bandits', *JSJ* 10: 37–63

HUMBERT, M. (1988) 'Le tribunat de la plèbe et le tribunal du peuple: remarques sur l'histoire de la provocatio ad populum', *MEFR* 100: 431–503

HUMPHREYS, S. C. (1984/85) 'Law as discourse', *History & Anthropology* 1: 241–64

HUNT, E. D. (1985) 'Christians and christianity in Ammianus Marcellinus', *CQ* 35: 186–200

HUNTER, V. J. (1994) *Policing Athens. Social Control in the Attic Lawsuits, 420–320 B.C.* Princeton

IGNATIEFF, M. (1978) *A Just Measure of Pain. The Penitentiary in the Industrial Revolution 1750–1850.* London

INGRAM, M. (1984) 'Ridings, rough music and the "reform of popular culture" in early modern England', *P & P* 105: 79–113

INNES, J. (1990) 'Politics and morals. The reformation of manners movement in later eighteenth-century England', in E. Hellmuth, ed., 1990: 58–118

INNES, J. and STYLES, J. (1986) 'The crime wave; recent writing on crime and criminal justice in eighteenth century England', *Journal of British Studies* 25: 380–435

ISAAC, B. (1984) 'Bandits in Judaea and Arabia', *HSPh* 88: 171–203

(1990) *The Limits of Empire. The Roman Army in the East.* Oxford

JOHNSON, L. T. (1990) 'Charivari. A European folk ritual on the American plains', *Journal of Interdisciplinary History* 20, 3: 371–88

JOHNSTON, D. (1989) 'The conduct of trials at Urso', in J. González, ed., *Estudios sobre Urso. Colonia Iulia Genetiva.* Sevilla: 11–22

JONES, A. H. M. (1940) *The Greek City. From Alexander to Justinian.* Oxford

(1960) 'The Roman civil service (clerical and sub-clerical grades)', in *Studies in Roman Government and Law.* Oxford: 151–75, 201–13

(1964) *The Later Roman Empire 284–602. A Social, Economic, and Administrative Survey.* Oxford

(1972) *The Criminal Courts of the Roman Republic and Principate.* Oxford

JONES, C. P. (1978) *The Roman World of Dio Chrysostom.* Cambridge, Mass.

(1987) 'A note on diogmitae', *ICS* 12: 179–80

JONES, D. J. V. (1983) 'The new police, crime and people in England and Wales, 1829–1888', *Transactions of the Royal Historical Society* ser. V, 33: 151–68

JORY, E. J. (1984) 'The early pantomime riots', in A. Moffatt, ed., *Maistor. Classical, Byzantine and Renaissance Studies for Robert Browning.* Canberra: 57–66

JUNG, J. H. (1982) 'Die Rechtsstellung der römischen Soldaten. Ihre Entwicklung von den Anfängen Roms bis auf Diokletian', *ANRW* II, 14: 882–1013

KAPLAN, S. L. (1976) *Bread, Politics and Political Economy in the Reign of Louis XV*. 2 vols. The Hague

KASER, M. (1963) 'Die Jurisdiktion der kurulischen Ädilen', in *Mélanges Ph. Meylan, vol. I*, Lausanne: 173–91

KASHER, A. (1985) *The Jews in Hellenistic and Roman Egypt. The Struggle for Equal Rights*. Tübingen

KAUFMANN, E. (1979) 'Zur Lehre von der Friedlosigkeit im Germanischen Recht', in *Beiträge zur Rechtsgeschichte. Gedächtnisschrift H. Conrad*. Paderborn: 329–66

KELLY, J. M. (1966) *Roman Litigation*. Oxford
(1976) *Studies in the Civil Judicature of the Roman Republic*. Oxford

KENT, J. R. (1983) ' "Folk justice" and royal justice in early seventeenth-century England: a "charivari" in the Midlands', *Midland History* 8: 70–85

KEPPIE, L. (1984) *The Making of the Roman Army. From Republic to Empire*. London and Totowa, N.J.

KERESZTES, P. (1967) 'The massacre at Lugdunum in 177 A.D.', *Historia* 16: 75–86
(1979) 'The Imperial Roman government and the Christian church. I: From Nero to the Severi', *ANRW* II, 23/1: 247–315

KING, P. (1984) 'Decision-makers and decision-making in the English criminal law, 1750–1800', *Historical Journal* 27: 25–58

KINSEY, T. E. (1965) 'Cicero, pro Murena 71', *RBPh* 43: 57–59

KLINGENBERG, E. (1983) 'Die Aufgaben der städtischen Verwaltungsbeamten in Griechenland', in *Symposion 1979*. Cologne: 219–35

KLOFT, H. (1980) 'Caesar und die Amtsentsetzung der Volkstribunen im Jahre 44 v. Chr.', *Historia* 29: 315–44

KNEISSL, P. (1994) 'Die fabri, fabri tignarii, fabri subaedandi, centonarii und dolabrarii als Feuerwehren in den Städten Italiens und der westlichen Provinzen', in *E fontibus haurire. Festschrift H. Chantraine*. Paderborn: 133–46

KNEMEYER, F.-L. (1978) ' "Polizei" ', in *Geschichtliche Grundbegriffe*, vol. 4. Stuttgart: 875–97

KNEPPE, A. (1979) *Untersuchungen zur städtischen Plebs des 4. Jahrhunderts n. Chr.* Bonn
(1988) 'Die Gefährdung der securitas. Angst vor Angehörigen sozialer Randgruppen der römischen Kaiserzeit', in Weiler, ed. (1988): 165–76

KÖNIG, I. (1984) ' "Exire de imperio" – "cedere imperio" ', in *Sodalitas* (see Bauman 1984): 295–314

KOHNS, H. P. (1961) *Versorgungskrisen und Hungerrevolten im spätantiken Rom*. Bonn

(1993) 'Anstifter von Demonstrationen und städtischen Unruhen in der römischen Kaiserzeit', in *Klassisches Altertum, Spätantike und frühes Christentum. A. Lippold zum 65. Geburtstag gewidmet.* Würzburg: 257–62

(1994) 'Innerstädtische Krisen in der römischen Kaiserzeit', in K. Rosen, ed., *Macht und Kultur im Rom der Kaiserzeit.* Bonn: 165–79

KOLB, F. (1980) 'Der Bußakt von Mailand', in *Geschichte und Gegenwart. Festschrift K. D. Erdmann.* Neumünster: 41–74

KOOL, P. (1954) 'De Phylakieten in Grieks-Romeins Egypte'. Diss. Amsterdam

KRAUSE, J.-U. (1987) *Spätantike Patronatsformen im Westen des Römischen Reiches.* Munich

KUHN, H.-W. (1982) 'Die Kreuzesstrafe während der frühen Kaiserzeit. Ihre Wirklichkeit und Wertung in der Umwelt des Urchristentums', *ANRW* II, 25/1: 648–793

KUNKEL, W. (1962) *Untersuchungen zur Entwicklung des römischen Kriminalverfahrens in vorsullanischer Zeit.* Munich

(1974) *Kleine Schriften. Zum römischen Strafverfahren und zur römischen Verfassungsgeschichte.* Weimar

LABRUNA, L. (1971) *Vim fieri veto. Alle radici di una ideologia.* Naples

(1972) 'Les racines de l'idéologie répressive de la violence dans l'histoire du droit romain', *Index* 3: 525–38

(1991) 'La violence, instrument de lutte politique à la fin de la République', *DHA* 17: 119–37

LANATA, G. (1987) 'Henkersbeil oder Chirurgenmesser? Eine falsche Alternative bei Palladas, Anth. Pal. XI 280', *RJ* 6: 293–306

LANDAU, N. (1984) *The Justices of the Peace, 1679–1760.* Berkeley

LATTE, K. (1968) *Kleine Schriften zu Religion, Recht, Literatur und Sprache der Griechen und Römer.* Munich

LAVELLE, B. M. (1992) 'Herodotos, Skythian archers, and the doryphoroi of the Peisistratids', *Klio* 74: 78–97

LE GALL, J. (1939) 'Notes sur les prisons de Rome à l'époque républicaine', *MEFR* 56: 60–80

LE GOFF, J. and SCHMITT, J. C., eds. (1981) *Le Charivari.* Paris

LE ROY LADURIE, E. (1981) *Carnival in Romans. A People's Uprising at Romans 1579–1580.* Harmondsworth

LEBEK, W. D. (1990a) 'Standeswürde und Berufsverbot unter Tiberius. Das SC der Tabula Larinas', *ZPE* 81: 37–96

(1990b) 'Welttrauer um Germanicus: das neugefundene Originaldokument und die Darstellung des Tacitus', *A & A* 36: 93–102

(1992) 'Die zwei Ehrenbeschlüsse für Germanicus und einer der "seltsamsten Schnitzer" des Tacitus (Ann. 2, 83, 2)', *ZPE* 90: 65–86

LENMAN, B. and PARKER, G. (1980) 'The state, the community and the criminal law in early modern Europe', in Gatrell, Lenman and Parker, eds. (1980): 11–48

LEPPIN, H. (1992) *Histrionen. Untersuchungen zur sozialen Stellung von Bühnen-*

künstlern im Westen des Römischen Reiches zur Zeit der Republik und des Prinzipats. Bonn

LEVICK, B. (1976) *Tiberius the Politician*. London

(1983) 'The senatus consultum from Larinum', *JRS* 73: 97–115

LEVICK, B. ed. (1985) *The Government of the Roman Empire. A Sourcebook*. London

LEVINE, L. I. (1974) 'The Jewish-Greek conflict in first century Caesarea', *Journal of Jewish Studies* 25: 381–97

LÉVY, Y. (1965) 'Police and policy', *Government and Opposition* 1: 487–510

LIEB, H. (1986) 'Die constitutiones für die stadtrömischen Truppen', in W. Eck and H. Wolff, eds. *Heer und Integrationspolitik. Die römischen Militärdiplome als historische Quelle*. Cologne: 322–46

LIEBESCHUETZ, J. H. W. G. (1972) *Antioch. City and Imperial Administration in the Later Roman Empire*. Oxford

LIEBS, D. (1980) 'Der Schutz der Privatsfäre (sic!) in einer Sklavenhaltergesellschaft. Aussagen von Sklaven gegen ihre Herren nach römischem Recht', *BIDR* 83: 147–89

(1981) 'Das ius gladii der römischen Provinzgouverneure in der Kaiserzeit', *ZPE* 43: 217–23

(1985) 'Unverhohlene Brutalität in den Gesetzen der ersten christlichen Kaiser', in *Römisches Recht in der europäischen Tradition. Symposion aus Anlaß des 75. Geb. v. F. Wieacker*. Ebelsbach: 89–116

LIND, L. R. (1986) 'The idea of the Republic and the foundations of Roman political liberty', in C. Deroux, ed. *Studies in Latin Literature and Roman History*, vol. IV. Brussels: 44–108

LINDERSKI, J. (1968) 'Der Senat und die Vereine', in *Gesellschaft und Recht im griechisch-römischen Altertum*. Berlin: 94–132

(1983) 'A witticism of Appuleius Saturninus', *RFIC* 111: 452–9

(1984a) 'Rome, Aphrodisias and the Res Gestae: the genera militiae and the status of Octavian', *JRS* 74: 74–80

(1984b) 'Rev. of *Le délit religieux*', *CPh* 79: 174–7

(1986) 'The augural law', *ANRW* II, 16/3: 2146–312

LINTOTT, A. W. (1967) 'P. Clodius Pulcher – Felix Catilina?', *G&R* 14: 157–69

(1968) *Violence in Republican Rome*. Oxford

(1972) 'Provocatio. From the struggle of the orders to the Principate', *ANRW* I, 2: 226–67

(1974) 'Cicero and Milo', *JRS* 64: 62–78

(1982) *Violence, Civil Strife and Revolution in the Classical City*. London

(1987) 'Democracy in the middle Republic', *ZRG* 104: 34–52

(1988) 'Rev. of Virlouvet 1985', *CR* n.s. 38: 171–2

(1990) 'Le procès devant les recuperatores d'après les données épigraphiques jusqu'au règne d'Auguste', *RD* 68: 1–11

(1993) *Imperium Romanum. Politics and Administration*. London

LONG, T. (1986) *Barbarians in Greek Comedy*. Carbondale and Edwardsville

ŁOPOSZKO, T. (1979) 'La famine à Rome en 57 avant J.-C.', *QS* 10: 101–21

LOPUSZANSKI, G. (1951) 'La police romaine et les chrétiens', *A C* 20: 5–46

ŁUKASZEWICZ, A. (1983) 'Petition concerning a theft. P. Berol. 7306', *JJP* 19: 107–19

MACCORMACK, G. (1972) 'Criminal liability for fire in early and classical Roman law', *Index* 3: 382–96

MACDOWELL, D. M. (1978) *The Law in Classical Athens*. London

MCGINN, T. A. J. (1992) 'The SC from Larinum and the repression of adultery at Rome', *ZPE* 93: 273–95

MCGOWEN, R. (1987) 'The body and punishment in eighteenth-century England', *Journal of Modern History* 59: 651–79

MACKIE, N. (1983) *Local Administration in Roman Spain AD 14–212*. Oxford (1992) 'Popularis ideology and popular politics in the first century B.C.', *RhM* 135: 49–73

MACMULLEN, R. (1963) *Soldier and Civilian in the Later Roman Empire*. Cambridge, Mass.

(1966) *Enemies of the Roman Order. Treason, Unrest and Alienation in the Empire*. Cambridge, Mass. [reissued with new Preface, London 1992]

(1974) *Roman Social Relations 50 B.C. to A.D. 284*. New Haven

(1984) *Christianizing the Roman Empire A.D. 100–400*. New Haven

(1986) 'Judicial savagery in the Roman empire', *Chiron* 16: 147–66

(1988) *Corruption and the Decline of Rome*. New Haven

MAGIE, D. (1950) *Roman Rule in Asia Minor to the end of the third century after Christ*. Princeton

MANN, J. C. (1988) 'The organization of the frumentarii', *ZPE* 74: 149–50

MANN, M. (1993) *The Sources of Social Power*. Vol. II: *The Rise of Classes and Nation-States, 1760–1914*. Cambridge

MARASCO, G. (1981) 'Sacrifici umani e cospirazioni politiche', *Sileno* 7: 167–78

MARSHALL, A. J. (1984) 'Symbols and showmanship in Roman public life: the fasces', *Phoenix* 38: 120–41

MARSHALL, B. A. (1985a) *A Historical Commentary on Asconius*. Columbia, Miss.

(1985b) 'Catilina and the execution of M. Marius Gratidianus', *CQ* 35: 124–33

MARTIN, J. (1970) 'Die Provokation in der klassischen und späten Republik', *Hermes* 98: 72–96

MARTIN, S. (1985) 'Images of power: the imperial senate', *JRS* 75: 222–8

MASŁOWSKI, T. (1976) 'Domus Milonis Oppugnata', *Eos* 64: 23–30

MATTHEWS, J. (1975) *Western Aristocracies and the Imperial Court, A.D. 364–425*. Oxford

(1987) 'Peter Valvomeres, re-arrested', in *Homo Viator: Classical Essays for J. Bramble*. Bristol: 277–84

(1989) *The Roman Empire of Ammianus*. London

MAXWELL-STUART, P. G. (1976) 'Per lancem et licium. A note', *G & R* 23: 1–4

MAYER-MALY, T. (1956) 'Der rechtsgeschichtliche Gehalt der "Christenbriefe" von Plinius und Trajan', *SDHI* 22: 311–28

MEIER, C. (1964) 'Rev. of Adcock, Roman Political Ideas', *GGA* 216: 37–52

(1966) *Res publica Amissa. Eine Studie zu Verfassung und Geschichte der späten römischen Republik.* Wiesbaden

(1968) 'Die loca intercessionis bei Rogationen. Zugleich ein Beitrag zum Problem der Bedingungen der tribunicischen Intercession', *MH* 25: 86–100

(1975) 'Das Kompromiss-Angebot an Caesar i. J. 59 v. Chr.', *MH* 32: 197–208

MEIGGS, R. (1973) *Roman Ostia.* 2nd edn. Oxford

MEIJER, F. J. (1983) 'Ordehandhaving in Rome tijdens de republiek', *Lampas* 12: 155–73

(1990) 'The financial aspects of the leges frumentariae of 123–58 BC', *MBAH* 9, no. 2: 14–23

MELLINKOFF, R. (1983) 'Riding backwards: theme of humiliation and symbol of evil', *Viator* 4: 153–76

MEULI, K. (1975) *Gesammelte Schriften*, vol. 1. Basel

MILLAR, F. G. B. (1977) *The Emperor in the Roman World (31 BC–AD 37).* London [reissued with new Afterword, 1992]

(1981) 'The world of the Golden Ass', *JRS* 71: 63–75

(1983) 'Empire and City, Augustus to Julian: obligations, excuses and status', *JRS* 73: 76–96

(1984) 'Condemnation to hard labour in the Roman Empire, from the Julio-Claudians to Constantine', *PBSR* 52: 128–47

(1986) 'Italy and the Roman Empire: Augustus to Constantine', *Phoenix* 40: 295–318

(1989) 'Political power in mid-republican Rome: curia or comitium?' (Review article), *JRS* 79: 138–50

MILLER, J. A. (1992) 'Politics and urban provisioning crises. Bakers, police, and parlements in France, 1750–1793', *Journal of Modern History* 24: 227–62

MILLER, W. R. (1977) 'Never on Sunday: moralistic reformers and the police in London and New York City 1830–1870', in D. Bayley, ed., *Police and Society.* London: 127–48

MOELLER, W. O. (1970) 'The riot of A.D. 59 at Pompeii', *Historia* 19: 84–95

MOLTHAGEN, J. (1991) 'Die ersten Konflikte der Christen in der griechisch-römischen Welt', *Historia* 40: 42–76

MOMIGLIANO, A. D. (1942) 'Rev. of L. Robinson, "Freedom of Speech in the Roman Republic", Diss. Baltimore 1940', *JRS* 32: 120–4

MOMMSEN, T. (1871–88) *Römisches Staatsrecht*, 3 vols. (in 5). Berlin

(1871b) 'Sp. Cassius, M. Manlius, Sp. Maelius, die drei Demagogen des 3. und 4. Jahrhunderts der römischen Republik', *Hermes* 5: 228–80

(1899) *Römisches Strafrecht.* Leipzig

(1907) 'Die Popularklagen', in *Gesammelte Schriften,* vol. III, Berlin: 375–85

MOREAU, P. (1987) 'La lex Clodia sur le banissement de Cicéron', *Athenaeum* 65: 465–92

(1989) 'La rogation des huit tribuns de 58 av. J.-C. et les clauses de sanctio réglementant l'abrogation des lois', *Athenaeum* 67: 151–78

MOROSI, R. (1981) 'I saiones. Speciali agenti di polizia presso i Goti', *Athenaeum* 58: 150–65

MUIR, E. (1981) *Civic Ritual in Renaissance Venice.* Princeton

NICHOLAS, B. (1962) *An Introduction to Roman Law.* Oxford

NICOLET, C. (1960) ' "Consul togatus". Remarques sur le vocabulaire politique de Cicéron et de Tite-Live', *REL* 38: 236–63

(1976a) *Le métier de citoyen dans la Rome républicaine.* Paris [English translation, London 1980]

(1976b) 'Le temple des Nymphes et les distributions frumentaires à Rome à l'époque républicaine d'après des découvertes récentes', *CRAI*: 29–51

(1980) 'La lex Gabinia-Calpurnia de insula Delo et la loi "annonaire" de Clodius (58 av. J.-C.)', *CRAI*: 260–87

(1985) 'Plèbe et tribus: les statues de Lucius Antonius et le testament d'Auguste', *MEFR* 97: 799–839

(1988) *L'inventaire du monde: géographie et politique aux origines de l'empire romain.* Paris

NIPPEL, W. (1981) 'Die plebs urbana und die Rolle der Gewalt in der späten römischen Republik', in H. Mommsen and W. Schulze, eds., *Vom Elend der Handarbeit. Probleme historischer Unterschichtenforschung.* Stuttgart: 70–92

(1984) 'Policing Rome', *JRS* 74: 20–9

(1984/85) 'Reading the Riot Act: the discourse of law-enforcement in eighteenth-century England', *History & Anthropology* 1: 401–26

(1988) *Aufruhr und "Polizei" in der römischen Republik.* Stuttgart

(1990) *Griechen, Barbaren und "Wilde". Alte Geschichte und Sozialanthropologie.* Frankfurt

NOETHLICHS, K. L. (1986) ' "Heidenverfolgung" ', *RAC* 13: 1149–90

NÖRR, D. (1977) 'Planung in der Antike. Über die Ehegesetze des Augustus', in *Freiheit und Sachzwang. Beiträge zu Ehren H. Schelskys.* Opladen: 309–34

(1982) 'C. Cassius Longinus: Der Jurist als Rhetor (Bemerkungen zu Tacitus, Ann. 14.42–45)', in *Althistorische Studien. Hermann Bengtson zum 70. Geb.* Wiesbaden: 187–222

(1986) *Causa Mortis. Auf den Spuren einer Redewendung.* Munich

NORTH, J. A. (1979) 'Religious toleration in republican Rome', *PCPhS* 205 (n.s. 25): 85–103

(1986) 'Religion and politics, from republic to principate' (review article), *JRS* 76: 251–8

(1990) 'Democratic politics in republican Rome', *P&P* 126: 3–21

NOWAK, K.-J. (1973) 'Der Einsatz privater Garden in der späten römischen Republik'. Diss. Munich

OBERWITTLER, D. (1990) 'Crime and authority in eighteenth century England. Law enforcement on the local level', *Historical Social Research* 15, no. 2: 3–34

OERTEL, F. (1917) *Die Liturgie. Studien zur ptolemäischen und kaiserlichen Verwaltung Ägyptens.* Leipzig

OSBORNE, R. (1990) 'Vexatious litigation in classical Athens: sykophancy and the sykophant', in *Nomos* (see Harvey 1990): 83–102

OSTWALD, M. (1955) 'The Athenian legislation against tyranny and subversion', *TAPhA* 86: 103–28

OWENS, E. J. (1983) 'The koprologoi at Athens in the fifth and fourth centuries B.C.', *CQ* 33: 44–50

PAILLER, J.-M. (1985) 'Rome aux cinq régions?', *MEFR* 97: 785–97

(1988) *Bacchanalia: la répression de 186 av. J.C. à Rome et en Italie.* Rome

PALMER, S. H. (1988) *Police and Protest in England and Ireland 1780–1850.* Cambridge

PASQUINO, P. (1991) 'Theatrum politicum: The genealogy of capital-police and the state of prosperity', in G. Burchell, C. Gordon and P. Miller, eds., *The Foucault Effect. Studies in Governmentality.* London: 105–18

PATLAGEAN, E. (1977) *Pauvreté économique et pauvreté sociale à Byzance IVe–VIIe siècles.* Paris

(1981) 'Les "jeunes" dans les villes byzantines, émeutiers et miliciens', in Le Goff and Schmitt, eds. (1981): 123–9

PATTERSON, J. R. (1992) 'The city of Rome: from republic to empire' (Review article), *JRS* 82: 186–215

PAVAN, E. (1980) 'Police des mœurs, société et politique à Venise à la fin du Moyen Age', *RH* 264: 241–88

PAVIS D'ESCURAC, H. (1976) *La préfecture de l'annone: service administratif impérial d'Auguste à Constantin.* Rome

PEASE, A. S. (1907) 'Notes on stoning among the Greeks and Romans', *TAPhA* 38: 5–18

PEKÁRY, T. (1985) *Das römische Kaiserbildnis in Staat, Kult und Gesellschaft.* Berlin

(1987) 'Seditio. Unruhen und Revolten im römischen Reich von Augustus bis Commodus', *AncSoc* 18: 133–50

PENNITZ, M. (1991) *Der 'Enteignungsfall' im römischen Recht der Republik und des Prinzipats. Eine funktional-rechtsvergleichende Problemstellung.* Cologne

PERELLI, L. (1982) *Il movimento popolare nell'ultimo secolo della Repubblica.* Torino

PETIT, P. (1955) *Libanius et la vie municipale à Antioche au IVe siècle après J.-C.* Paris

PHILIPS, D. (1977) *Crime and Authority in Victorian England. The Black Country 1835–1860.* London

　(1980) ' "A new engine of power and authority": the institutionalization of law-enforcement in England, 1780–1830', in Gatrell, Lenman, Parker, eds. (1980): 155–89

　(1983) ' "A just measure of crime, authority, hunters and blue Locusts": the "revisionist" social history of crime and the law in Britain, 1780–1850', in S. Cohen and A. Scull, eds., *Social Control and the State.* Oxford: 50–74

　(1989) 'Good men to associate and bad men to conspire. Associations for the prosecution of felons in England 1760–1860', in Hay and Snyder, eds. (1989a): 113–51

PIAZZA, M. P. (1980) 'Tabulae novae. Osservazioni sul problema dei debiti negli ultimi decenni della repubblica', in *Atti del II Seminario Romanistico Gandesano, 12–14 giugno 1978.* Milan: 39–107

PICARD, G.-CH. (1965) 'L'aedes libertatis de Clodius au Palatin', *REL* 43: 229–37

PICKARD-CAMBRIDGE, A. (1968) *The Dramatic Festivals of Athens.* 2nd edn revised J. Gould and D. M. Lewis. Oxford [repr. with addenda, 1988]

PINON, R. (1969) 'Qu'est-ce qu'un charivari? Essai en vue d'une définition opératoire', in *Kontakte und Grenzen. Festschrift f. G. Heilfurth zum 60. Geburtstag.* Göttingen: 393–405

PLASSART, A. (1913) 'Les archers d'Athènes', *REG* 26: 151–213

PLAUMANN, G. (1913) 'Das sogenannte senatus consultum ultimum, die Quasidiktatur der späten römischen Republik', *Klio* 13: 321–86

POLAY, E. (1971) 'Das "regimen morum" des Zensors und die sogenannte Hausgerichtsbarkeit', in *Studi in onore di E. Volterra,* vol. III. Milan: 263–317

PULLAN, B. (1971) *Rich and Poor in Renaissance Venice: The Social Institutions of a Catholic state, to 1620.* Oxford

PURCELL, N. (1983) 'The apparitores. A study in social mobility', *PBSR* 51: 125–73

　(1994) 'The city of Rome and the *plebs urbana* in the late republic', in J. A. Crook, A. Lintott and E. Rawson, eds., *The Cambridge Ancient History.* 2nd edn. Vol. IX: *The Last Age of the Roman Republic, 146–43 B.C.* Cambridge: 644–88

RAAFLAUB, K. A., ed. (1986) *Social Struggles in Archaic Rome. New Perspectives on the Conflict of the Orders.* Berkeley

RABER, F. (1969) *Grundlagen klassischer Injurienansprüche.* Wien

RADZINOWICZ, L. (1948) *A History of English Criminal Law and Its Administration from 1750.* Vol. I: *The Movement for Reform.* London
(1956) *A History of English Criminal Law and its Administration from 1750.* Vol. III: *Cross-Currents in the Movement for the Reform of the Police.* London

RAEFF, M. (1975) 'The well-ordered police state and the development of modernity in seventeenth- and eighteenth-century Europe: an attempt at a comparative approach', *AHR* 80: 1221–43

RAINBIRD, J. S. (1986) 'The fire stations of Imperial Rome', *PBSR* 54: 147–69

RAMAGE, E. S. (1983) 'Urban problems in ancient Rome', in T. Marchese, ed., *Aspects of Greco-Roman Urbanism.* Oxford: 61–92

RAWSON, E. (1974) 'Religion and politics in the late second century B.C. at Rome', *Phoenix* 28: 193–212
(1985) 'Theatrical life in republican Rome and Italy', *PBSR* 53: 97–113
(1987) 'Discrimina ordinum: the lex Julia theatralis', *PBSR* 55: 83–114

REYNOLDS, J. (1988) 'Cities', in D. Braund, ed., *The Administration of the Roman Empire 241 BC–AD 193.* Exeter: 15–51

RICH, J. W. (1991) 'Rev. of Nippel 1988', *JRS* 81: 193–5

RICHLIN, A. (1983) *The Garden of Priapus. Sexuality and Aggression in Roman Humor.* New Haven [2nd edn. 1992]

RICKMAN, G. (1980) *The Corn Supply of Ancient Rome.* Oxford

RIDLEY, R. T. (1983) 'Pompey's commands in the 50s; how cumulative?', *RhM* 126: 136–48

RILINGER, R. (1988) *Humiliores-Honestiores. Zu einer sozialen Dichotomie im Strafrecht der römischen Kaiserzeit.* Munich
(1989) ' "Loca intercessionis" und Legalismus in der späten Republik', *Chiron* 19: 481–98

RINI, A. (1983) 'La plebe urbana a Roma della morte di Cesare alla sacrosancta potestas di Ottaviano', in *Epigrafia e territorio. Politica e società.* Bari: 161–90

ROBERT, L. (1937) *Etudes anatoliennes. Recherches sur les inscriptions grecques de l'Asie Mineure.* Paris

ROBERTS, M. J. D. (1983) 'The Society for the Suppression of Vice and its early critics, 1802–1812', *Historical Journal* 26: 159–76

ROBINSON, O. F. (1977) 'Fire prevention at Rome', *RIDA* 24: 377–88
(1981) 'Slaves and the criminal law', *ZRG* 98: 213–54
(1992) *Ancient Rome. City Planning and Administration.* London

ROCK, P. (1983) 'Law, order and power in late seventeenth and early eighteenth century England', in S. Cohen and A. Scull, eds., *Social Control and the State.* Oxford: 191–221

ROGERS, N. (1990) 'Crowd and people in the Gordon Riots', in E. Hellmuth, ed. (1990): 39–55

ROLLIN, J. P. (1979) *Untersuchungen zu Rechtsfragen römischer Bildnisse.* Bonn

ROOT, H. L. (1990) 'Politiques frumentaires et violence collective en Europe au XVIIIe siècle', *Annales (ESC)* 45: 167–89

ROSEN, K. (1990) 'Index und Officium. Kollektivstrafe, Kontrolle und Effizienz in der spätantiken Provinzialverwaltung', *AncSoc* 21: 273–92

ROSIVACH, V. J. (1987) 'Execution by stoning in Athens', *ClAnt* 6: 232–48

ROSTOVTZEFF, M. I. (1905) 'Die Domänenpolizei in dem römischen Kaiserreiche', *Philologus* 64: 297–307

(1957) *The Social and Economic History of the Roman Empire.* 2 vols. 2nd edn, rev. P. M. Fraser. Oxford

ROUECHÉ, C. (1993) *Performers and Artisans in Aphrodisias in the Roman and Late Roman Periods.* London (*JRS* Monographs No. 6)

ROXAN, M. and ECK, W. (1993) 'A military diploma of AD 85 for the Rome cohorts', *ZPE* 96: 67–74

ROYDEN, H. L. (1988) *The Magistrates of the Roman Professional Collegia in Italy from the First to the Third Century A.D.* Pisa

RUDÉ, G. (1964) *The Crowd in History.* New York

RUGGIERO, G. (1980) *Violence in Early Renaissance Venice.* New Brunswick, N.J.

RÜPKE, J. (1990) *Domi Militiae. Die religiöse Konstruktion des Krieges in Rom.* Stuttgart

STE CROIX, G. E. M. de (1974) 'Why were the Early Christians persecuted', in M. I. Finley, ed., *Studies in Ancient Society.* London: 210–49

(1981) *The Class Struggle in the Ancient Greek World.* London

SALERNO, F. (1984) 'Collegia adversus rem publicam?', in *Sodalitas* (see Bauman 1984): 615–31

(1990) *Dalla 'consecratio' alla 'publicatio bonorum': forme giuridiche e uso politico dalle origini a Cesare.* Naples

SALLER, R. P. (1986) 'Patria potestas and the stereotype of the Roman family', *Continuity & Change* 1: 7–22

(1988) 'Pietas, obligation and authority in the Roman family', in *Alte Geschichte und Wissenschaftsgeschichte. Festschrift für K. Christ zum 65. Geb.* Darmstadt: 393–410

(1991) 'Corporal punishment, authority, and obedience in the Roman household', in B. Rawson, ed., *Marriage, Divorce, and Children in Ancient Rome.* Oxford: 144–65

SALMON, E. T. (1982) *The Making of Roman Italy.* London

SCHÄFER, T. (1989) *Imperii Insignia. Sella curulis und fasces. Zur Repräsentation römischer Magistrate.* Mainz

SCHÄFKE, W. (1979) 'Frühchristlicher Widerstand', *ANRW* II, 23/1: 464–723

SCHEID, J. (1981) 'Le délit religieux dans la Rome tardo-républicaine', in *Le délit religieux dans la cité antique.* Rome: 117–71

(1985) *Religion et piété à Rome.* Paris

SCHETTER, W. (1984) 'Aequentur Vulnera Membris', *Hermes* 112: 127–8

SCHILLER, A. A. (1949) 'The jurists and the praefects of Rome', *RIDA* ser. I, 3: 319–59

SCHMIDLIN, B. (1963) *Das Rekuperatorenverfahren. Eine Studie zum römischen Prozeß.* Fribourg

SCHMITT-PANTEL, P. (1981) 'L'âne, l'adultère et la cité', in Le Goff and Schmitt, eds. (1981): 117–22

SCHNEIDER, H. (1982/83) 'Die politische Rolle der plebs urbana während der Tribunate des L. Appuleius Saturninus', *AncSoc* 13/14: 193–221

(1983) 'Die Getreideversorgung der Stadt Antiochia im 4. Jh. n. Chr.', *MBAH* 2, no. 1: 59–72

(1986) 'Infrastruktur und politische Legitimation im frühen Principat', *Opus* 5: 23–51

SCHREINER, K. (1989) 'Gregor VIII., nackt auf einem Esel. Entehrende Entblößung und schandbares Reiten im Spiegel einer Miniatur der "Sächsischen Weltchronik"', in D. Berg and H.-W. Goetz, eds., *Ecclesia et Regnum.* Bochum: 155–202

SCHULLER, W. (1975) 'Grenzen des spätrömischen Staates: Staatspolizei und Korruption', *ZPE* 16: 1–21

SCHULZE, W. (1933) 'Beiträge zur Wort- und Sittengeschichte (II)', in *Kleine Schriften.* Göttingen: 160–89

SCHUMACHER, L. (1982) *Servus Index. Sklavenverhör und Sklavenanzeige im republikanischen und kaiserzeitlichen Rom.* Wiesbaden

SCHWARTZ, R. M. (1988) *Policing the Poor in Eighteenth-Century France.* Chapel Hill

SCHWENK, C. J. (1985) *Athens in the Age of Alexander. The Dated Laws and Decrees of "The Lycourgan Era" 338–322 B.C.* Chicago

SCHWERHOFF, G. (1992) 'Verordnete Schande? Spätmittelalterliche und frühneuzeitliche Ehrenstrafen zwischen Rechtsakt und sozialer Sanktion', in A. Blauert and G. Schwerhoff, eds., *Mit den Waffen der Justiz. Zur Kriminalitätsgeschichte des späten Mittelalters und der Frühen Neuzeit.* Frankfurt: 158–88, 236–40

SCHWERIN, C. von (1924) *Die Formen der Haussuchung in indogermanischen Rechten.* Mannheim

SCOBIE, A. (1986) 'Slums, sanitation and mortality in the Roman world', *Klio* 68: 399–433

(1988) 'Spectator security and comfort at gladiatorial games', *Nikephoros* 1: 191–243

SHARPE, J. A. (1980) 'Enforcing the law in the seventeenth century English village', in Gatrell, Lenman, Parker, eds. (1980): 97–119

(1984) *Crime in Early Modern England 1550–1750.* London

SHAW, B. D. (1979) 'Rural periodic markets in Roman North Africa as mechanisms of social integration and control', *Research in Economic Anthropology* 2: 91–117

(1984) 'Bandits in the Roman Empire', *P & P* 105: 3–52

(1990) 'Bandit highlands and lowland peace: the mountains of Isauria-Cilicia', *JESHO* 33: 199–233

(1991) 'Der Bandit', in A. Giardina, ed., *Der Mensch der römischen Antike*. Frankfurt: 337–81 [= 'The Bandit', in *The Romans*. Chicago and London 1993, 300–41]

(1993) 'The passion of Perpetua', *P&P* 139: 3–45

SHELTON, W. J. (1973) *English Hunger and Industrial Disorders. A Study of Social Conflict during the First Decade of George III's Reign*. London

SHERK, R. K. (1970) *The Municipal Decrees of The Roman West*. Buffalo

SHERWIN-WHITE, A. N. (1963) *Roman Society and Roman Law in the New Testament*. Oxford

SHOEMAKER, R. A. (1987) 'The London "mob" in the early eighteenth century', *Journal of British Studies* 26: 273–304

SHUBERT, A. (1981) 'Private initiative in law enforcement: associations for the prosecution of felons', in V. Bailey, ed., *Policing and Punishment in Nineteenth-Century Britain*. London: 25–41

SILVER, A. (1967) 'The demand for order in civil society: a review of some themes in the history of urban crime, police, and riot', in D. J. Bordua, ed., *The Police*. New York: 1–24

SIMÉLON, P. (1985) 'A propos des émeutes de M. Caelius Rufus et de P. Cornelius Dolabella (48–47 av. J.C.)', *LEC* 53: 387–405

SIMSHÄUSER, W. (1973) *Iuridici und Municipalgerichtsbarkeit in Italien*. Munich

SINNIGEN, W. G. (1957) *The Officium of the Urban Prefecture during the Later Roman Empire*. Rome

SIRKS, A. J. B. (1991) 'The size of the grain distributions in Imperial Rome and Constantinople', *Athenaeum* 69: 215–37

SMALLWOOD, M. (1976) *The Jews under Roman Rule from Pompey to Diocletian*. Leiden

SMITH, R. E. (1977) 'The use of force in passing legislation in the late republic', *Athenaeum* 55: 150–74

SOLIN, H. (1981) 'Caesar und P. Clodius Pulcher in Tarracina', *ZPE* 43: 357–61

SOMAN, A. (1980) 'Deviance and criminal justice in Western Europe, 1300–1800: an essay in structure', *Criminal Justice History* 1: 3–28

SONNABEND, H. (1992) 'Stadtverkehr im antiken Rom. Probleme und Lösungsversuche', *Die Alte Stadt* 19: 183–94

SPAETH, B. S. (1990) 'The goddess Ceres and the death of Tiberius Gracchus', *Historia* 39: 182–95

SPEIDEL, M. P. (1984) 'Germani Corporis Custodes', *Germania* 62: 31–45

SPERBER, D. (1970) 'On pubs and policemen in Roman Palestine', *ZDMG* 120: 257–63

STAHL, M. (1978) *Imperiale Herrschaft und provinziale Stadt. Strukturprobleme der römischen Reichsorganisation im 1.–3. Jh. der Kaiserzeit*. Göttingen

STANLEY, P. V. (1979) '*Agoranomoi* and *metronomoi*: Athenian market officials and regulations', *AncW* 2: 13–19

STEVENSON, J. (1974) 'Food Riots in England 1792–1818', in J. Stevenson and R. Quinault, eds., *Popular Protest and Public Order. Six Studies in British History, 1790–1820*. London: 33–79

(1977) 'Social control and the prevention of riots in England, 1789–1829', in A. P. Donajgrodzki, ed., *Social Control in Nineteenth Century Britain*. London: 27–50

(1979) *Popular Disturbances in England, 1700–1870*. London

STORCH, R. D. (1975) 'The plague of the blue locusts. Police reform and popular resistance in northern England, 1840–1857', *Intern. Review of Social History* 20: 61–90

(1976) 'The policeman as domestic missionary: urban discipline and popular culture in northern England, 1850–1880', *Journal of Social History* 9: 481–509

(1989) 'Policing rural southern England before the police: public opinion and practice', in Hay and Snyder, eds. (1989a): 211–64

STRACHAN-DAVIDSON, J. L. (1912) *Problems of the Roman Criminal Law*. 2 vols. Oxford

STROUX, J. (1929) 'Eine Gerichtsreform des Kaisers Claudius (BGU 611)', *SBAW* no. 8

(1938) 'Die Versäumnisbuße der Senatoren', *Philologus* 93: 85–101

STYLES, J. (1983) 'Sir John Fielding and the problem of criminal investigation in eighteenth-century England', *Transactions of the Royal Historical Society* ser. V, 33: 127–49

(1987) 'The emergence of the police – explaining police reform in eighteenth and nineteenth century England', *British Journal of Criminology* 27: 15–22

TAJRA, H. W. (1989) *The Trial of Paulus. A Juridical Exegesis of the Second Half of the Acts of Apostles*. Tübingen

TALBERT, R. J. A. (1984) *The Senate of Imperial Rome*. Princeton

TATUM, W. J. (1990a) 'The Lex Clodia de censoria notione', *CPh* 85: 34–43

(1990b) 'Cicero's opposition to the lex Clodia de collegiis', *CQ* 40: 187–94

(1990c) 'P. Clodius Pulcher and Tarracina', *ZPE* 83: 299–304

(1993) 'The lex Papiria de dedicationibus', *CPh* 88: 319–28

TAYLOR, L. R. (1949) 'Foreign groups in Roman politics of the late republic', in *Hommages J. Bidez and F. Cumont*. Brussels: 323–30

(1960) *The Voting Districts of the Roman Republic*. Rome

(1962) 'Forerunners of the Gracchi', *JRS* 52: 19–27

TENGSTRÖM, E. (1974) *Bread for the People. Studies of the Corn-Supply of Rome during the Late Empire*. Stockholm

(1977) 'Theater and Politik im kaiserzeitlichen Rom', *Eranos* 75: 43–56

TERRILL, R. J. (1980) 'Police theorists and the "new enlightenment"',
    Anglo-American Law Review 9: 48–64
THOMAS, Y. (1984) 'Vitae necisque potestas. Le père, la cité, la mort', in
    Du châtiment dans la cité (see David 1984): 499–548
THOMMEN, L. (1989) *Das Volkstribunat der späten römischen Republik*. Stutt-
    gart
THOMPSON, E. P. (1971) 'The moral economy of the English crowd in the
    eighteenth century', *P & P* 50: 76–136
    (1972) ' "Rough Music". Le charivari anglais', *Annales (ESC)* 27: 285–
    312
    (1974) 'Patrician society, plebeian culture', *Journal of Social History* 7:
    382–405
    (1985) 'Ridings, rough music and mocking rhymes in early modern
    England', in B. Reay, ed., *Popular Culture in Seventeenth Century England*.
    London: 166–97
TILLY, C., ed. (1975a) *The Formation of National States in Western Europe*.
    Princeton: 380–455
    (1975b) 'Food supply and public order in modern Europe', in (1975a):
    380–455
TILLY, L. A. (1971) 'The food riot as a form of political conflict in France',
    Journal of Interdisciplinary History 2: 23–57
TIMPE, D. (1990) 'Das Kriegsmonopol des römischen Staates', in Eder,
    ed. (1990): 368–87
TINNEFELD, F. (1977) *Die frühbyzantinische Gesellschaft*. Munich
TONDO, S. (1963) 'Il "sacramentum militiae" nell' ambiente culturale
    romano-italico', *SDHI* 29: 1–123
TREGGIARI, S. (1969) *Roman Freedmen during the Late Republic*. Oxford
    (1980) 'Urban labour in Rome: mercennarii and tabernarii', in P.
    Garnsey, ed., *Non-Slave Labour in the Greco-Roman World*. Cambridge:
    48–64
TREXLER, R. C. (1984a) 'Follow the flag. The Ciompi revolt seen from the
    streets', *Bulletin d'Humanisme et Renaissance* 46: 357–92
    (1984b) 'Correve la terra: collective insults in the late Middle Ages',
    MEFRM 96: 845–902
UNDERDOWN, D. (1987) *Revel, Riot and Rebellion. Popular Politics and Culture
    in England 1603–1660*. Oxford
UNGERN-STERNBERG, J. v. (1970) *Untersuchungen zum spätrepublikanischen
    Notstandsrecht. Senatus consultum ultimum und hostis-Erklärung*. Munich
    (1984) 'Die beiden Fragen des Titus Annius Luscus', in *Sodalitas* (see
    Bauman 1984): 339–48
    (1991) 'Die politische und soziale Bedeutung der spätrepublikanischen
    leges frumentariae', in Giovannini, ed. (1991): 19–42
    (1993) 'Romulus-Bilder: Die Begründung der Republik im Mythos', in
    F. Graf, ed., *Mythos in mythenloser Gesellschaft. Das Paradigma Roms*.
    Stuttgart: 88–108

USENER, H. (1913) 'Italische Volksjustiz', in *Kleine Schriften*, vol. IV. Leipzig: 356–82

VAN BERCHEM, D. (1939) *Les distributions de blé et d'argent à la plèbe romaine sous l'empire*. Geneva

(1982) 'Nyon et son praefectus arcendis latrociniis', in P. Ducrey and D. Paunier, eds., *Les routes et l'histoire*. Geneva: 47–53

VAN DAM, R. (1985) *Leadership and Community in Late Antique Gaul*. Berkeley

VAN HOOFF, A. J. L. (1988) 'Ancient robbers. Reflections behind the facts', *AncSoc* 19: 105–24

VANDERBROECK, P. J. J. (1987) *Popular Leadership and Collective Behavior in the Late Roman Republic (ca 80–50 B.C.)*. Amsterdam

VANZETTI, M. (1975) 'Iuvenes turbolenti', *Labeo* 21: 77–82

VERBRUGGHE, G. P. (1973) 'The elogium from Polla and the first slave war', *CPh* 68: 25–35

VERSNEL, H. S. (1980) 'Destruction, *devotio* and despair in a situation of anomy. The mourning for Germanicus in triple perspective', in *Perennitas. Studi in onore di A. Brelich*. Rome: 541–618

VEYNE, P. (1976) *Le pain et le cirque. Sociologie historique d'un pluralisme politique*. Paris

(1983) 'Le folklore à Rome et les droits de la conscience publique sur la conduite individuelle', *Latomus* 42: 3–30

(1987) 'The Roman Empire', in G. Duby and P. Ariès, eds., *A History of Private Life. Vol. I: From Pagan Rome to Byzantium* (ed. P. Veyne). Cambridge, Mass.: 1–234

VILLARI, R. (1985) 'Masaniello: contemporary and recent interpretations', *P & P* 108: 117–32

VIRLOUVET, C. (1985) *Famines et émeutes à Rome des origines de la République à la mort de Néron*. Rome

(1991) 'La plèbe frumentaire à l'époque d'Auguste', in Giovannini, ed. (1991): 43–65

VISSCHER, F. de (1966) 'Macro, Préfet des Vigiles et ses cohortes contre la tyrannie de Séjan', in *Mélanges A. Piganiol*. Paris: 761–8

VITTINGHOFF, F. (1936) *Der Staatsfeind in der römischen Kaiserzeit*. Berlin

(1984) '"Christianus sum" – Das "Verbrechen" von Aussenseitern der römischen Gesellschaft', *Historia* 33: 331–57

VITZTHUM, W. (1966) 'Untersuchungen zum materiellen Gehalt der "lex Plautia" und "lex Iulia de vi"'. Diss. München

WALDSTEIN, W. (1972) 'Zum Fall der "dos Licinniae"', *Index* 3: 343–61

WALLACE-HADRILL, A. (1981) 'Family and inheritance in the Augustan marriage laws', *PCPhS* 207 (n.s. 27): 58–80

(1982) 'Civilis princeps: between citizen and king', *JRS* 72: 32–48

(1988) 'The social structure of the Roman house', *PBSR* 56: 43–97

(1990) 'Roman arches and Greek Honours: the language of power at Rome', *PCPhS* 216 (n.s. 36): 143–81

WALLACE-HADRILL, A., ed. (1989) *Patronage in Ancient Society*. London

WALSH, J. (1972) 'Methodism and the mob in the eighteenth century', in G. J. Cumming and D. Baker, eds., *Popular Belief and Practice*. Cambridge: 213–27

WALTZING, J. P. (1895–1900) *Etude historique sur les corporations professionnelles chez les Romains*. 4 vols. Louvain

WATSON, A. (1974) 'Enuptio Gentis', in *Daube Noster*. Edinburgh: 331–41
(1987) *Roman Slave Law*. Baltimore
(1992) *The State, Law and Religion: Pagan Rome*. Athens, Ga.

WATSON, G. R. (1971) 'The pay of the urban Forces', in *Acta of the Fifth International Congress of Greek and Latin Epigraphy. Cambridge 1967*. Oxford: 413–16

WEBER, E. (1976) *Peasants into Frenchmen*. Stanford

WEBER, M. (1972) *Wirtschaft und Gesellschaft*. 5th edn. Tübingen

WEHRLI, C. (1962) 'Les gynéconomes', *MH* 19: 33–8

WEILER, I., ed. (1988) *Soziale Randgruppen und Außenseiter im Altertum*. Graz

WEISS, E. (1949) 'Proscriptio debitorum', *RIDA* ser. 1, 3: 501–6

WELWEI, K.-W. (1988) *Unfreie im antiken Kriegsdienst*, vol. III: *Rom*. Stuttgart

WESTERN, J. R. (1956) 'The volunteer movement as an anti-revolutionary force, 1793–1801', *EHR* 71: 603–14

WHITTAKER, C. R. (1964) 'The revolt of Papirius Dionysius A. D. 190', *Historia* 13: 348–69

WIEACKER, F. (1944) 'Endoplorare. Diebstahlsverfolgung und Gerüft im altrömischen Recht', in *Festschrift L. Wenger*, vol. I. Munich: 129–79
(1988) *Römische Rechtsgeschichte*, vol. I: *Einleitung, Quellenkunde. Frühzeit und Republik*. Munich

WIEDEMANN, T. (1992) *Emperors and Gladiators*. London

WILLIAMS, A. (1978) 'The police and the administration of eighteenth-century Paris', *Journal of Urban History* 4: 157–82

WILLIAMS, M. H. (1989) 'The expulsion of the Jews from Rome in AD 19', *Latomus* 48: 765–84

WINSLOW, C. (1975) 'Sussex smugglers', in Hay *et al*. (1975): 119–66

WINTERLING, A. (1991) 'Polisbegriff und Stasistheorie des Aeneas Tacticus. Zur Frage der Grenzen der griechischen Polisgesellschaften im 4. Jahrhundert v. Chr.', *Historia* 40: 193–229

WISEMAN, T. P. (1985) *Catullus and His World. A Reappraisal*. Cambridge
(1987) 'Conspicui postes tectaque digna deo: The public image of aristocratic and imperial houses in the late republic and early empire', in *L'urbs. Espaces urbaines et histoire ... Actes ... Rome 1985*. Rome: 393–413

WISTRAND, M. (1992) *Entertainment and Violence in Ancient Rome. The Attitudes of Roman Writers of the First Century A.D.* Göteborg

WITT, N. W. de (1926) 'Litigation in the forum in Cicero's Time', *CPh* 21: 218–24

WOESS, F. von (1931) 'Die Oratio des Claudius über Richteralter, Prozeß-verschleppung und Anklägertyrannei (BGU 611)', *ZRG* 51: 336–68

WOLF, J. G. (1970) 'Lanx und licium – Das Ritual der Haussuchung im altrömischen Recht', in *Sympotika Franz Wieacker*. Göttingen: 59–79

(1988) 'Das Senatusconsultum Silanianum und die Senatsrede des C. Cassius Longinus aus dem Jahre 61 n. Chr.', *Sitzungsberichte der Akademie der Wissenschaften Heidelberg*, no. 2

WOLFGANG, M. E. (1954) 'Political crimes and punishments in Renaissance Florence', *Journal of Criminal Law, Criminology and Police Science* 44: 555–81

WRIGHTSON, K. (1980) 'Two concepts of order: justices, constables and jurymen in seventeenth-century England', in Brewer and Styles, eds. (1980a): 21–46

WYATT-BROWN, B. (1982) *Southern Honor, Ethics and Behavior in the Old South*. Oxford

YAVETZ, Z. (1969) *Plebs and Princeps*. Oxford

(1983) *Julius Caesar and His Public Image*. London

(1986) 'The urban plebs in the days of the Flavians, Nerva and Trajan', in *Opposition et résistances ...* (see Giovannini 1986): 135–86

Index

Abbreviations: *cens.* = censor; *cos.* = consul; *dict.* = dictator; *mag. eq.* = *magister equitum* (master of the horse); *pr.* = praetor; *praef. pr.* = *praefectus praetorio* (praetorian prefect); *praef. u.* = *praefectus urbi* (city prefect); *procos.* = proconsul; *tr. pl.* = *tribunus plebis* (tribune of the people)